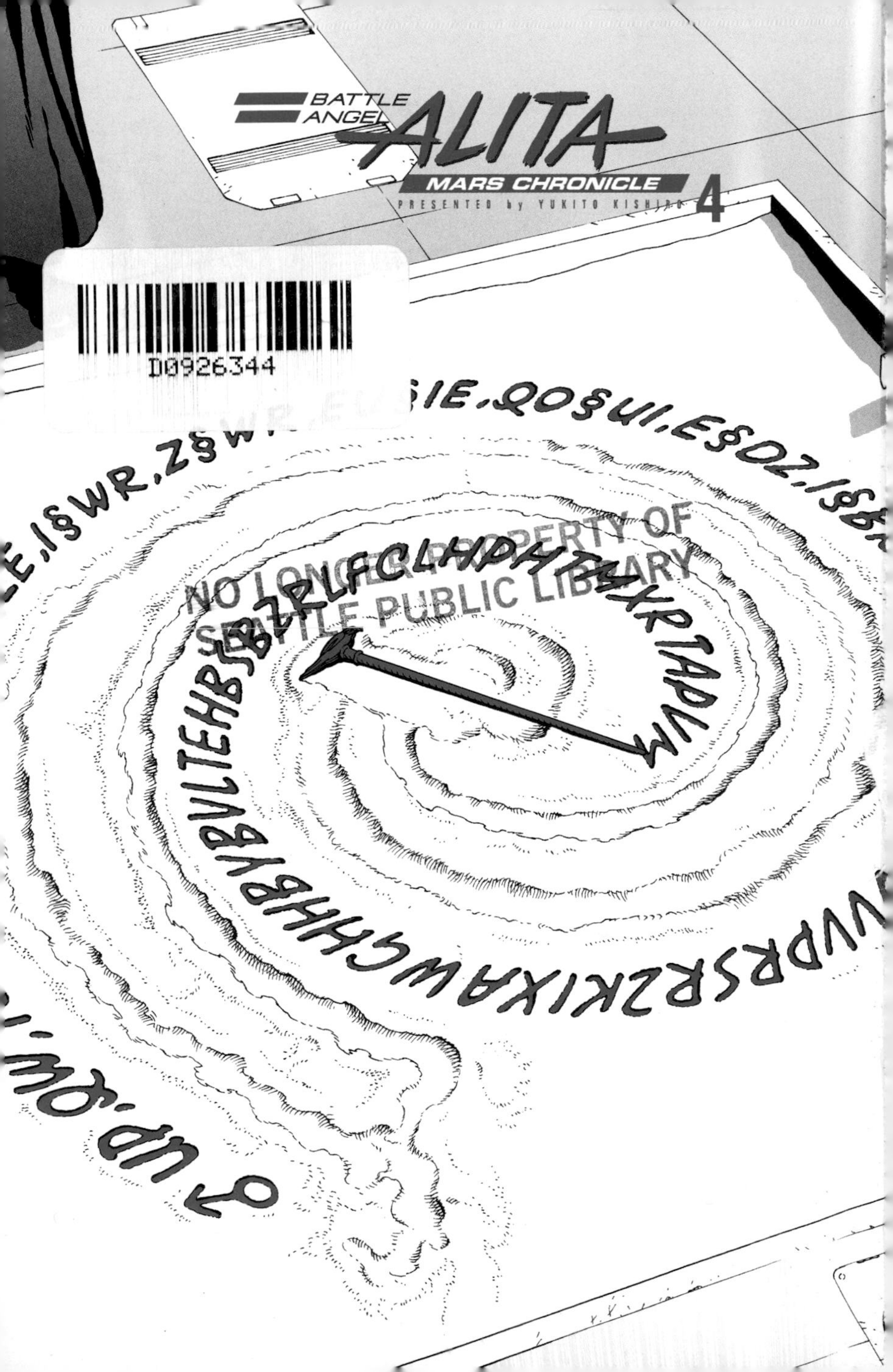
BATTLE ANGEL
ALITA
MARS CHRONICLE
PRESENTED by YUKITO KISHIRO
4

BATTLE ANGEL ALITA MARS CHRONICLE

PRESENTED by YUKITO KISHIRO

CONTENTS

ADDITIONAL STAFF:
TSUTOMU KISHIRO / EMIYA KINARI

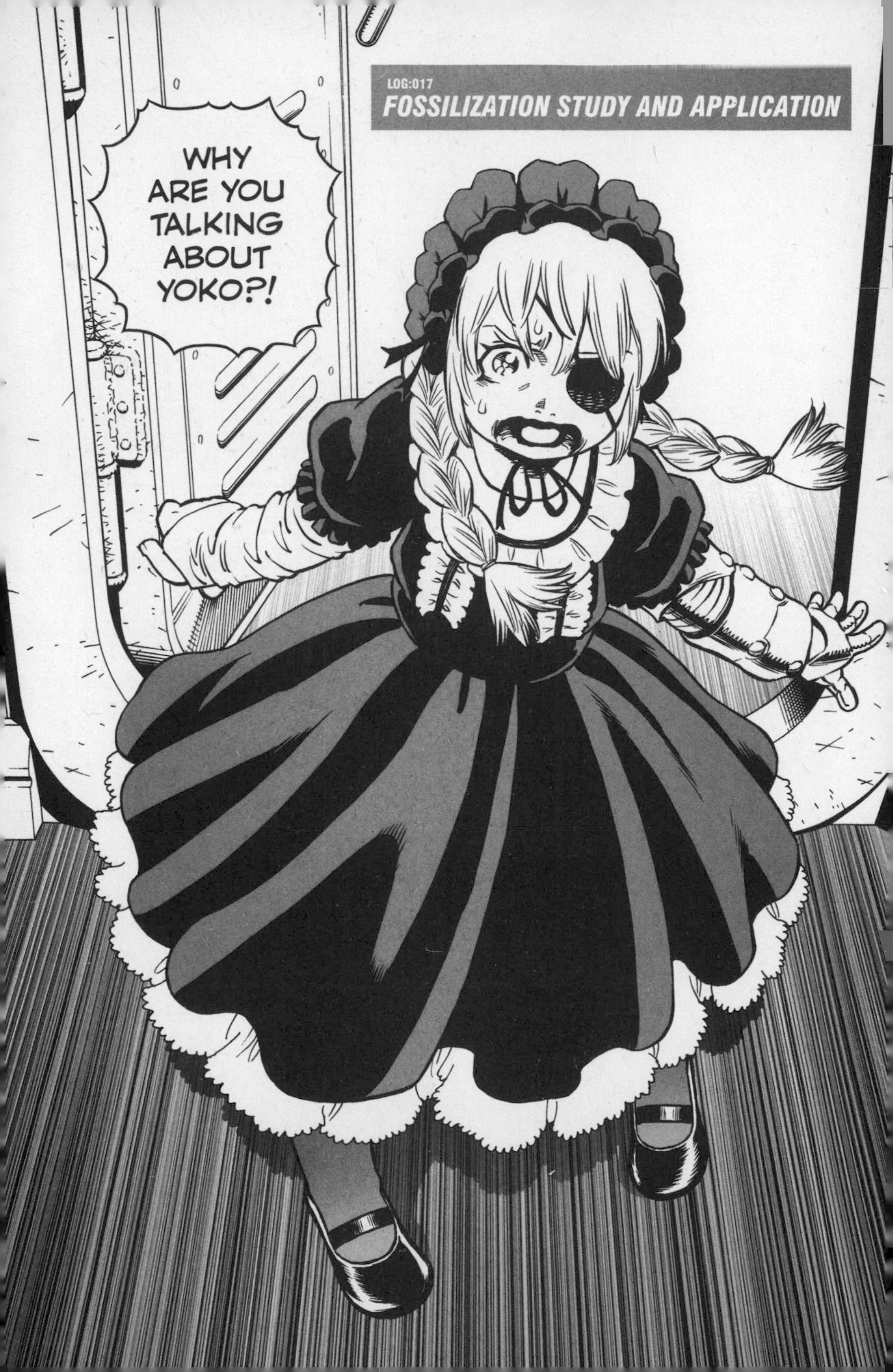
LOG:017
FOSSILIZATION STUDY AND APPLICATION
WHY ARE YOU TALKING ABOUT YOKO?!

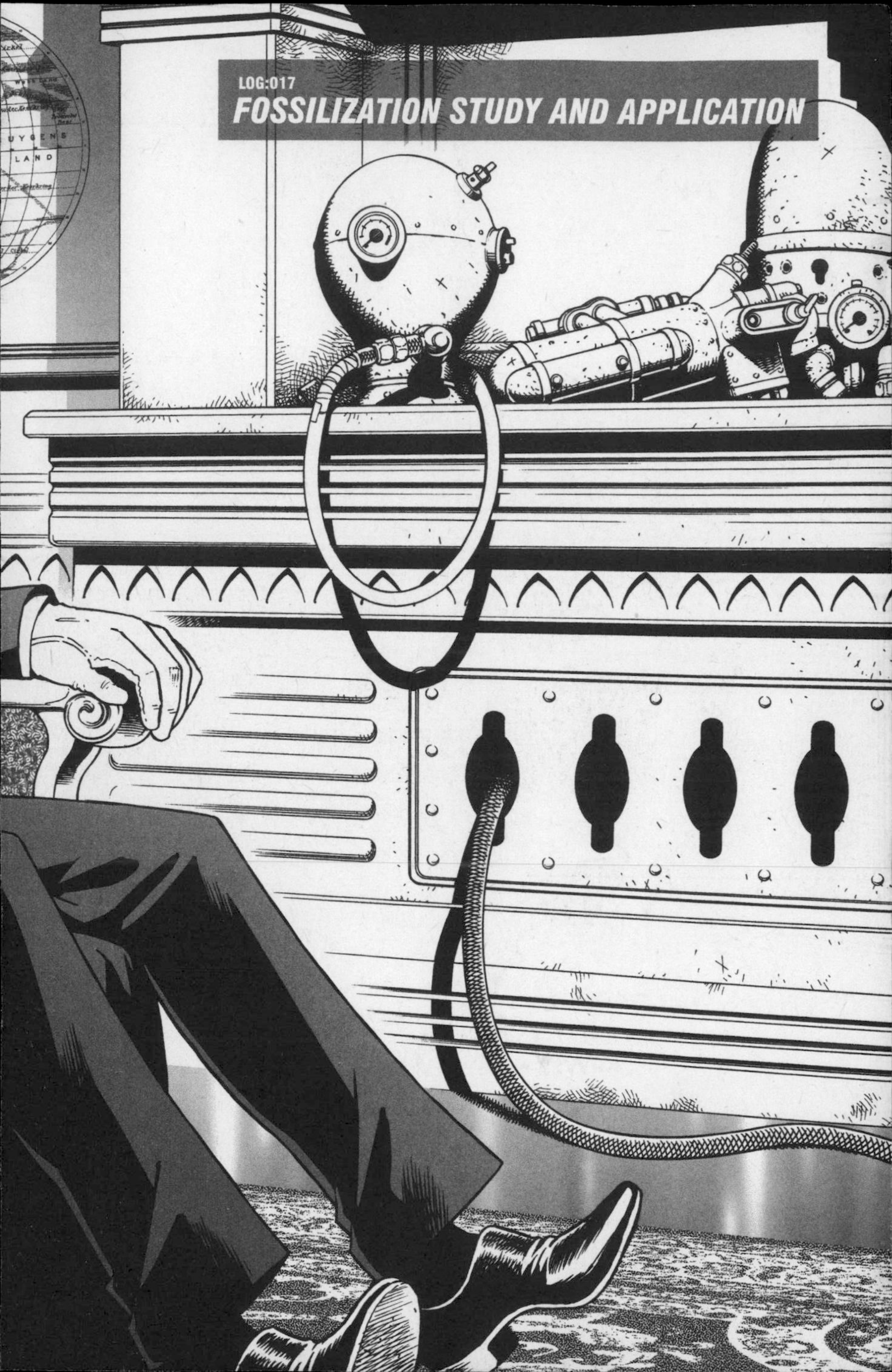
LOG:017
FOSSILIZATION STUDY AND APPLICATION

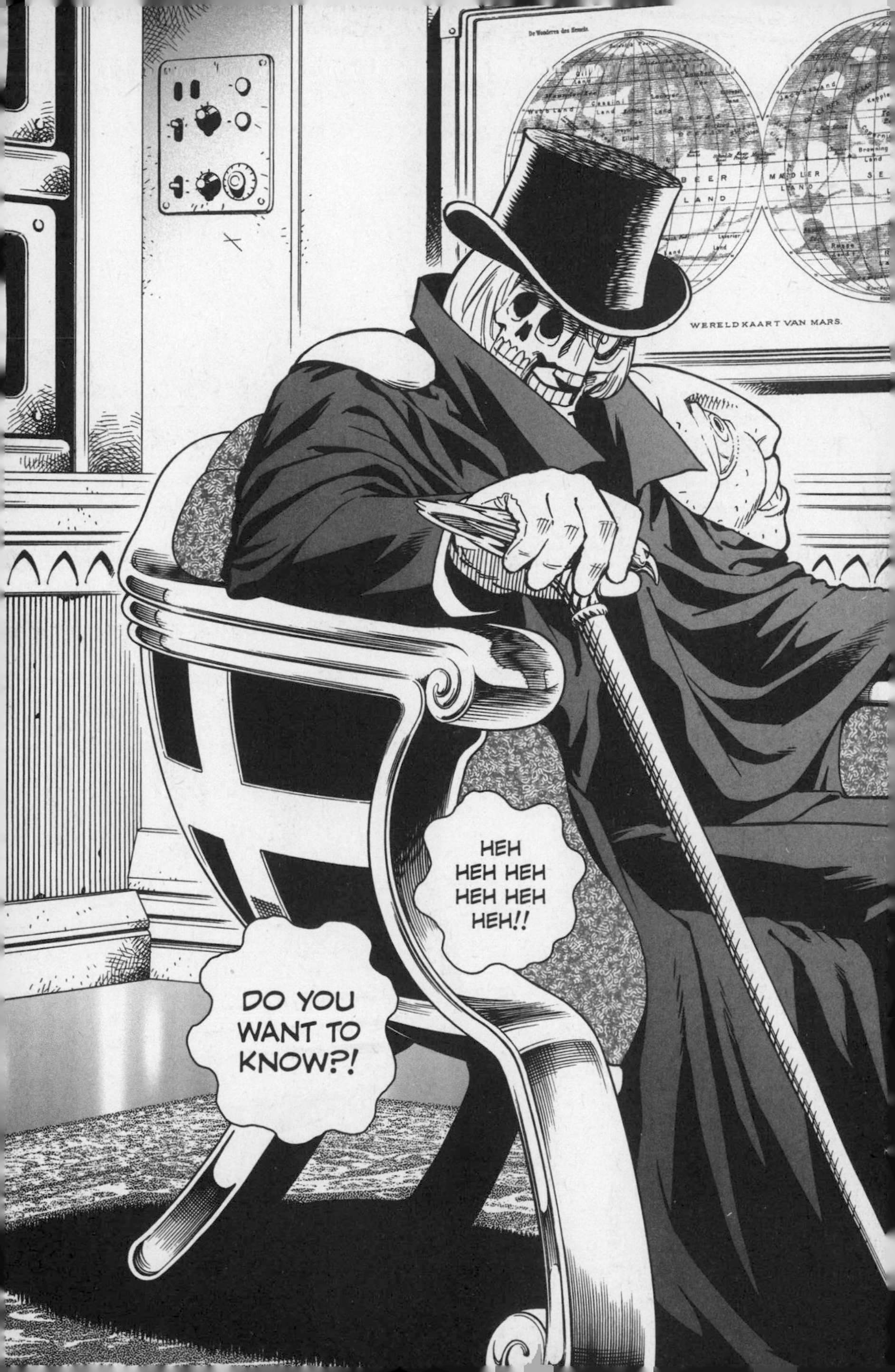
WERELDKAART VAN MARS.
HEH HEH HEH HEH HEH HEH!!
DO YOU WANT TO KNOW?!

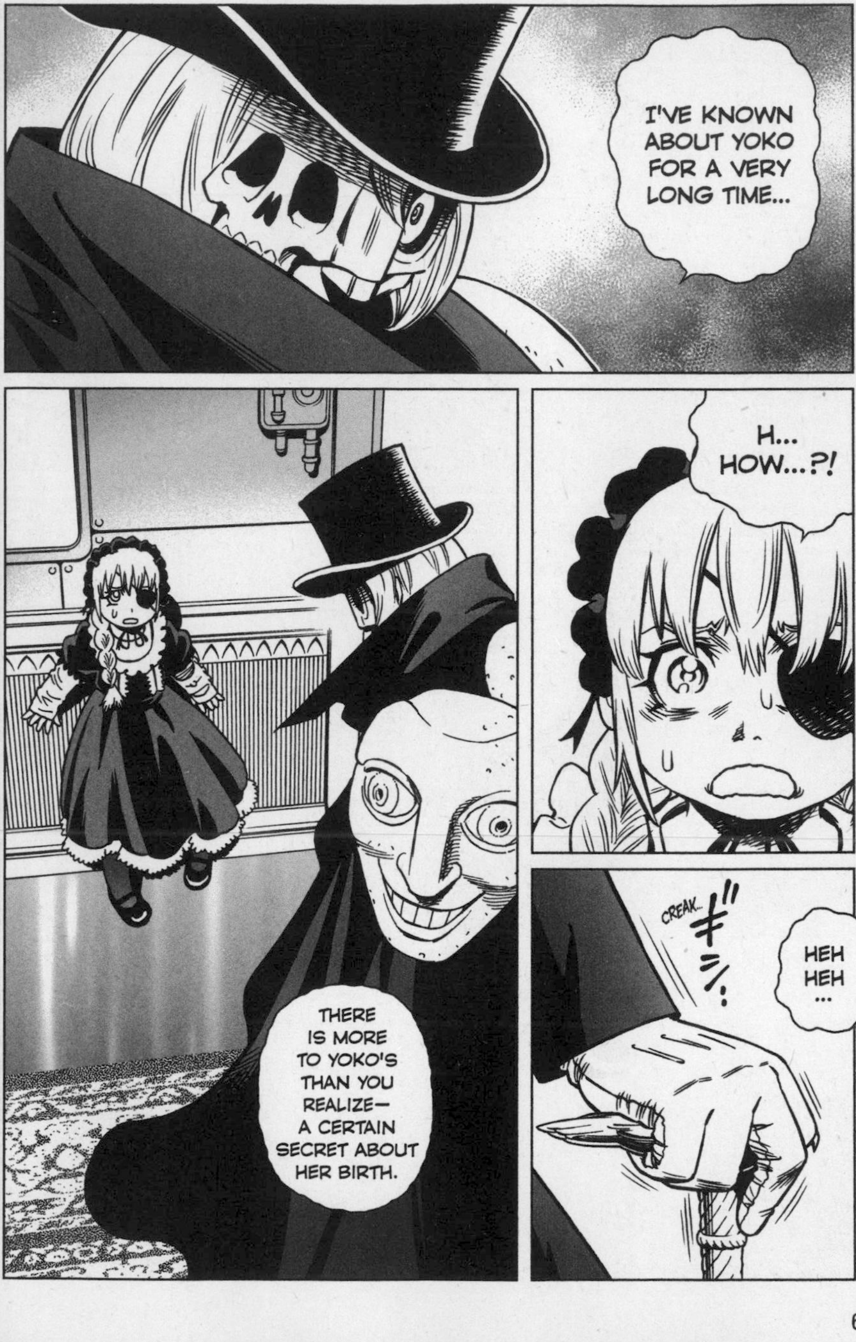

I'VE KNOWN ABOUT YOKO FOR A VERY LONG TIME...
H... HOW...?!
CREAK...
HEH HEH ...
THERE IS MORE TO YOKO'S THAN YOU REALIZE— A CERTAIN SECRET ABOUT HER BIRTH.

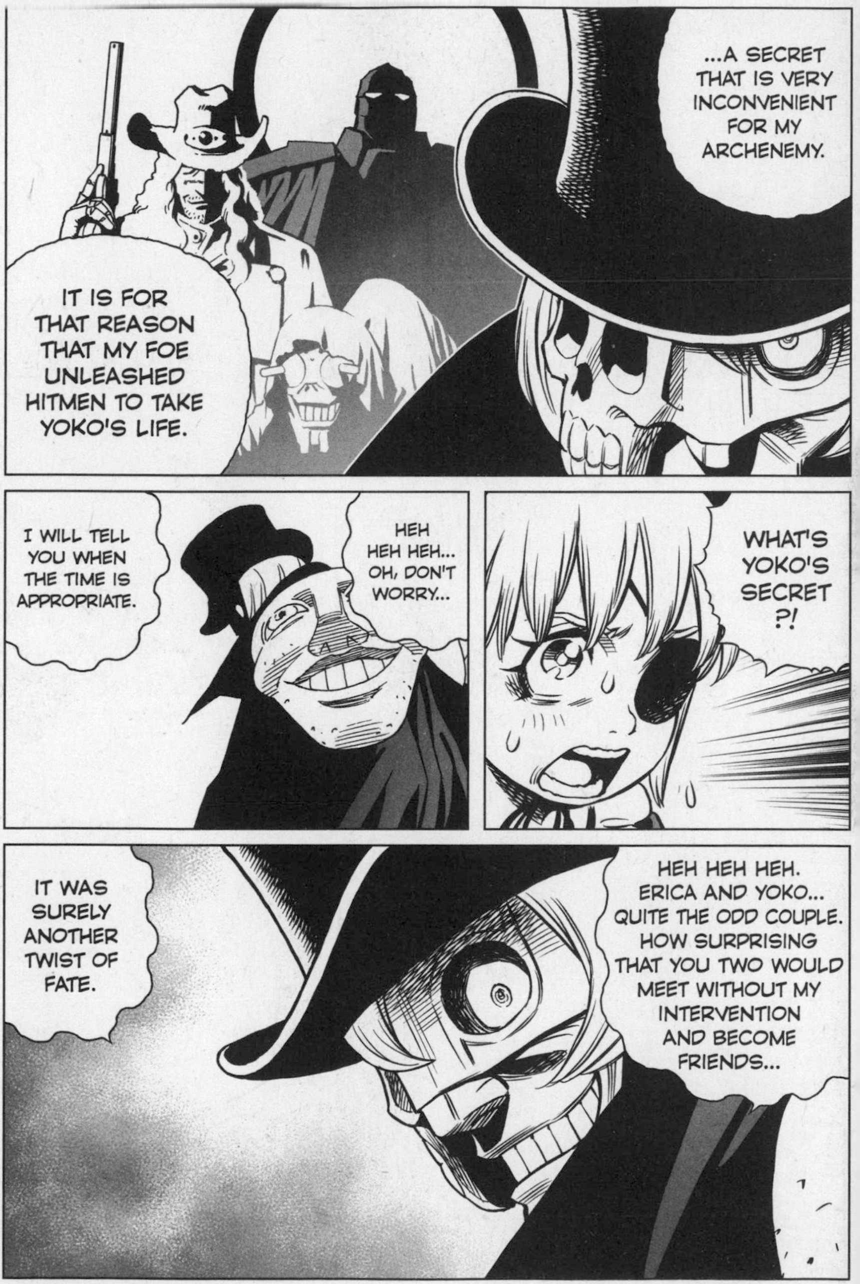
...A SECRET THAT IS VERY INCONVENIENT FOR MY ARCHENEMY.
IT IS FOR THAT REASON THAT MY FOE UNLEASHED HITMEN TO TAKE YOKO'S LIFE.
WHAT'S YOKO'S SECRET ?!
HEH HEH HEH... OH, DON'T WORRY...
I WILL TELL YOU WHEN THE TIME IS APPROPRIATE.
HEH HEH HEH. ERICA AND YOKO... QUITE THE ODD COUPLE. HOW SURPRISING THAT YOU TWO WOULD MEET WITHOUT MY INTERVENTION AND BECOME FRIENDS...
IT WAS SURELY ANOTHER TWIST OF FATE.

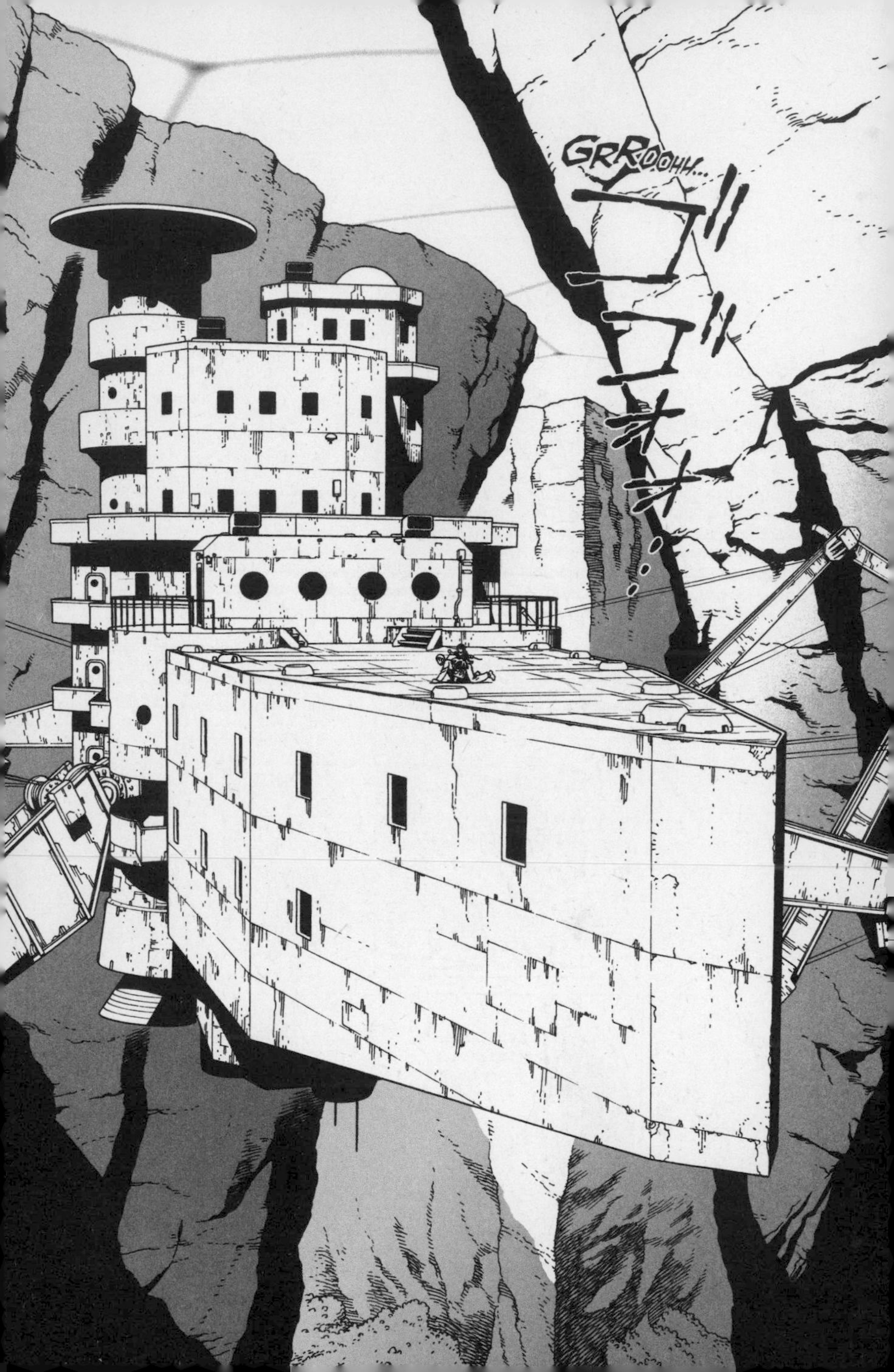
GRROOHH...
ゴゴオオ…

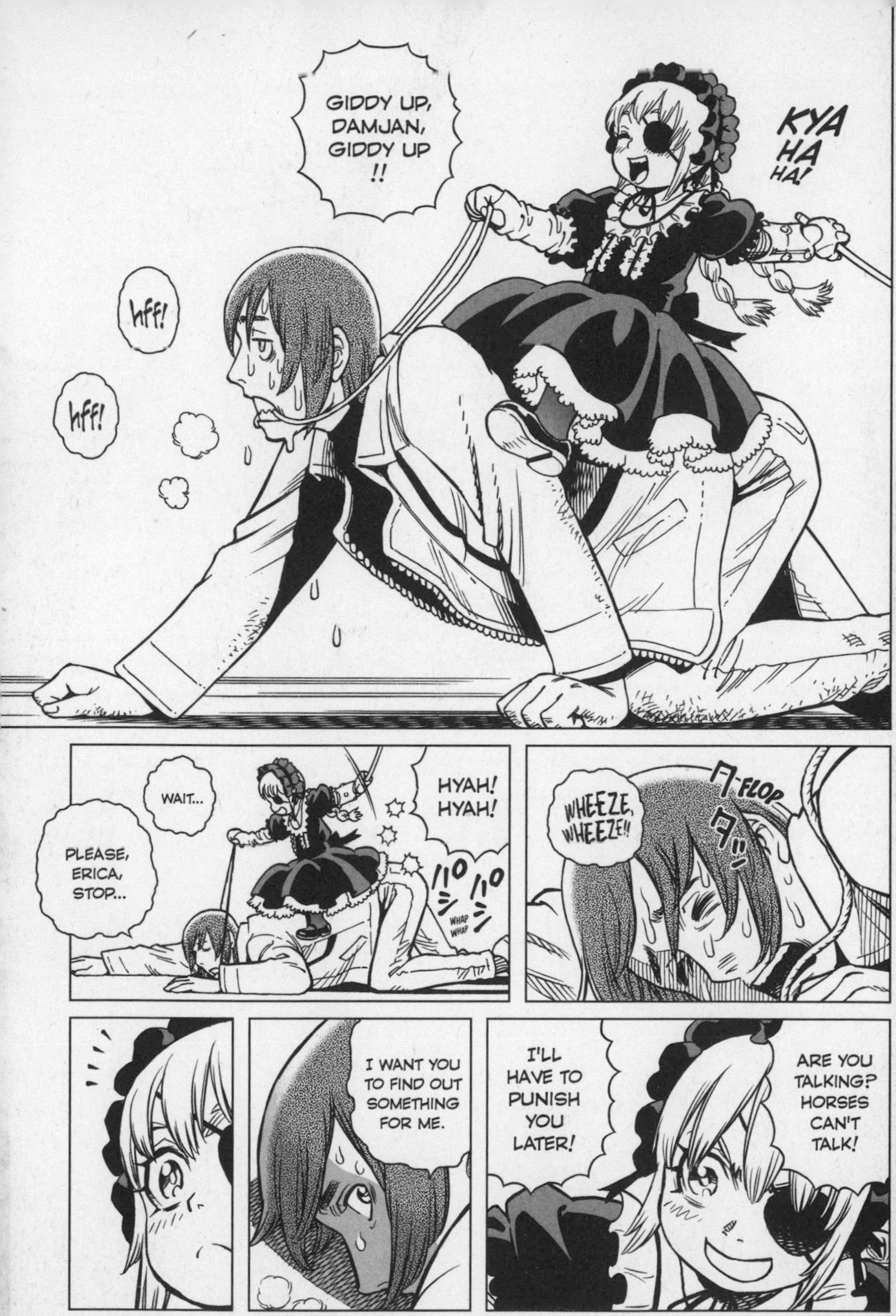
KYA HA HA!
GIDDY UP, DAMJAN, GIDDY UP !!
hff!
hff!
WHEEZE, WHEEZE!!
FLOP
HYAH! HYAH!
WAIT...
PLEASE, ERICA, STOP...
WHAP WHAP
ARE YOU TALKING? HORSES CAN'T TALK!
I'LL HAVE TO PUNISH YOU LATER!
I WANT YOU TO FIND OUT SOMETHING FOR ME.

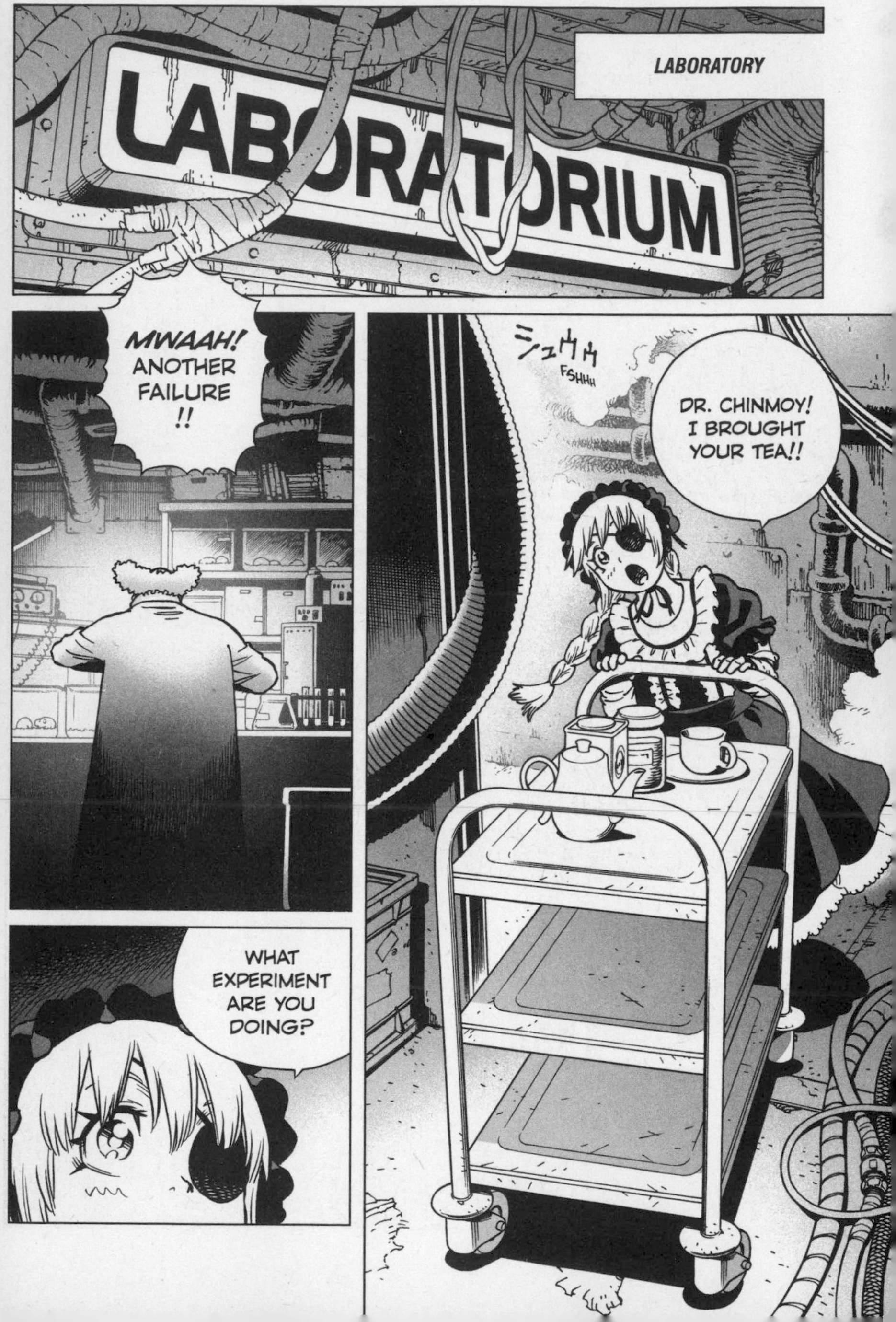
LABORATORY
LABORATORIUM
FSHHH
DR. CHINMOY! I BROUGHT YOUR TEA!!
MWAAH! ANOTHER FAILURE !!
WHAT EXPERIMENT ARE YOU DOING?

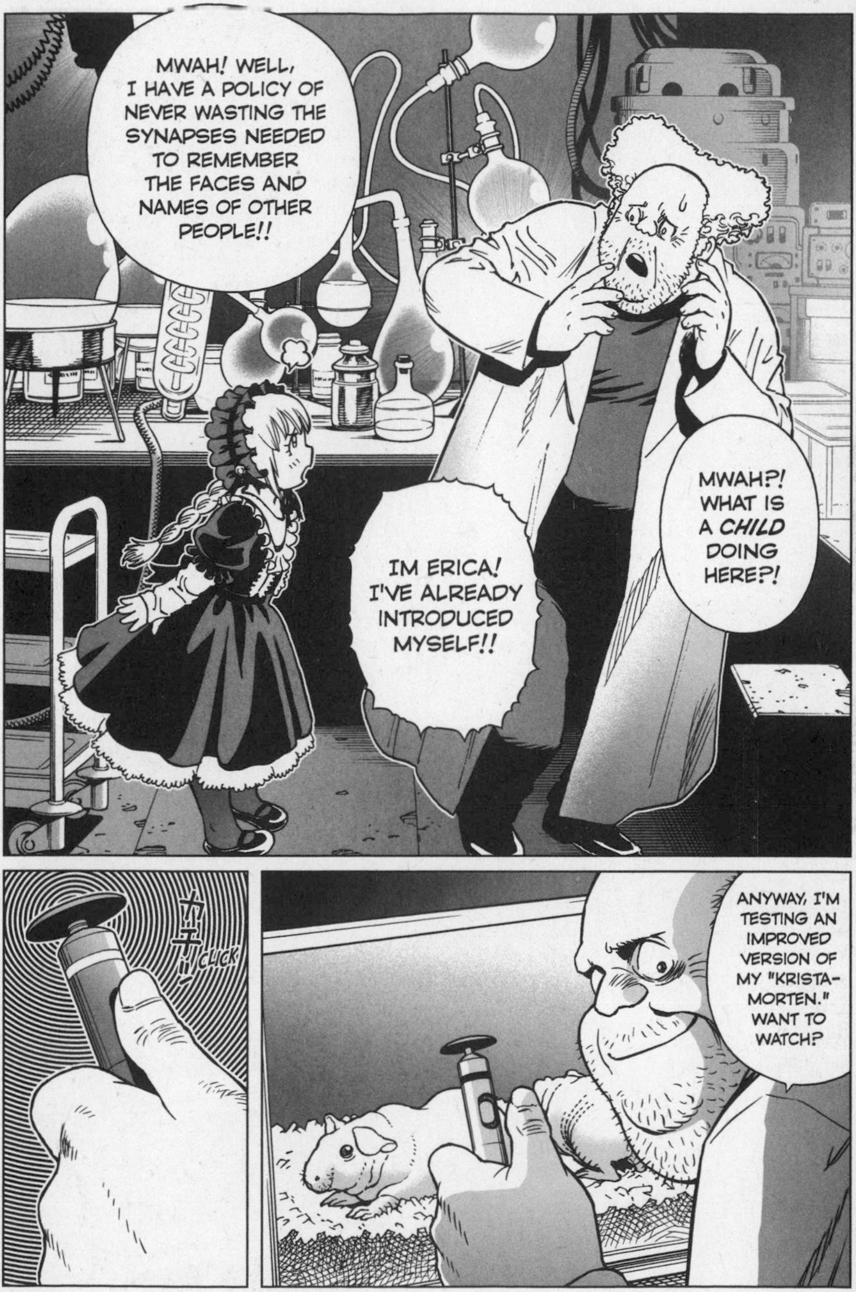
MWAH?! WHAT IS A *CHILD* DOING HERE?!
IM ERICA! I'VE ALREADY INTRODUCED MYSELF!!
MWAH! WELL, I HAVE A POLICY OF NEVER WASTING THE SYNAPSES NEEDED TO REMEMBER THE FACES AND NAMES OF OTHER PEOPLE!!
ANYWAY, I'M TESTING AN IMPROVED VERSION OF MY "KRISTA-MORTEN." WANT TO WATCH?
カチ!! CLICK

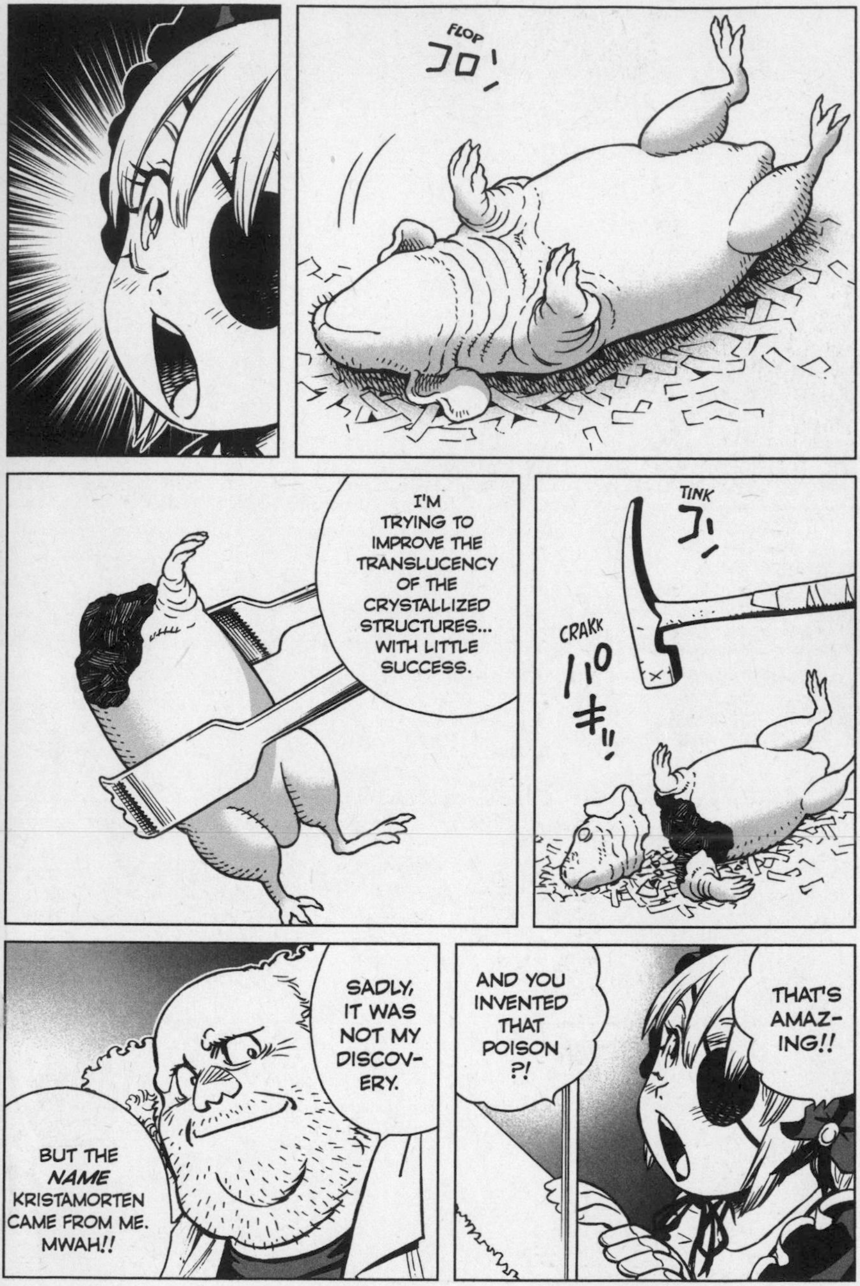
FLOP
コロン
TINK
コン
CRAKK
パキ!!
I'M TRYING TO IMPROVE THE TRANSLUCENCY OF THE CRYSTALLIZED STRUCTURES... WITH LITTLE SUCCESS.
THAT'S AMAZ-ING!!
AND YOU INVENTED THAT POISON ?!
SADLY, IT WAS NOT MY DISCOV-ERY.
BUT THE *NAME* KRISTAMORTEN CAME FROM ME. MWAH!!

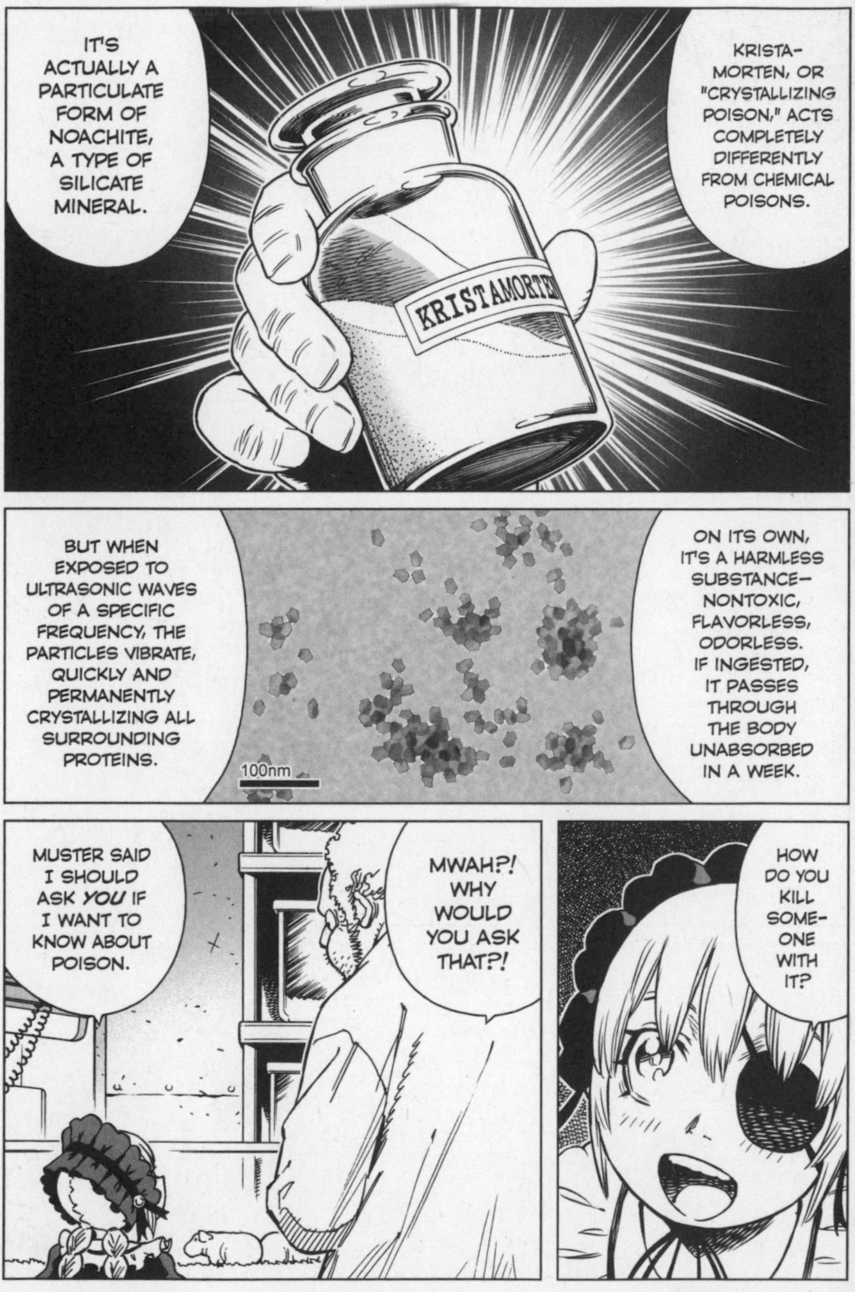
KRISTA-MORTEN, OR "CRYSTALLIZING POISON," ACTS COMPLETELY DIFFERENTLY FROM CHEMICAL POISONS.
KRISTAMORTEN
IT'S ACTUALLY A PARTICULATE FORM OF NOACHITE, A TYPE OF SILICATE MINERAL.
ON ITS OWN, IT'S A HARMLESS SUBSTANCE— NONTOXIC, FLAVORLESS, ODORLESS. IF INGESTED, IT PASSES THROUGH THE BODY UNABSORBED IN A WEEK.
100nm
BUT WHEN EXPOSED TO ULTRASONIC WAVES OF A SPECIFIC FREQUENCY, THE PARTICLES VIBRATE, QUICKLY AND PERMANENTLY CRYSTALLIZING ALL SURROUNDING PROTEINS.
HOW DO YOU KILL SOME-ONE WITH IT?
MWAH?! WHY WOULD YOU ASK THAT?!
MUSTER SAID I SHOULD ASK *YOU* IF I WANT TO KNOW ABOUT POISON.

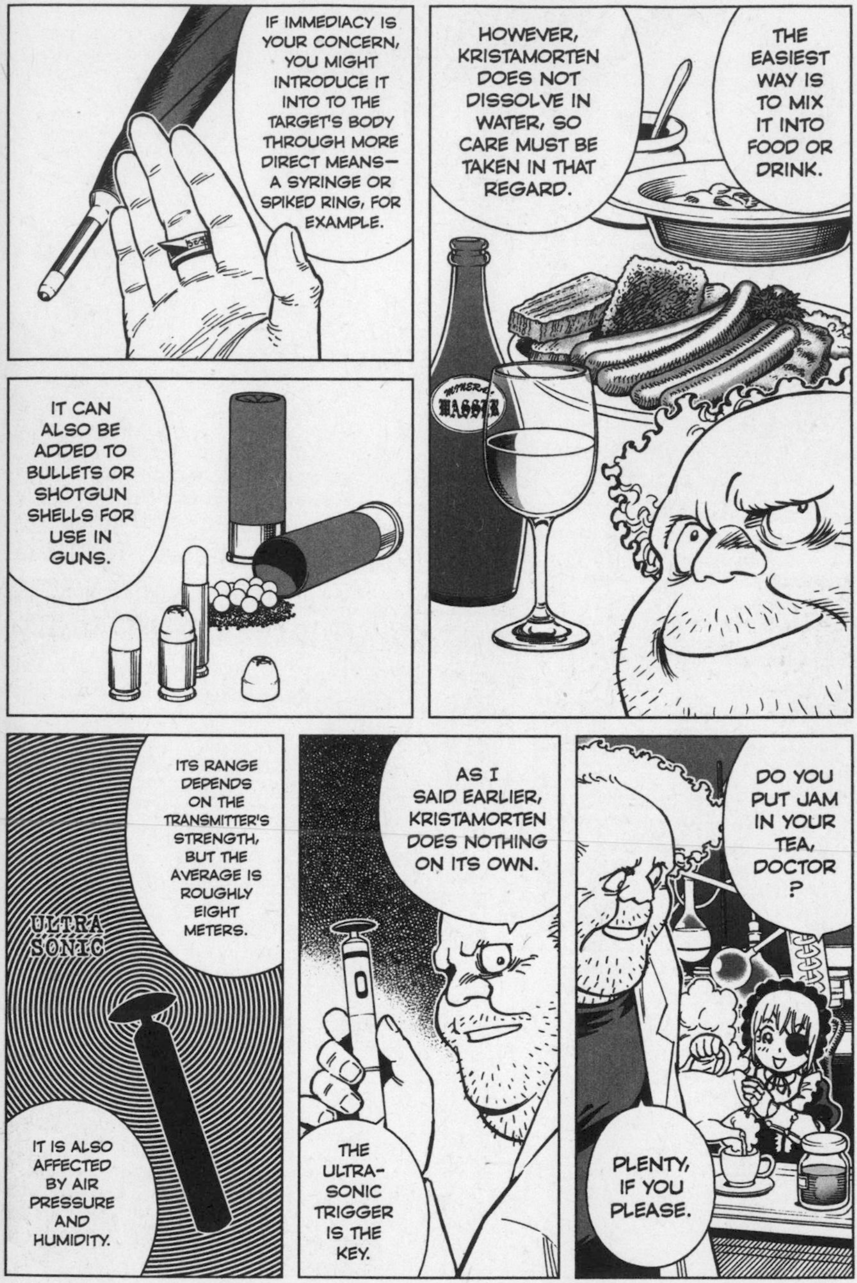
THE EASIEST WAY IS TO MIX IT INTO FOOD OR DRINK.
HOWEVER, KRISTAMORTEN DOES NOT DISSOLVE IN WATER, SO CARE MUST BE TAKEN IN THAT REGARD.
IF IMMEDIACY IS YOUR CONCERN, YOU MIGHT INTRODUCE IT INTO TO THE TARGET'S BODY THROUGH MORE DIRECT MEANS—A SYRINGE OR SPIKED RING, FOR EXAMPLE.
IT CAN ALSO BE ADDED TO BULLETS OR SHOTGUN SHELLS FOR USE IN GUNS.
DO YOU PUT JAM IN YOUR TEA, DOCTOR?
PLENTY, IF YOU PLEASE.
AS I SAID EARLIER, KRISTAMORTEN DOES NOTHING ON ITS OWN.
THE ULTRA-SONIC TRIGGER IS THE KEY.
ITS RANGE DEPENDS ON THE TRANSMITTER'S STRENGTH, BUT THE AVERAGE IS ROUGHLY EIGHT METERS.
ULTRA SONIC
IT IS ALSO AFFECTED BY AIR PRESSURE AND HUMIDITY.

*8 M = 26.25 FT.

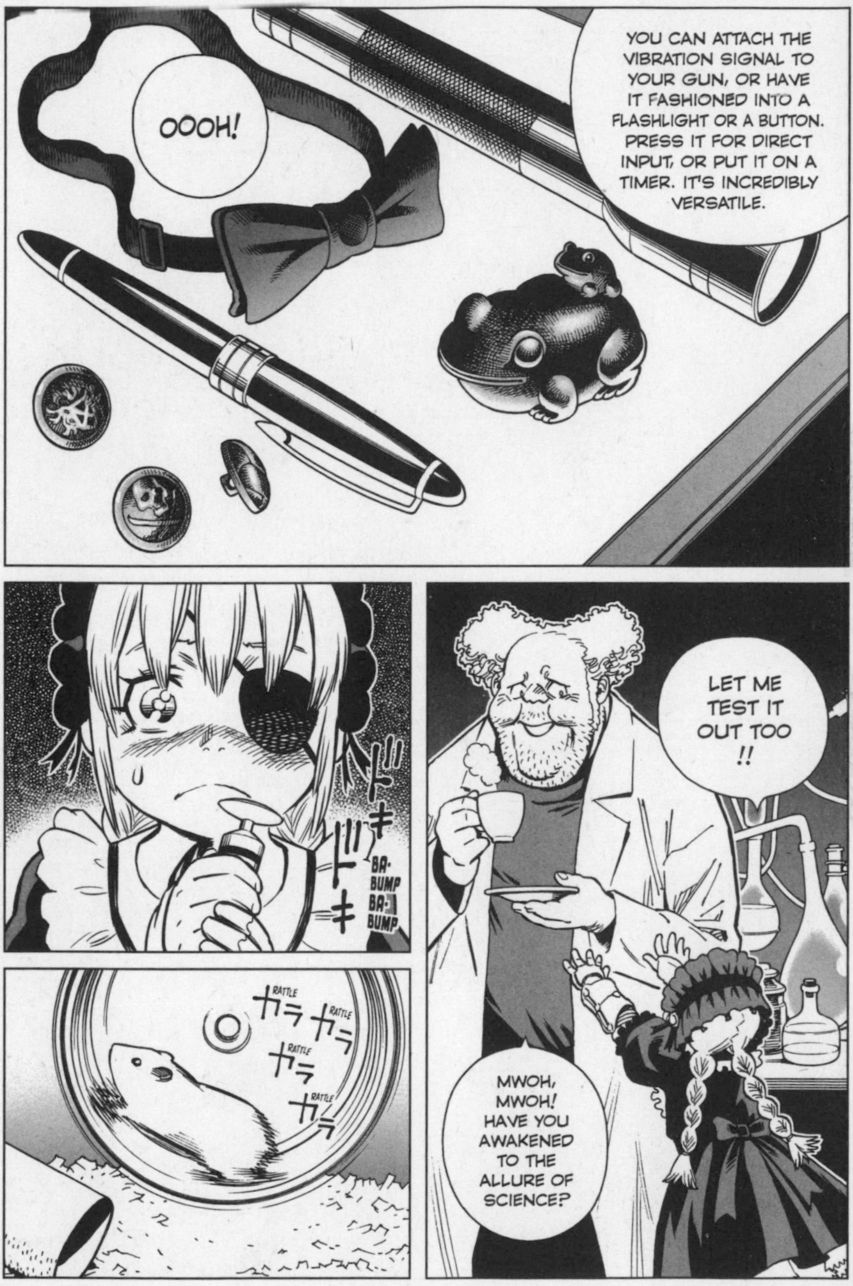
YOU CAN ATTACH THE VIBRATION SIGNAL TO YOUR GUN, OR HAVE IT FASHIONED INTO A FLASHLIGHT OR A BUTTON. PRESS IT FOR DIRECT INPUT, OR PUT IT ON A TIMER. IT'S INCREDIBLY VERSATILE.
OOOH!
LET ME TEST IT OUT TOO !!
MWOH, MWOH! HAVE YOU AWAKENED TO THE ALLURE OF SCIENCE?
ドキドキ
BA-BUMP BA-BUMP
RATTLE ガラ
RATTLE ガラ
RATTLE ガラ
RATTLE ガラ

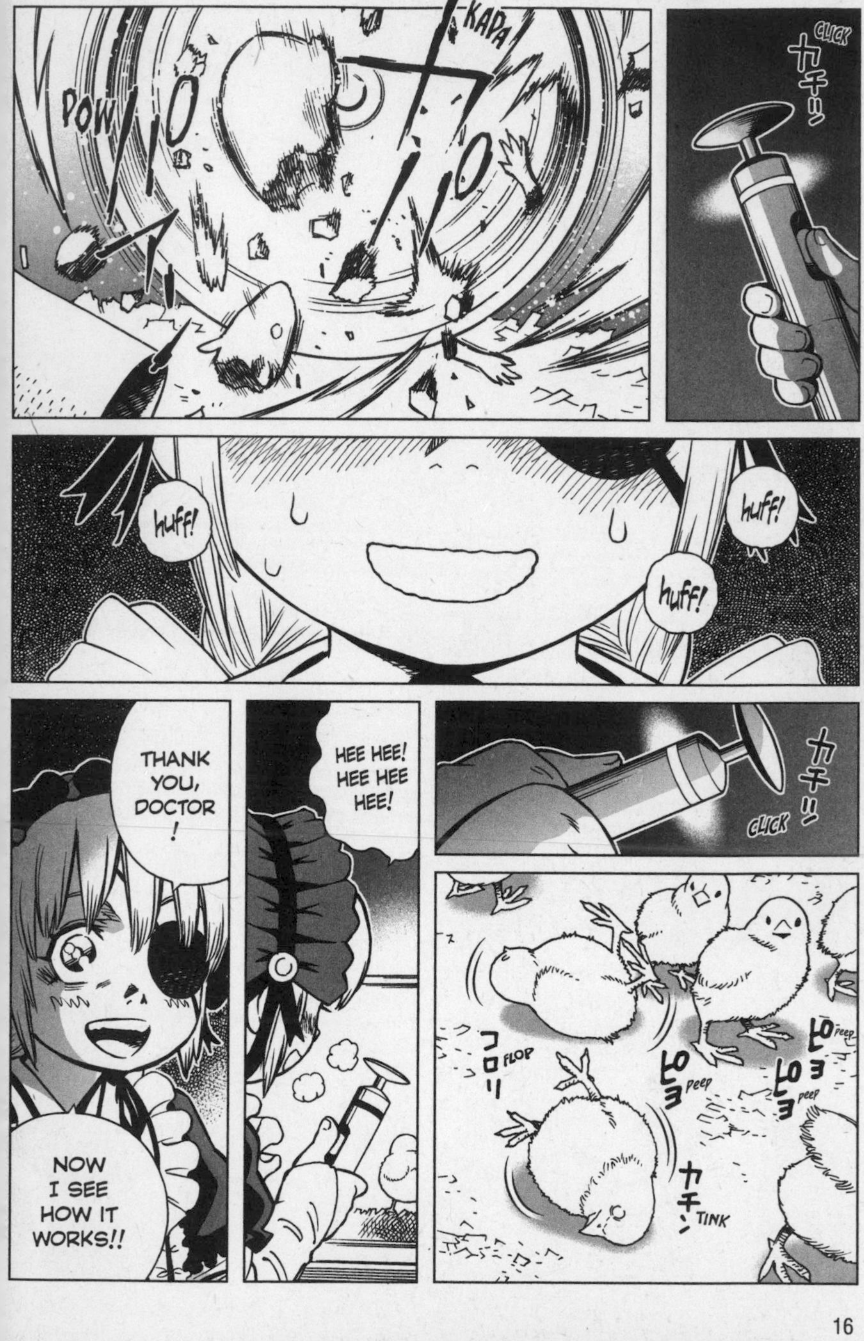
CLICK
カチッ
KAPA
POW
huff!
huff!
huff!
カチッ
CLICK
HEE HEE! HEE HEE HEE!
THANK YOU, DOCTOR!
NOW I SEE HOW IT WORKS!!
ピョ peep
ピョ peep
ピョ peep
コロリ FLOP
カチン TINK

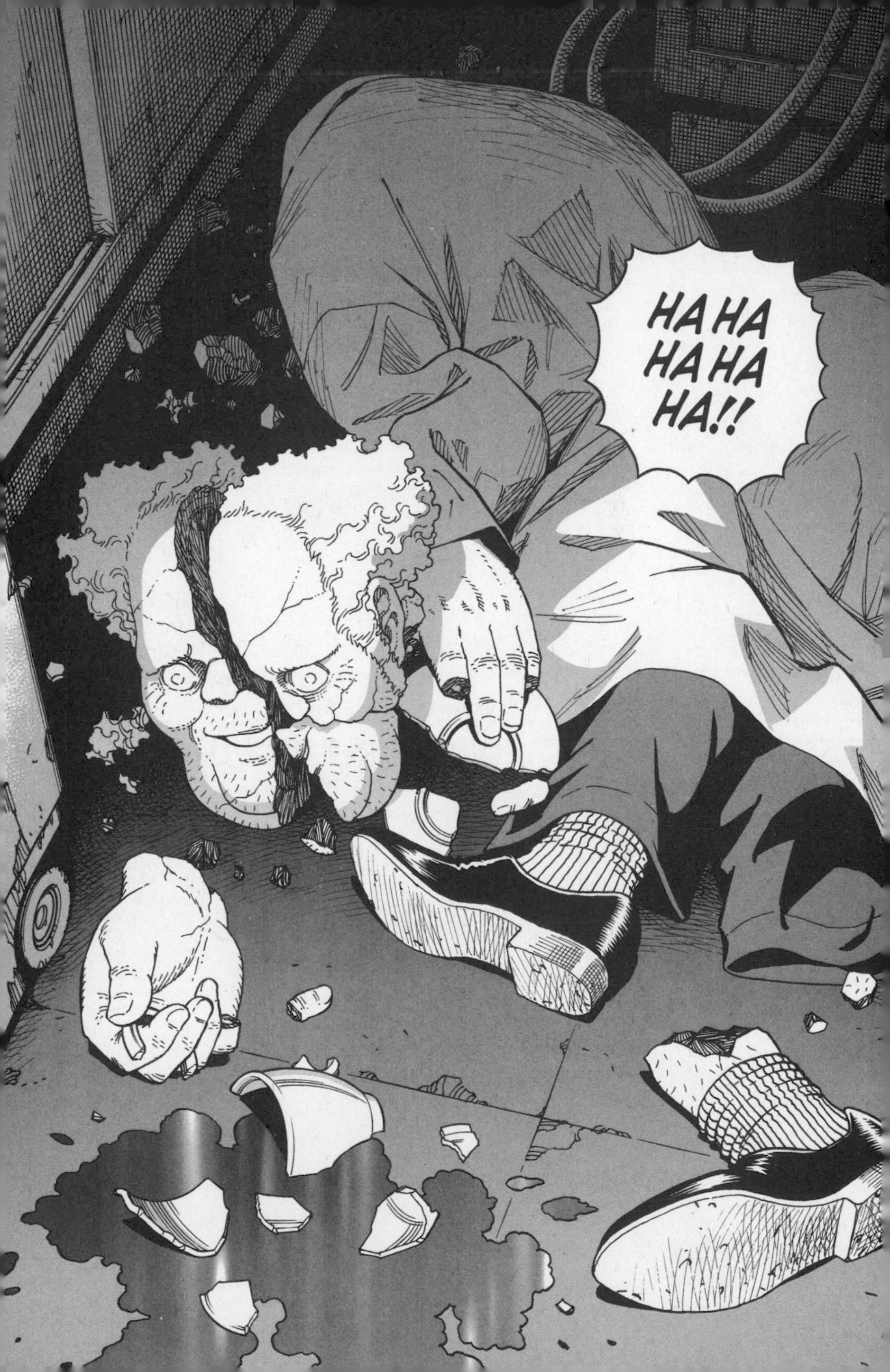
HA HA HA HA HA!!

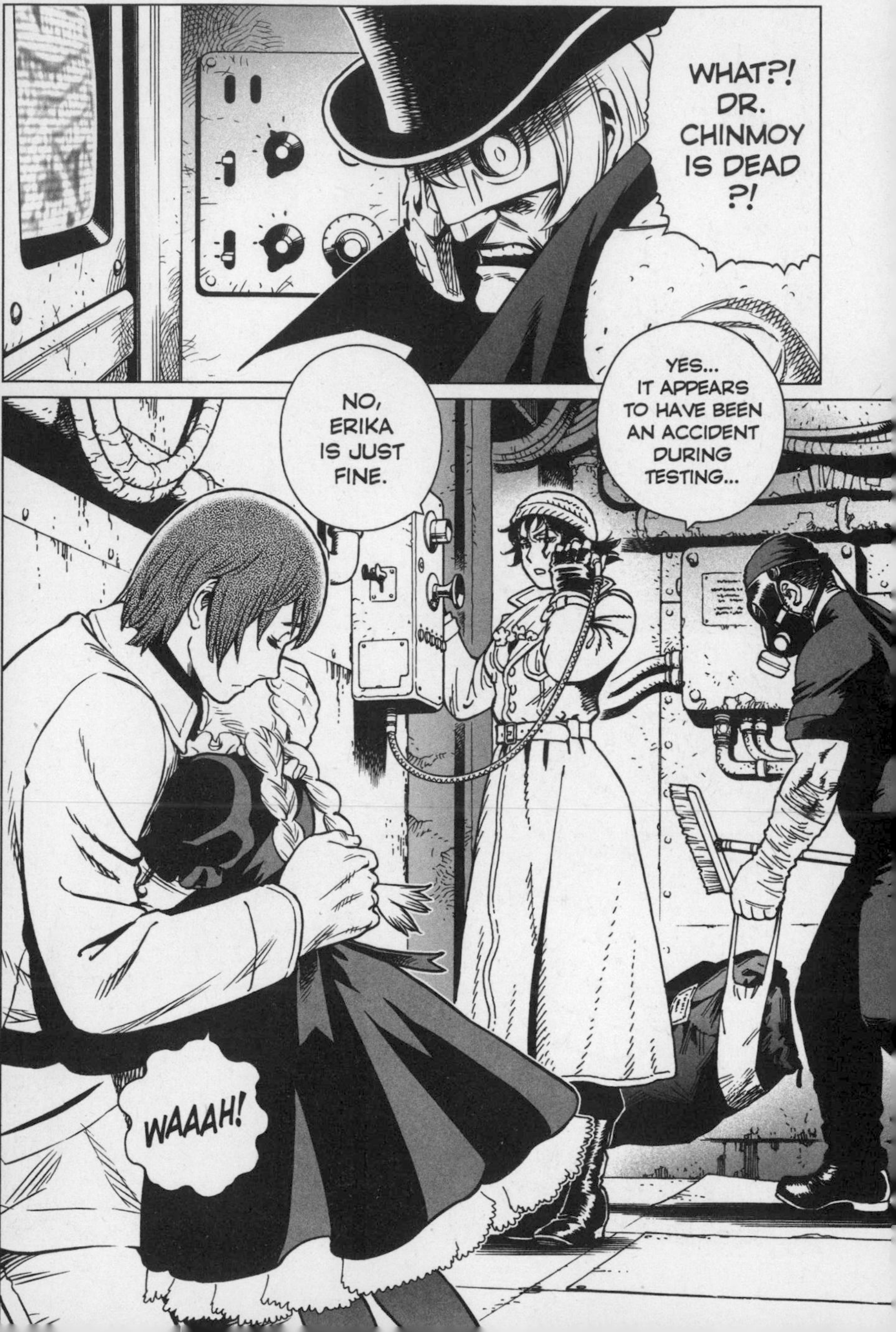
WHAT?! DR. CHINMOY IS DEAD ?!
YES... IT APPEARS TO HAVE BEEN AN ACCIDENT DURING TESTING...
NO, ERIKA IS JUST FINE.
WAAAH!

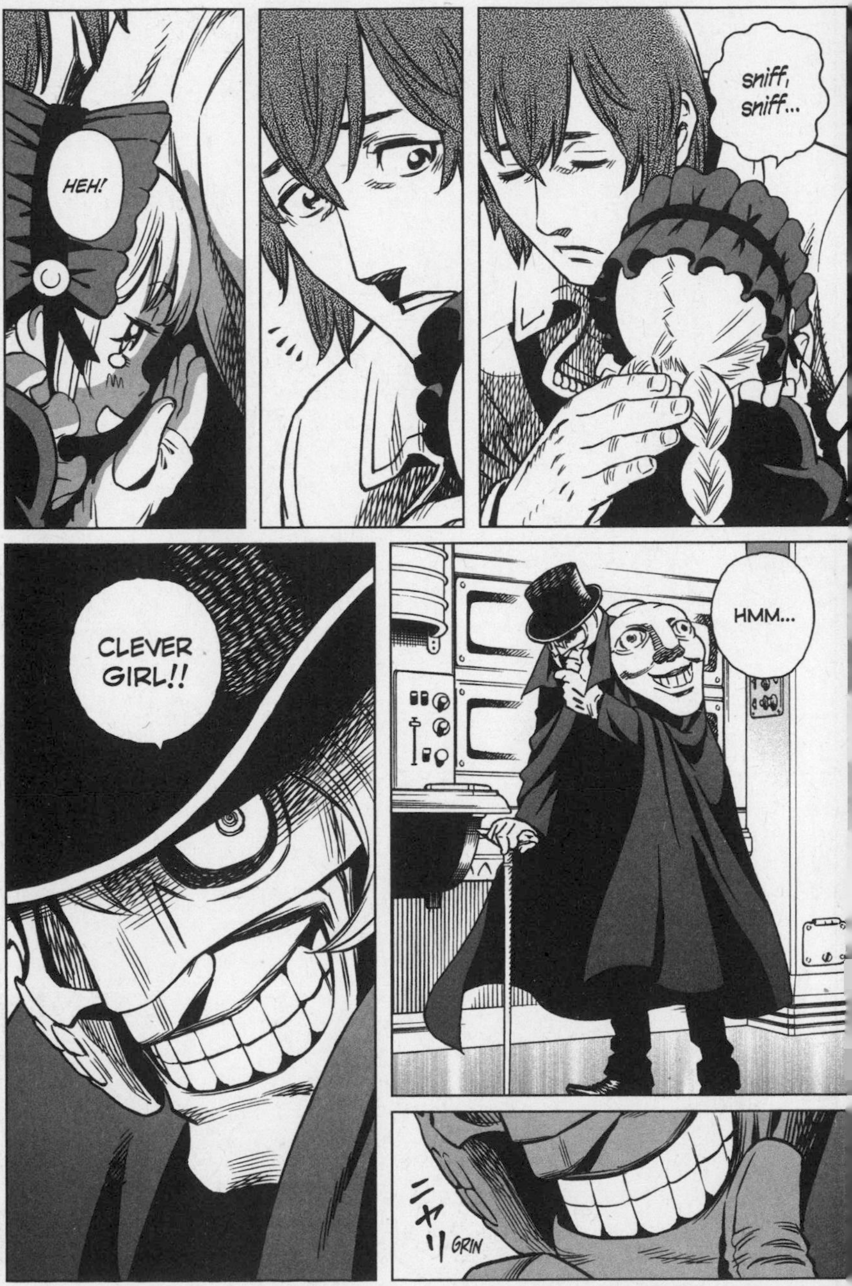
sniff, sniff...
HEH!
HMM...
ニヤリ GRIN
CLEVER GIRL!!

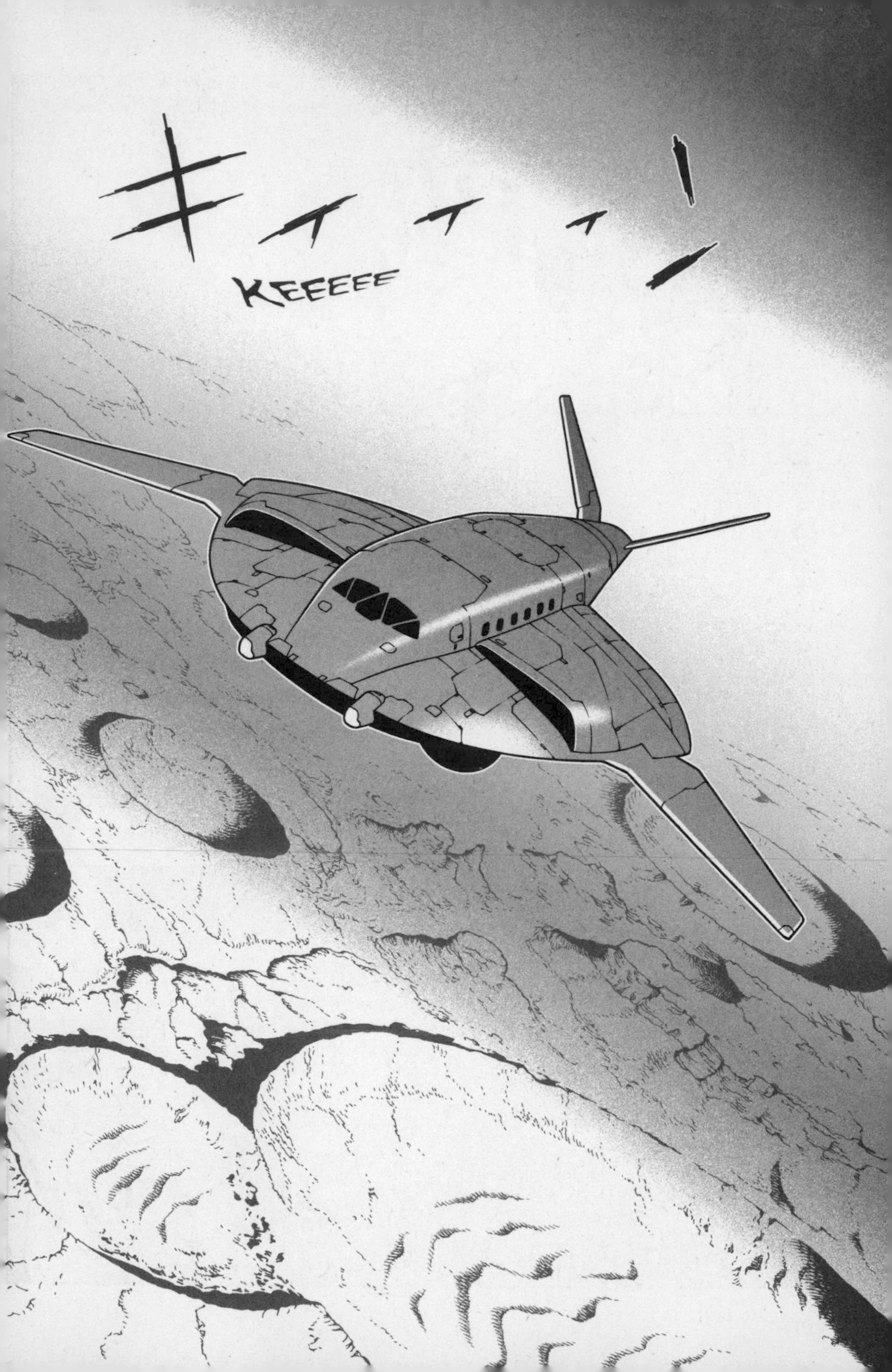
キィィィー
KEEEEEE

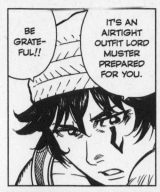

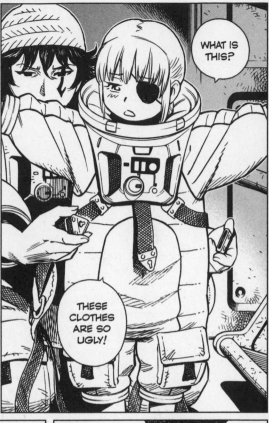

WHAT IS THIS?
THESE CLOTHES ARE SO UGLY!
IT'S AN AIRTIGHT OUTFIT LORD MUSTER PREPARED FOR YOU.
BE GRATE-FUL!!
WE'RE RUNNING A PRACTICAL TEST IN THE VOID TODAY.
VOID?
THE NATURAL, EXPOSED AREAS OF MARS WITH NO ATMOSPHERIC ENGINEERING. GOING OUT IN THAT WOULD QUICKLY KILL YOU.
THERE'S A JOB GOING ON OUT THERE, AND WE WANT YOU TO SEE IT.

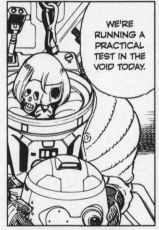

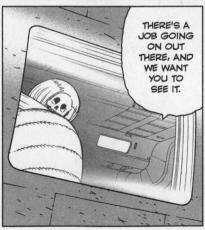

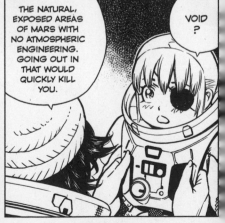

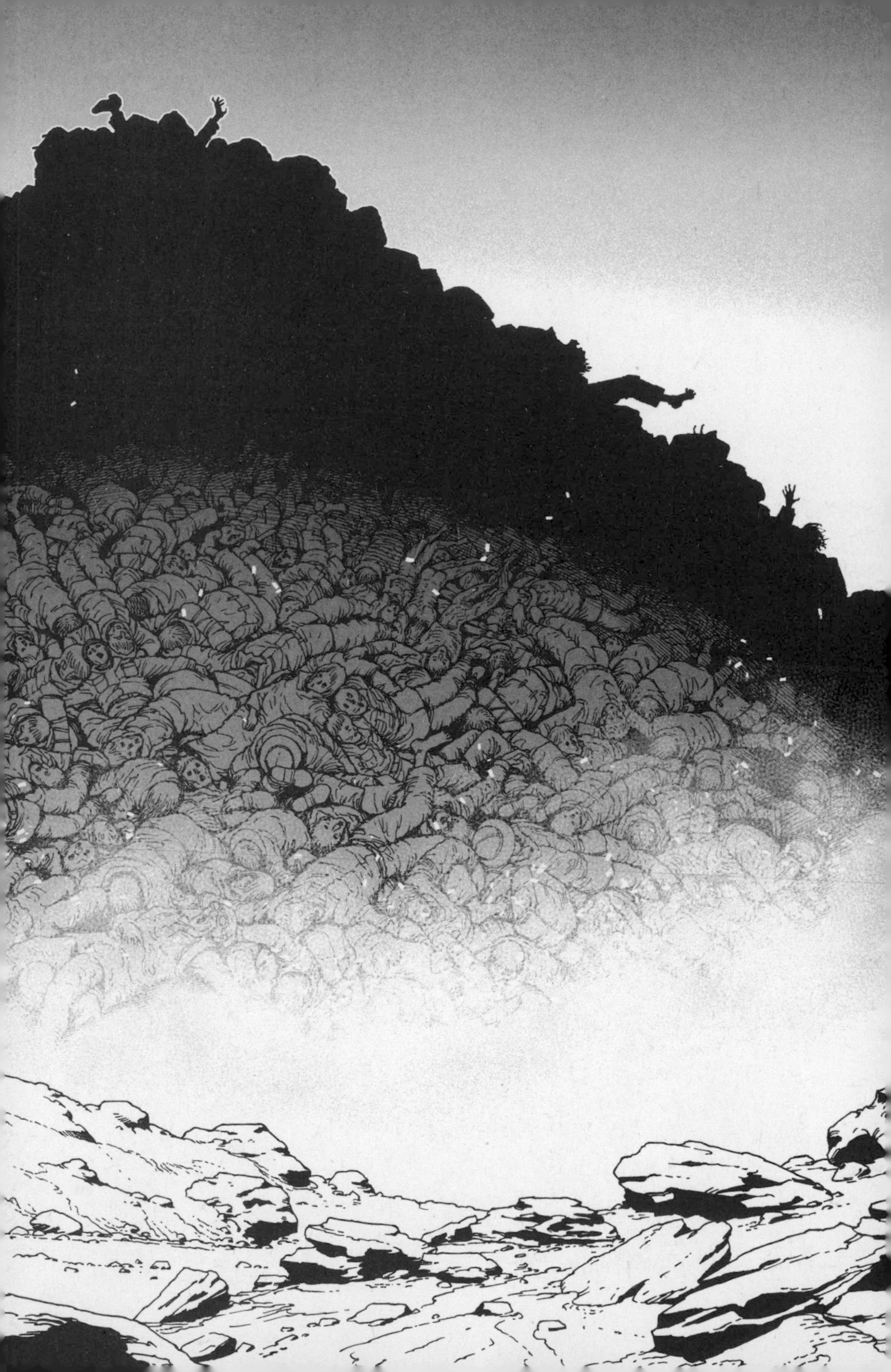

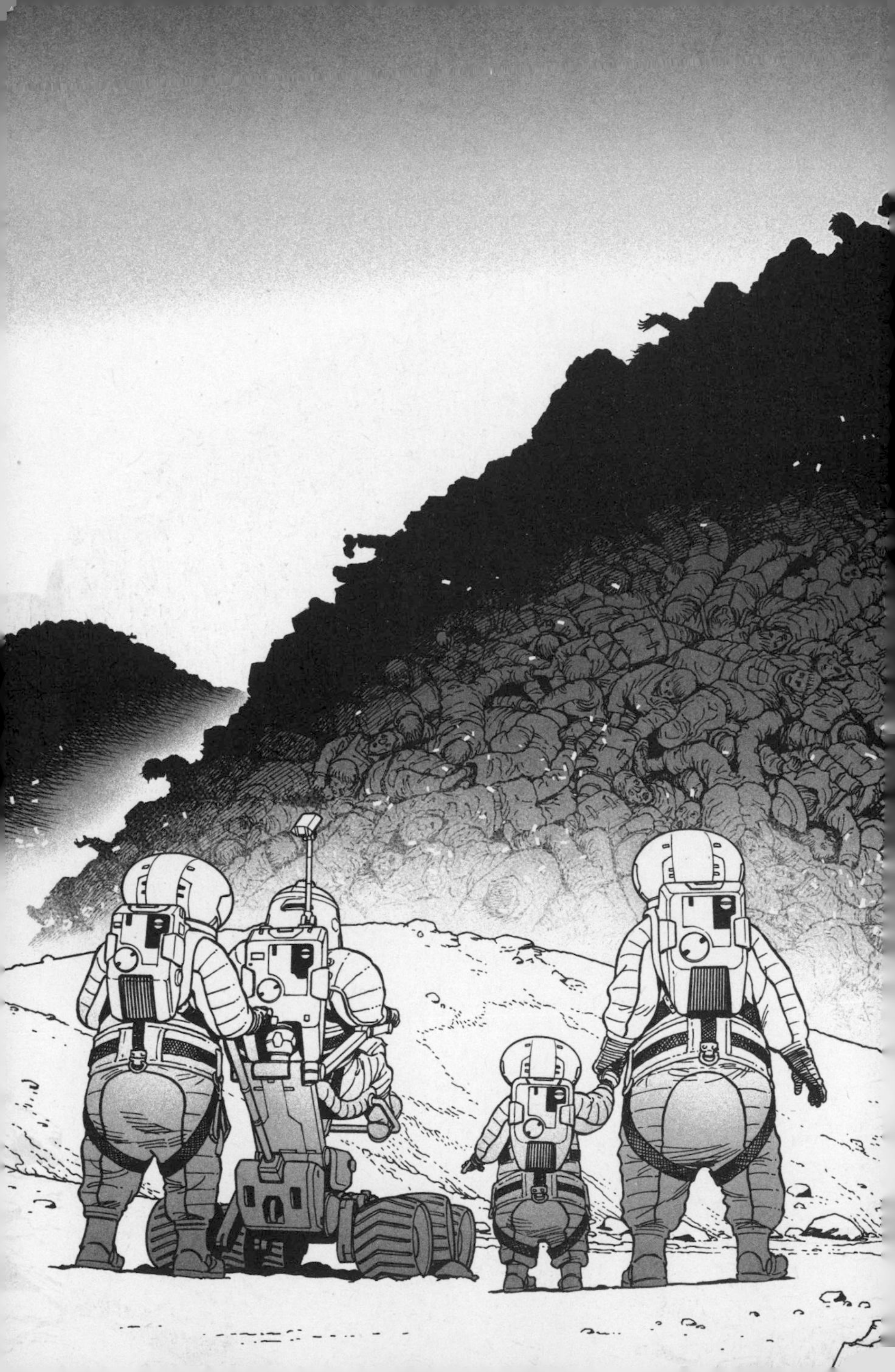

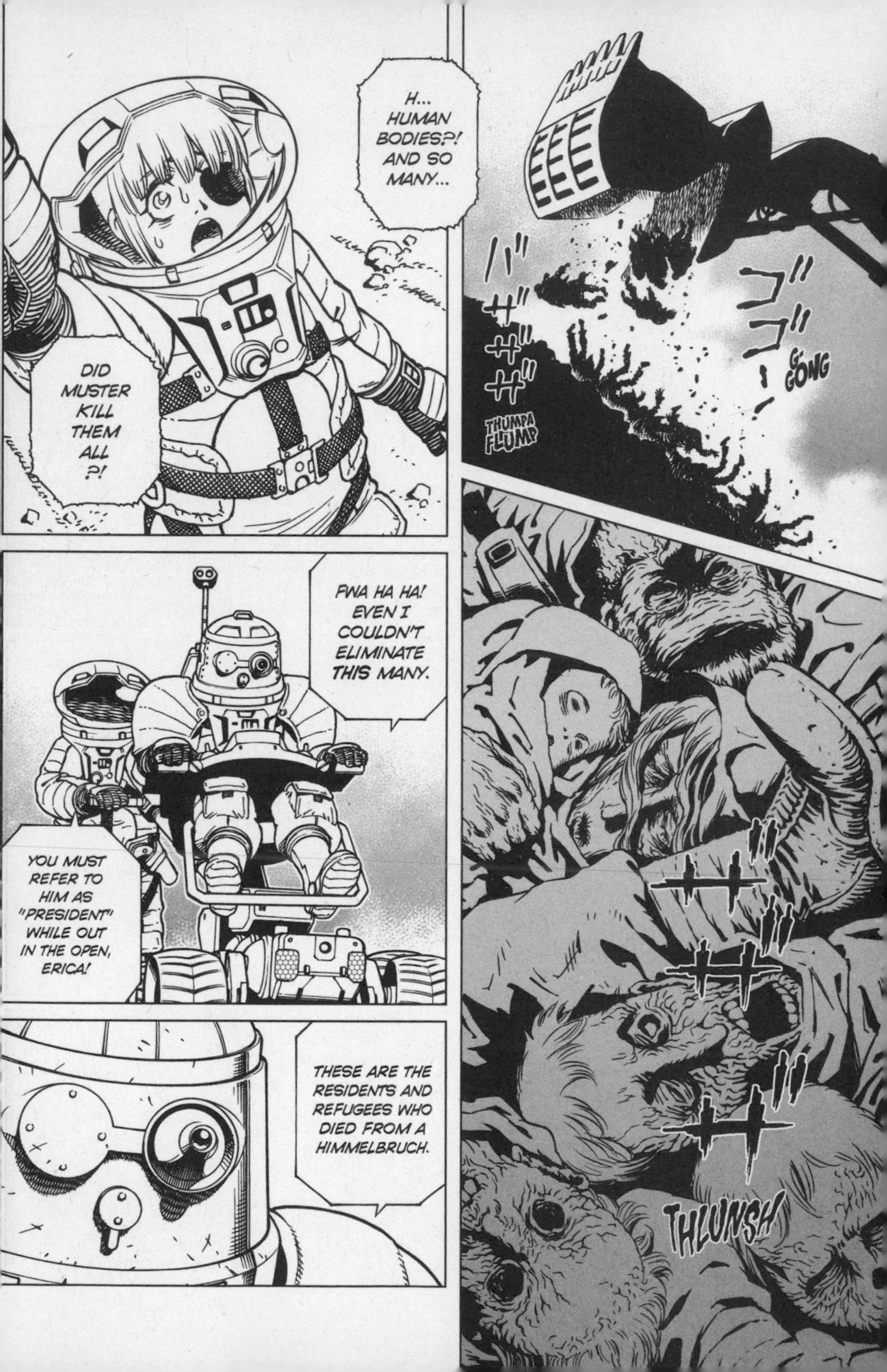
G-GONG
THUMPA FLUMP
THLUNSH
H... HUMAN BODIES?! AND SO MANY...
DID MUSTER KILL THEM ALL ?!
FWA HA HA! EVEN I COULDN'T ELIMINATE THIS MANY.
YOU MUST REFER TO HIM AS "PRESIDENT" WHILE OUT IN THE OPEN, ERICA!
THESE ARE THE RESIDENTS AND REFUGEES WHO DIED FROM A HIMMELBRUCH.

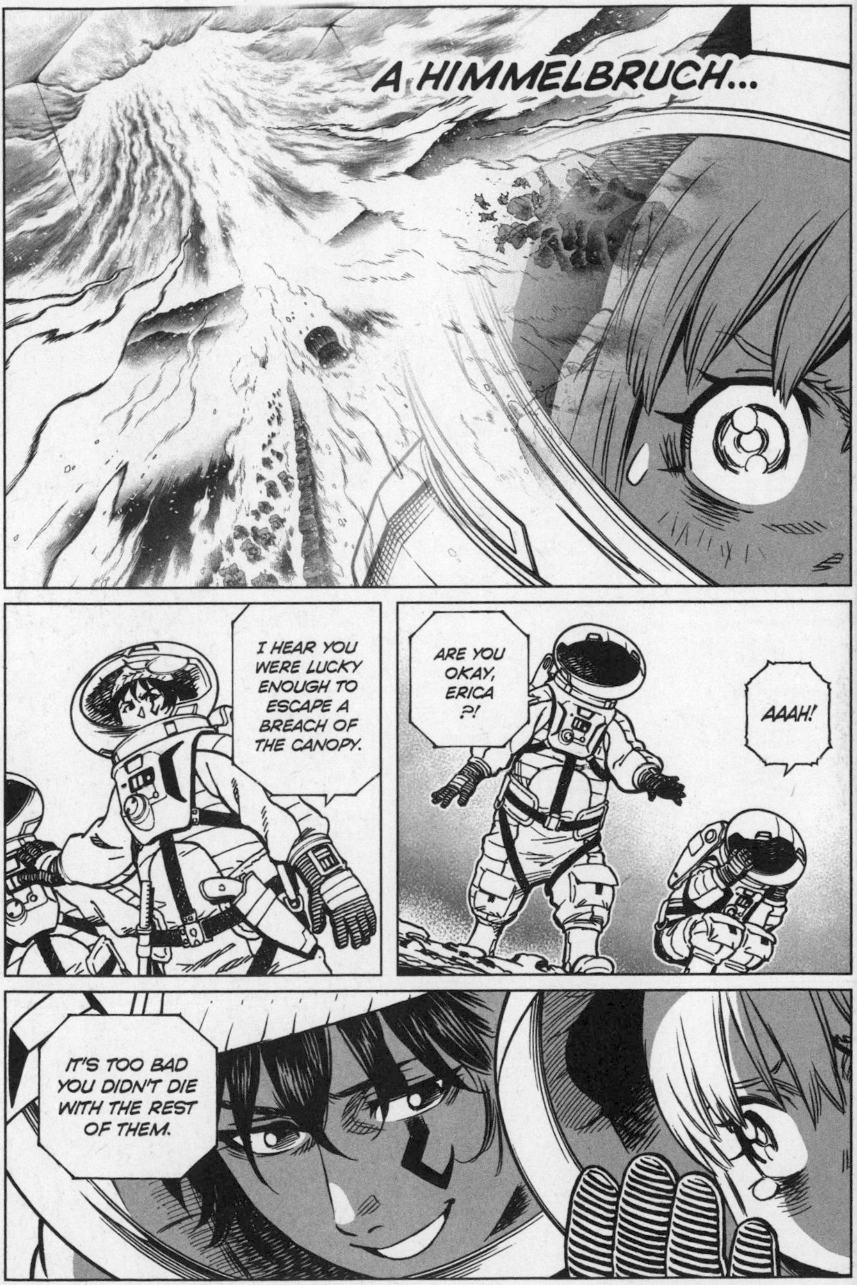
A HIMMELBRUCH...
AAAH!
ARE YOU OKAY, ERICA ?!
I HEAR YOU WERE LUCKY ENOUGH TO ESCAPE A BREACH OF THE CANOPY.
IT'S TOO BAD YOU DIDN'T DIE WITH THE REST OF THEM.

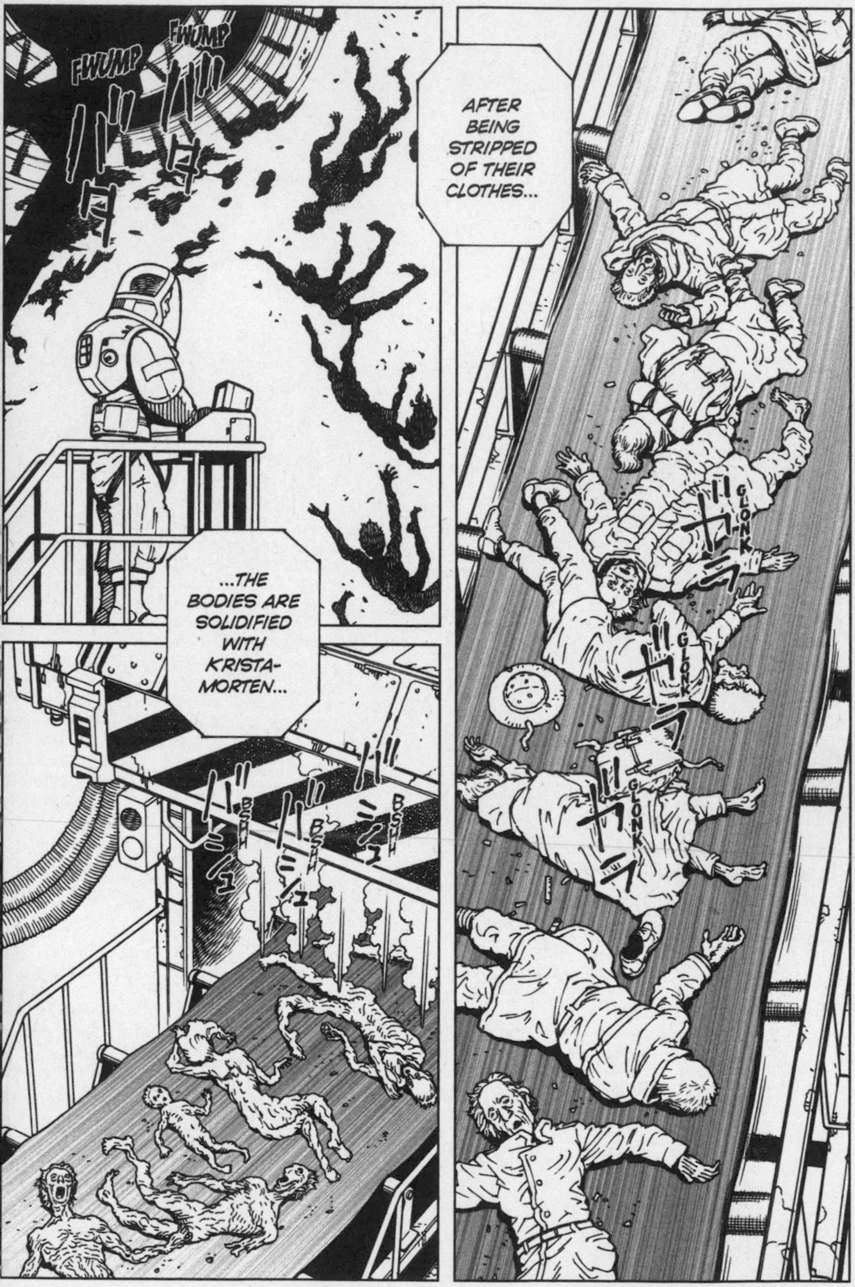
AFTER BEING STRIPPED OF THEIR CLOTHES...
GLONK
GLONK
GLONK
FWUMP
FWUMP
...THE BODIES ARE SOLIDIFIED WITH KRISTA-MORTEN...
BSHH
BSHH
BSHH

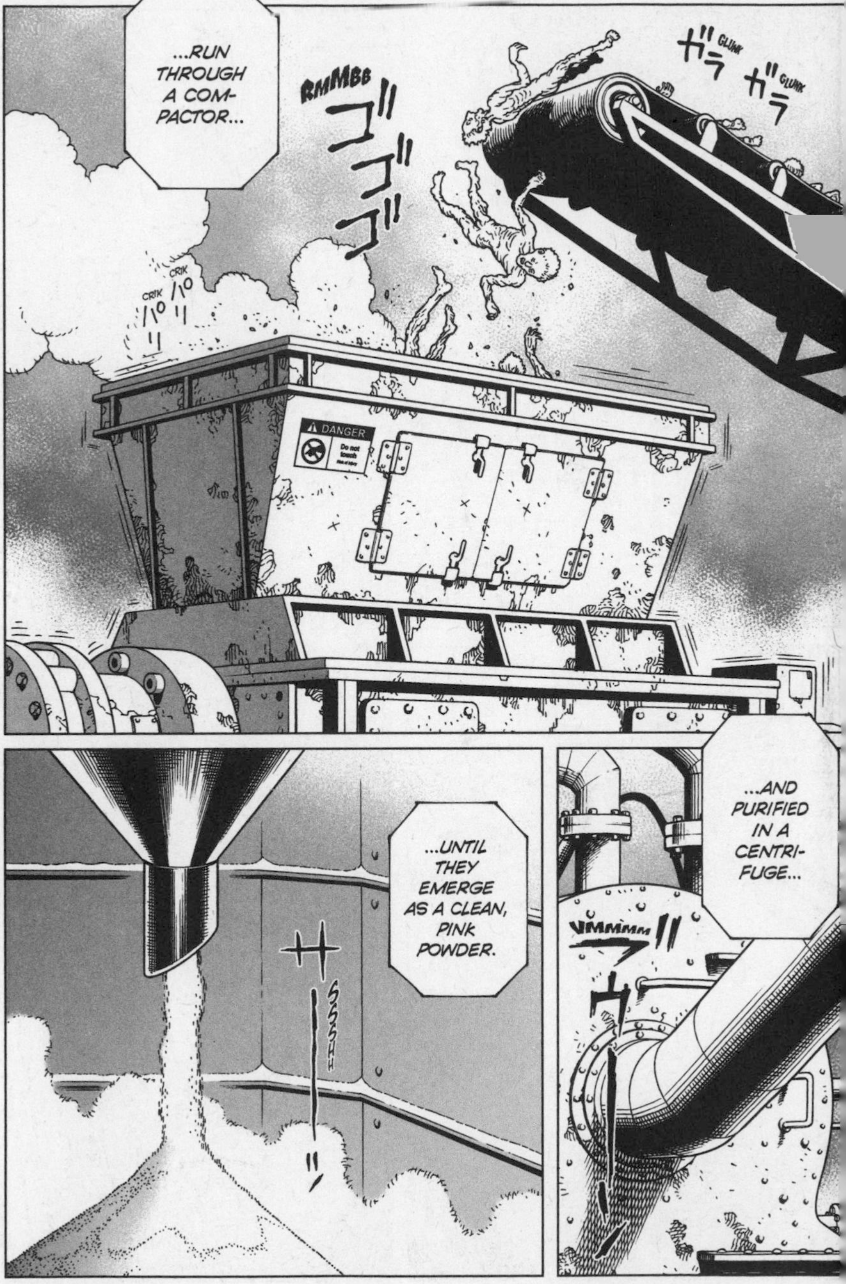
GLUNK ガラ
GLUNK ガラ
...RUN THROUGH A COMPACTOR...
RMMBB ゴゴゴ
CRIK パリ
CRIK パリ
DANGER
Do not touch
...AND PURIFIED IN A CENTRIFUGE...
VMMMMM ウ
...UNTIL THEY EMERGE AS A CLEAN, PINK POWDER.
サ SSSSHH

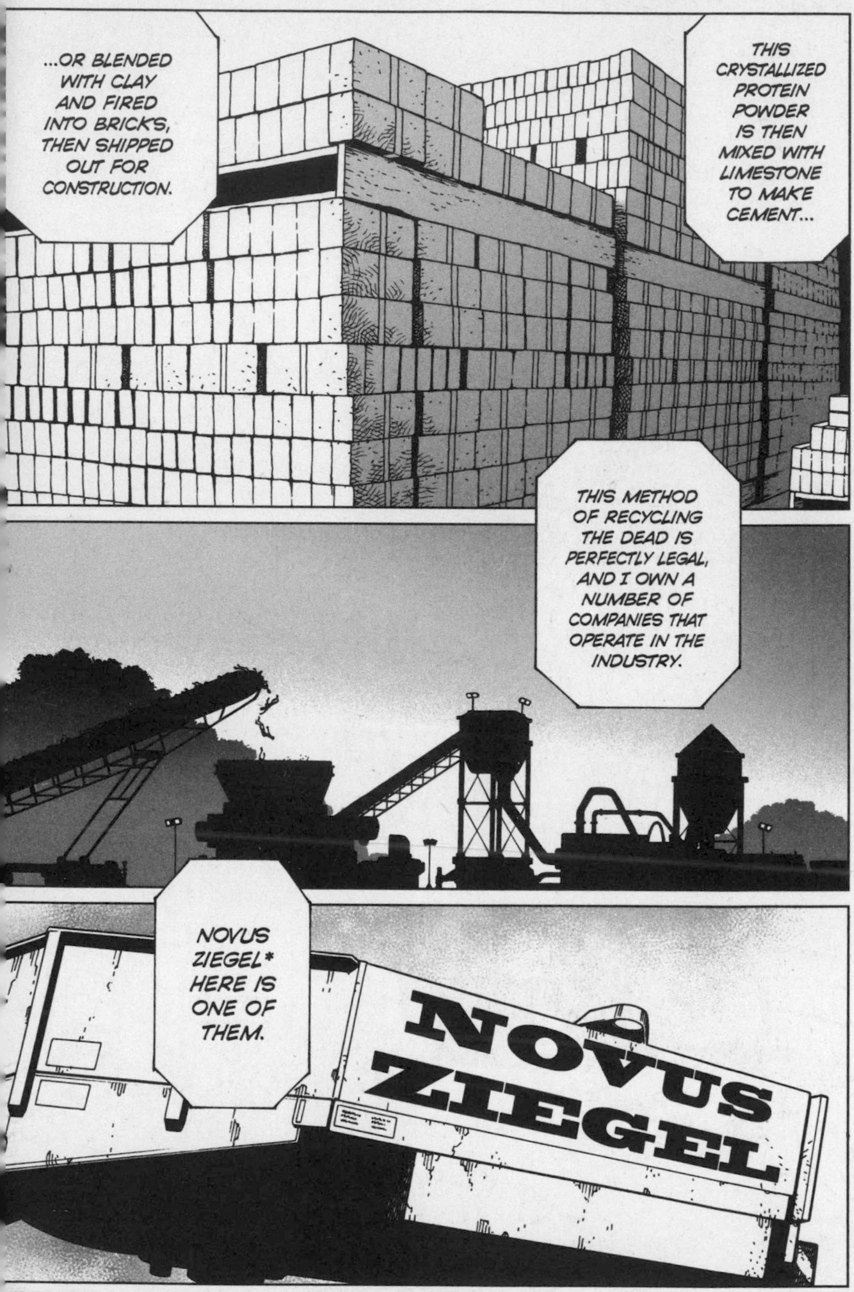
THIS CRYSTALLIZED PROTEIN POWDER IS THEN MIXED WITH LIMESTONE TO MAKE CEMENT...
...OR BLENDED WITH CLAY AND FIRED INTO BRICKS, THEN SHIPPED OUT FOR CONSTRUCTION.
THIS METHOD OF RECYCLING THE DEAD IS PERFECTLY LEGAL, AND I OWN A NUMBER OF COMPANIES THAT OPERATE IN THE INDUSTRY.
NOVUS ZIEGEL* HERE IS ONE OF THEM.
NOVUS ZIEGEL

NOVUS ZIEGEL: A combination of the Latin word for "new" and the German word for "bricks."

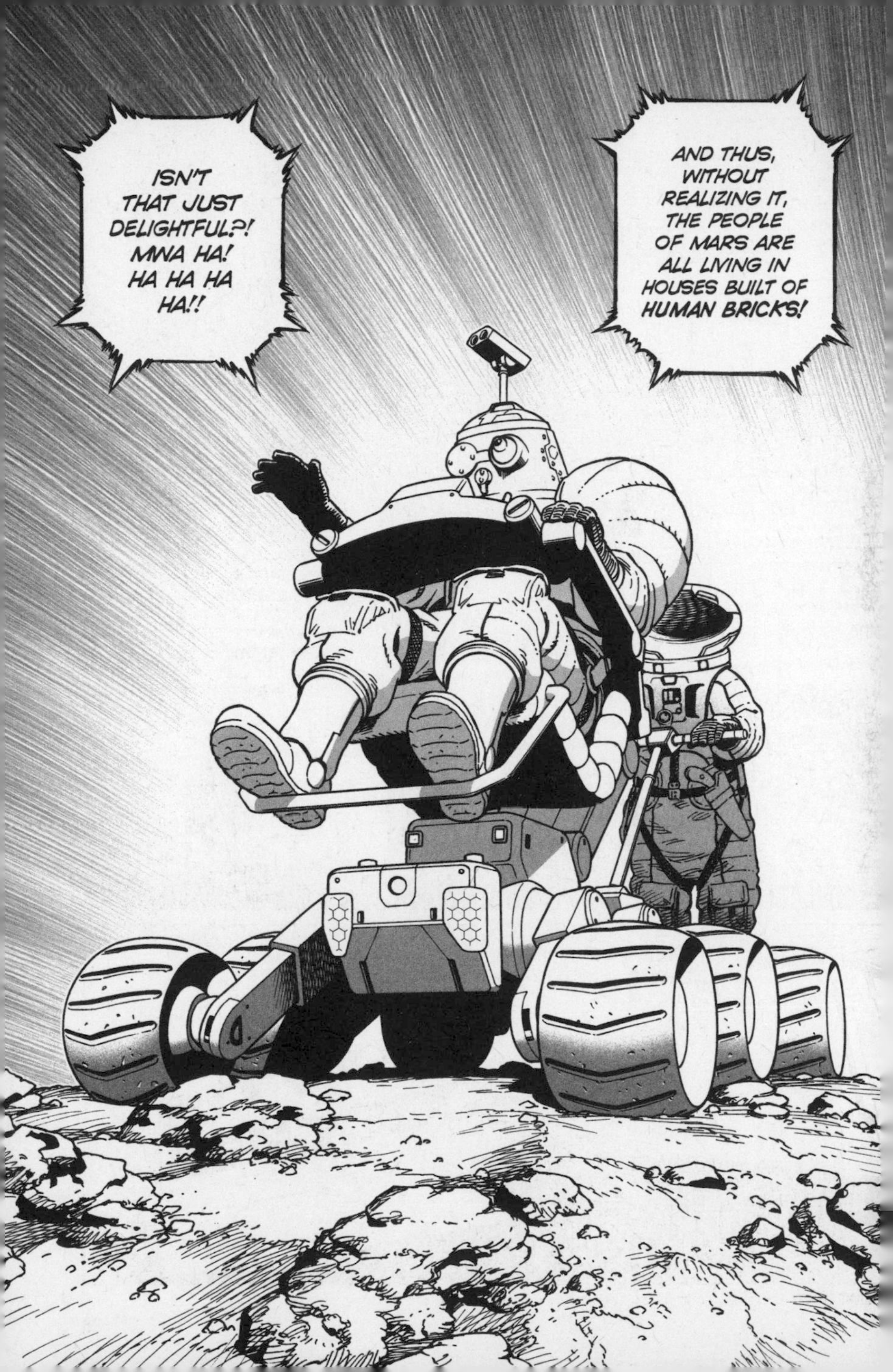
AND THUS, WITHOUT REALIZING IT, THE PEOPLE OF MARS ARE ALL LIVING IN HOUSES BUILT OF HUMAN BRICKS!
ISN'T THAT JUST DELIGHTFUL?! MWA HA! HA HA HA HA!!

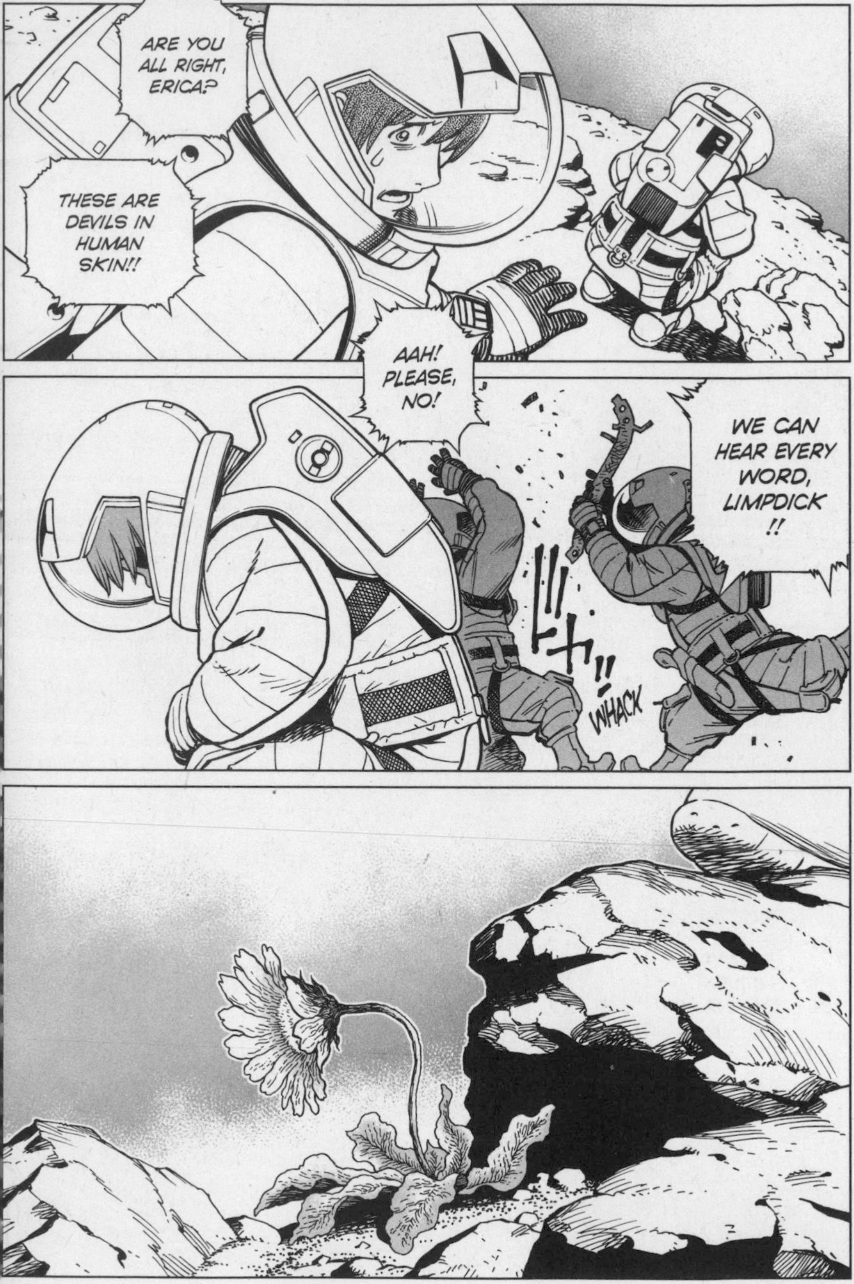
ARE YOU ALL RIGHT, ERICA?
THESE ARE DEVILS IN HUMAN SKIN!!
WE CAN HEAR EVERY WORD, LIMPDICK !!
AAH! PLEASE, NO!
WHACK

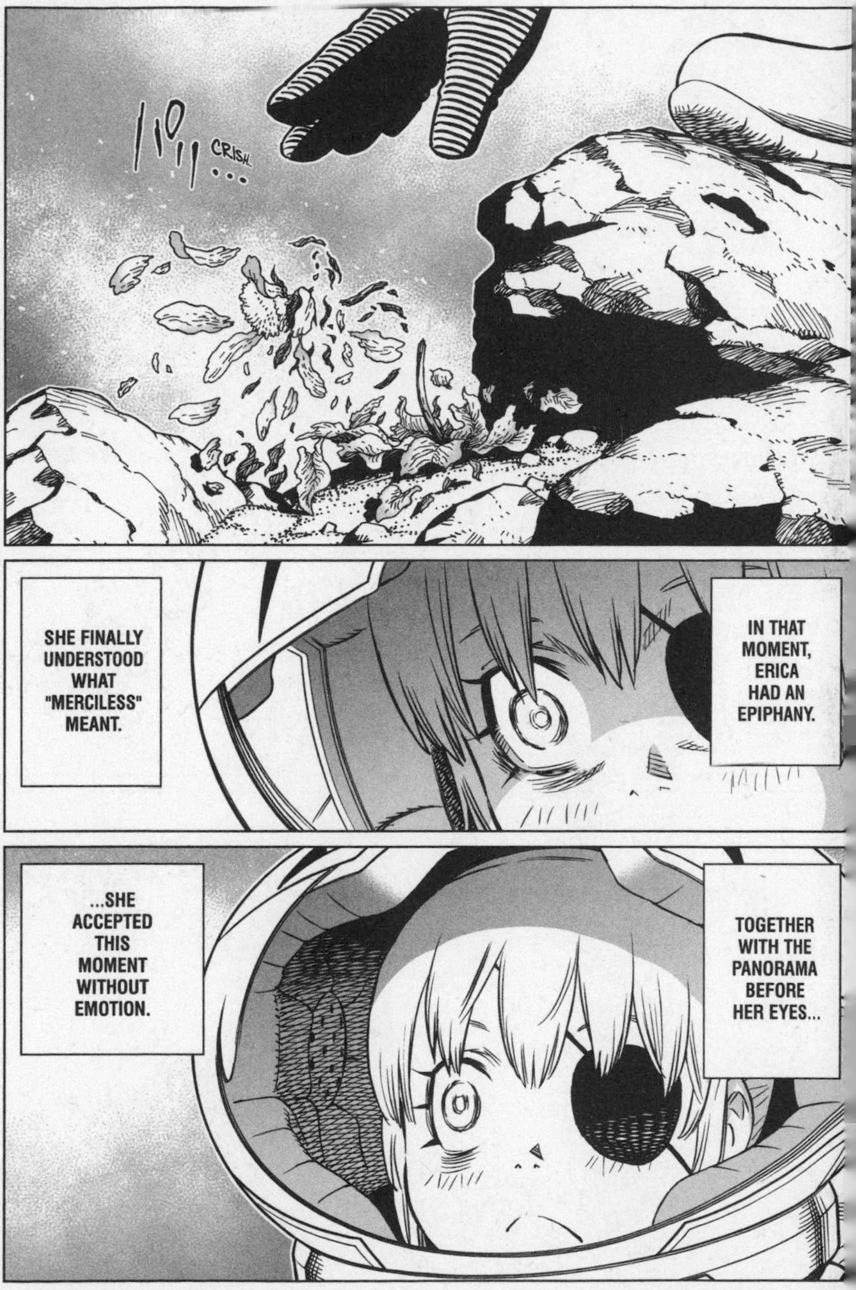
CRISH...
IN THAT MOMENT, ERICA HAD AN EPIPHANY.
SHE FINALLY UNDERSTOOD WHAT "MERCILESS" MEANT.
TOGETHER WITH THE PANORAMA BEFORE HER EYES...
...SHE ACCEPTED THIS MOMENT WITHOUT EMOTION.

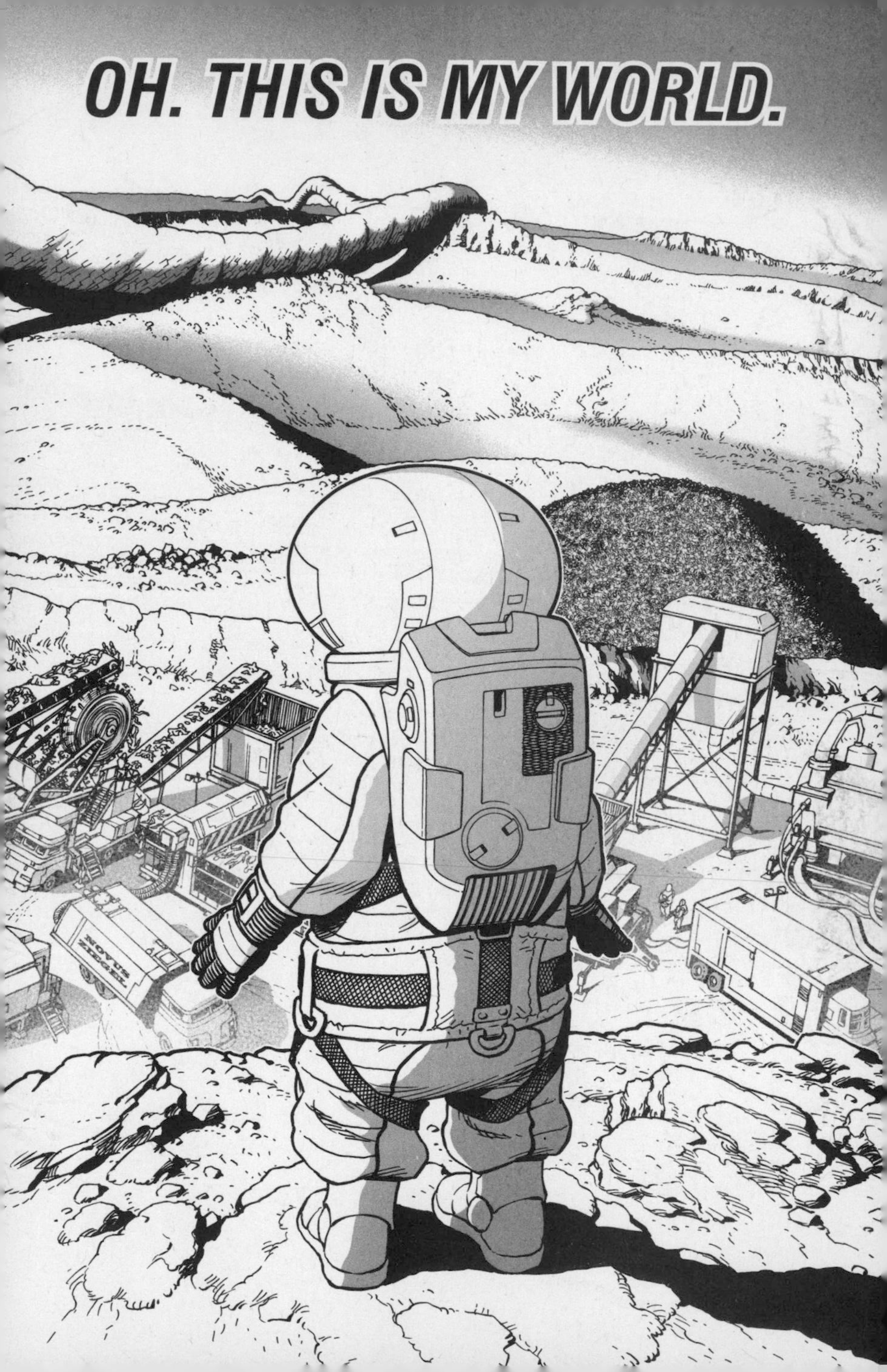
OH. THIS IS MY WORLD.
NOVUS ZIEGEL

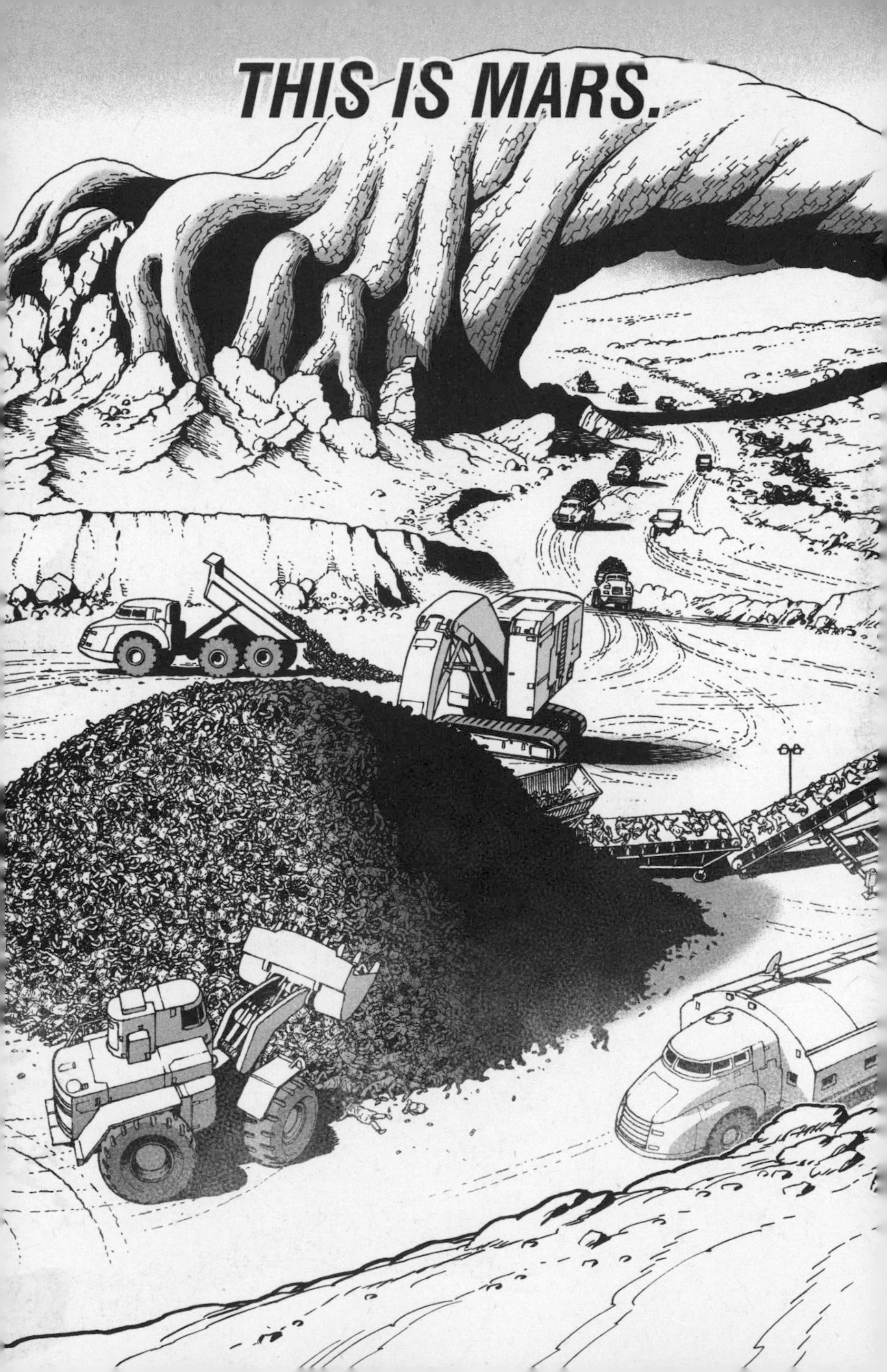
THIS IS MARS.

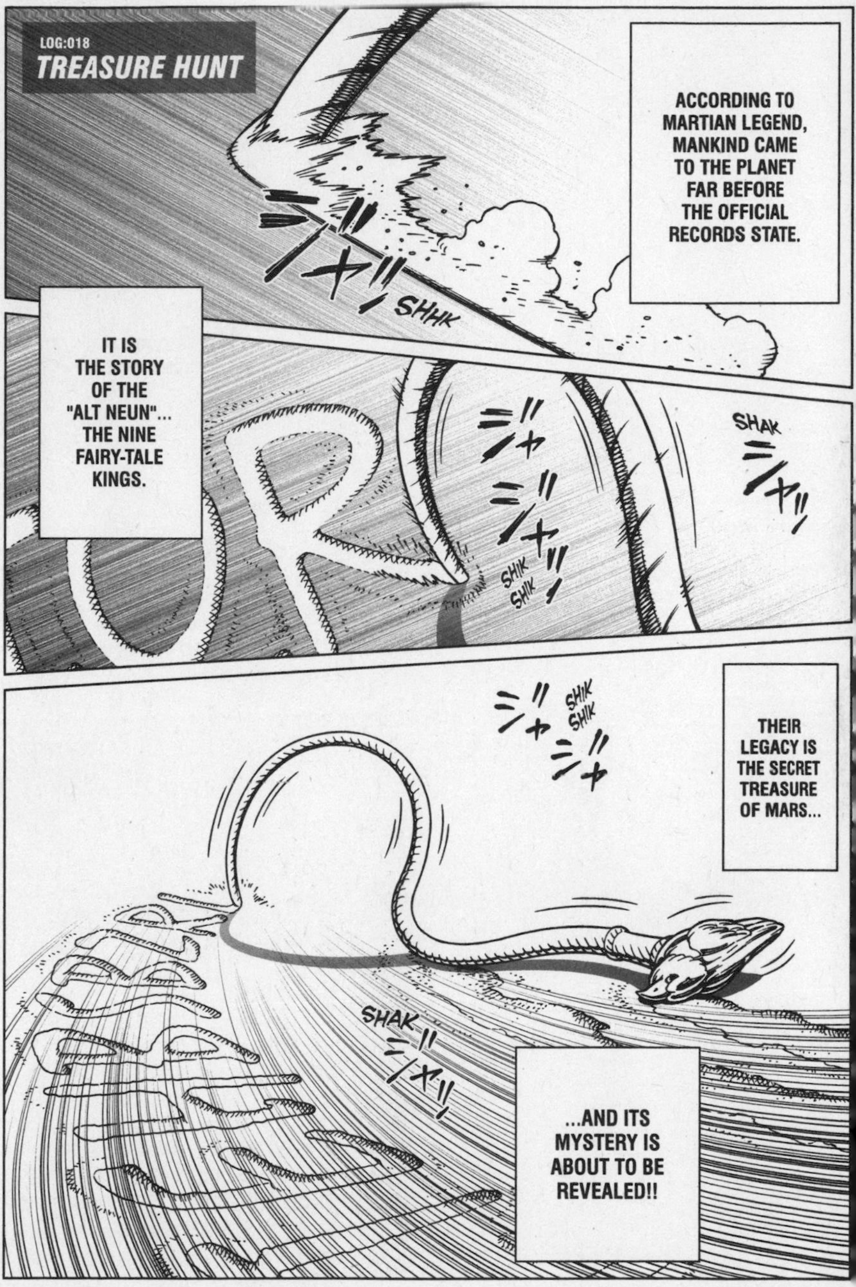

ACCORDING TO MARTIAN LEGEND, MANKIND CAME TO THE PLANET FAR BEFORE THE OFFICIAL RECORDS STATE.
LOG:018
TREASURE HUNT
SHHK
SHAK
SHIK SHIK
IT IS THE STORY OF THE "ALT NEUN"... THE NINE FAIRY-TALE KINGS.
THEIR LEGACY IS THE SECRET TREASURE OF MARS...
SHIK SHIK
SHAK
...AND ITS MYSTERY IS ABOUT TO BE REVEALED!!

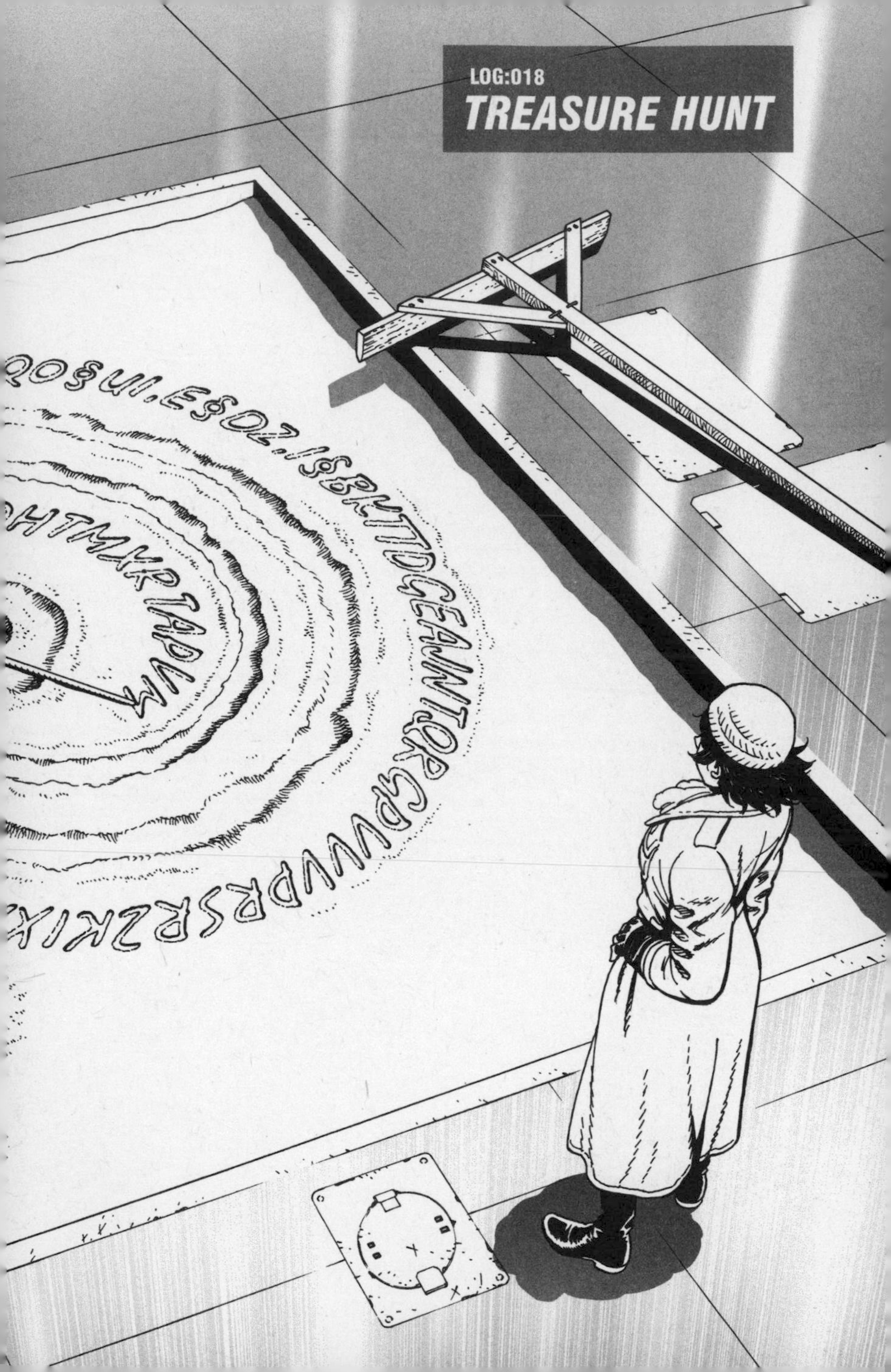
LOG:018
TREASURE HUNT

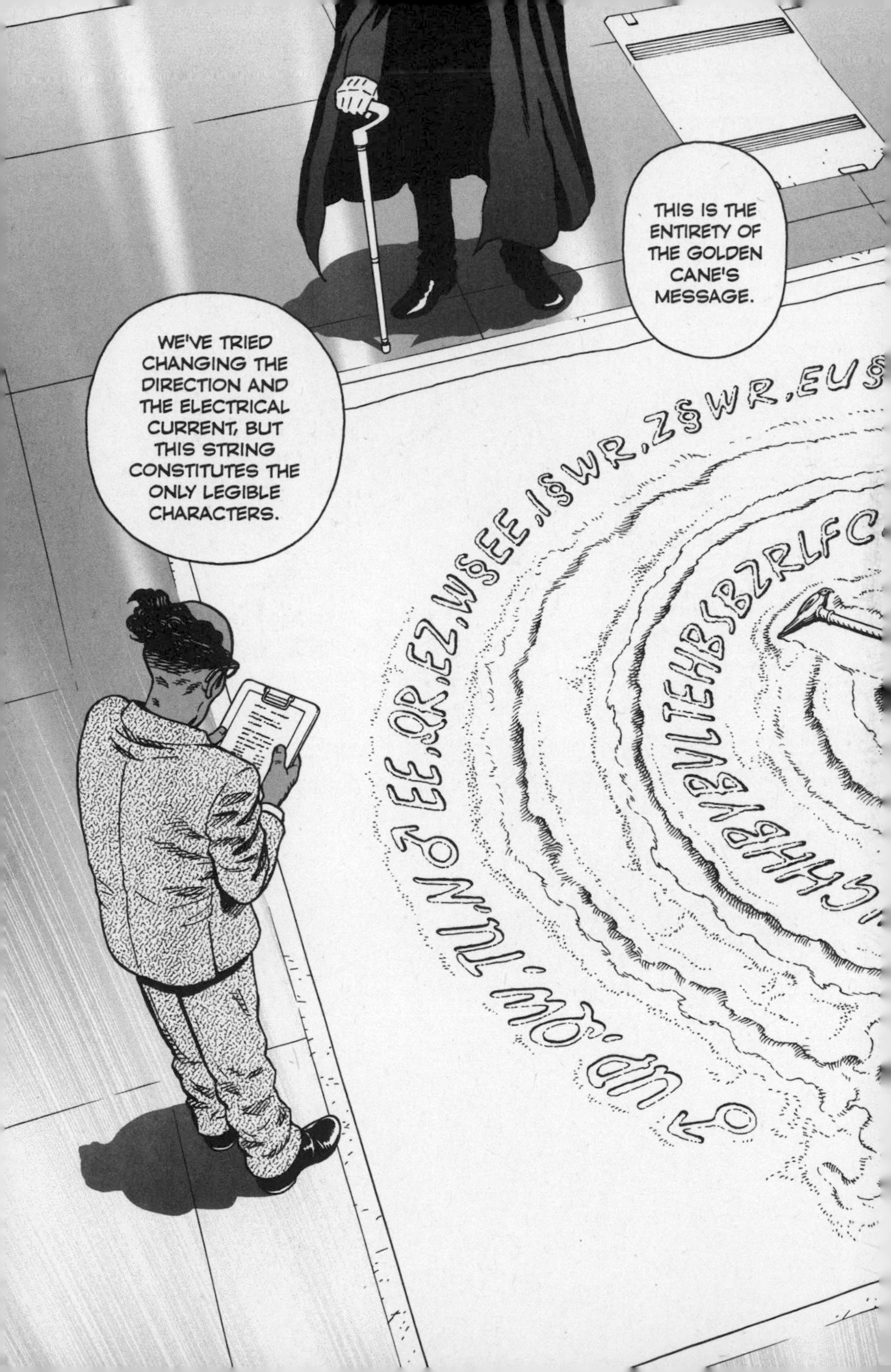
THIS IS THE ENTIRETY OF THE GOLDEN CANE'S MESSAGE.
WE'VE TRIED CHANGING THE DIRECTION AND THE ELECTRICAL CURRENT, BUT THIS STRING CONSTITUTES THE ONLY LEGIBLE CHARACTERS.

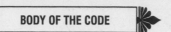

BODY OF THE CODE

♂UP,QW,TU,N♂EE,QR,EZ,W§EE,I§WR,Z§WR,EU

§IE,QO§UI,E§OZ,I§BKTTDGEAJNTQRGPVVVPRSRZ

KIXAWGHHBYBVLTEHBSBZRLFCLHPHTMXRTAPVM

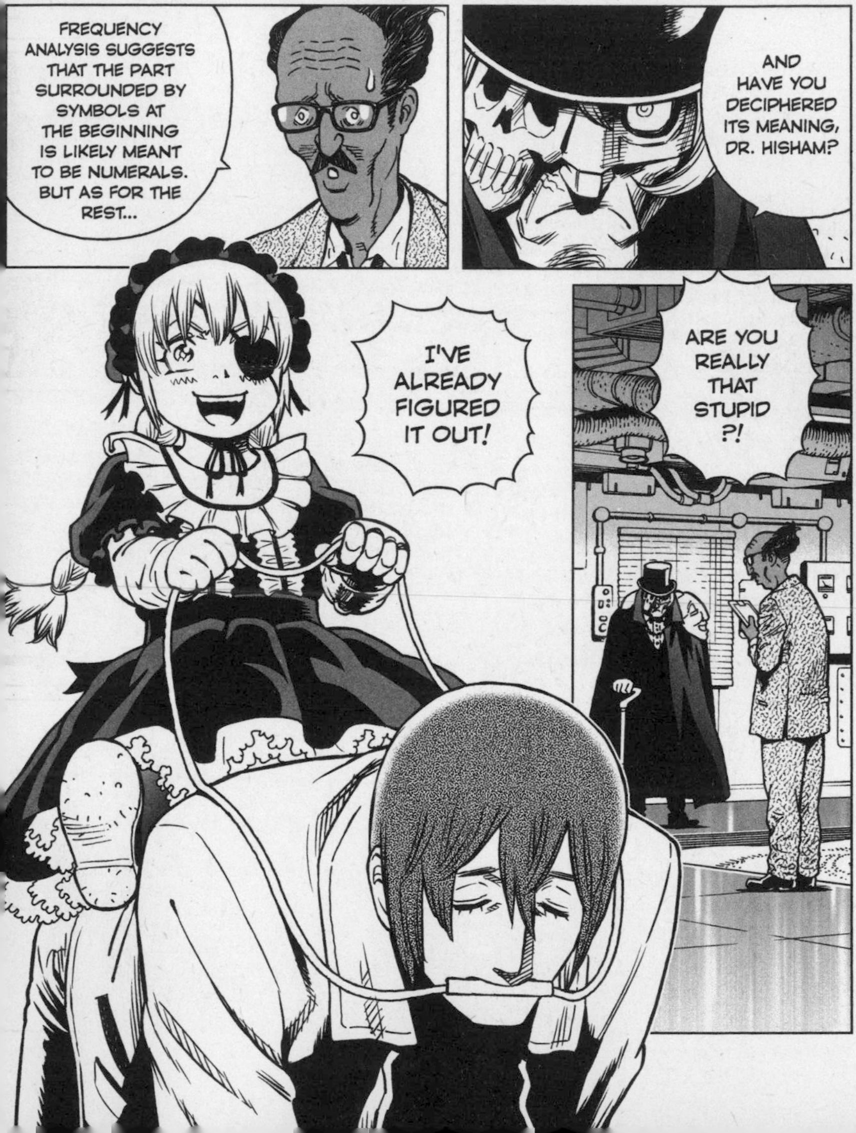
AND HAVE YOU DECIPHERED ITS MEANING, DR. HISHAM?
FREQUENCY ANALYSIS SUGGESTS THAT THE PART SURROUNDED BY SYMBOLS AT THE BEGINNING IS LIKELY MEANT TO BE NUMERALS. BUT AS FOR THE REST...
ARE YOU REALLY THAT STUPID?!
I'VE ALREADY FIGURED IT OUT!

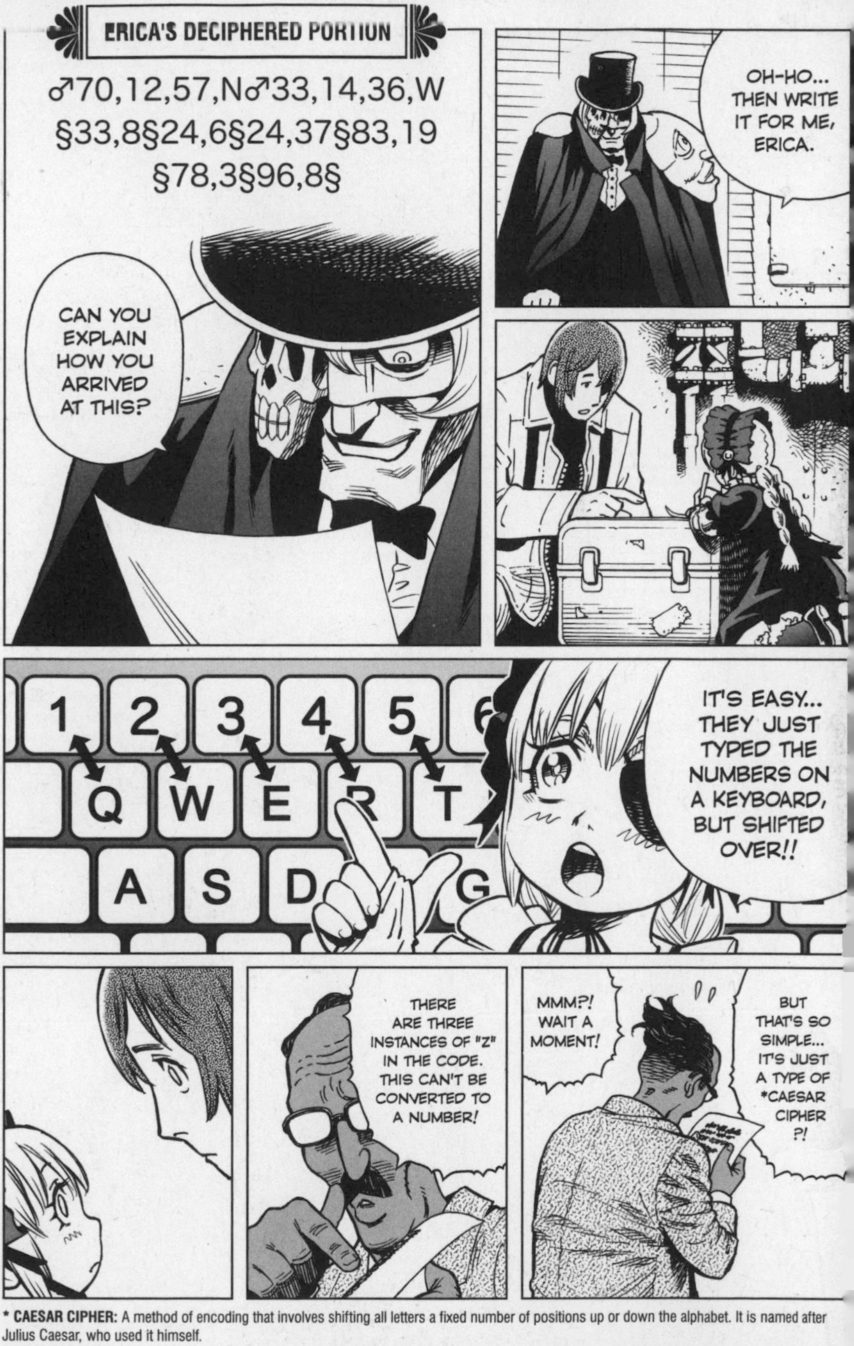
OH-HO... THEN WRITE IT FOR ME, ERICA.
ERICA'S DECIPHERED PORTION
♂70,12,57,N♂33,14,36,W
§33,8§24,6§24,37§83,19
§78,3§96,8§
CAN YOU EXPLAIN HOW YOU ARRIVED AT THIS?
IT'S EASY... THEY JUST TYPED THE NUMBERS ON A KEYBOARD, BUT SHIFTED OVER!!
1 2 3 4 5
Q W E R T
A S D G
BUT THAT'S SO SIMPLE... IT'S JUST A TYPE OF *CAESAR CIPHER ?!
MMM?! WAIT A MOMENT!
THERE ARE THREE INSTANCES OF "Z" IN THE CODE. THIS CAN'T BE CONVERTED TO A NUMBER!

*** CAESAR CIPHER:** A method of encoding that involves shifting all letters a fixed number of positions up or down the alphabet. It is named after Julius Caesar, who used it himself.

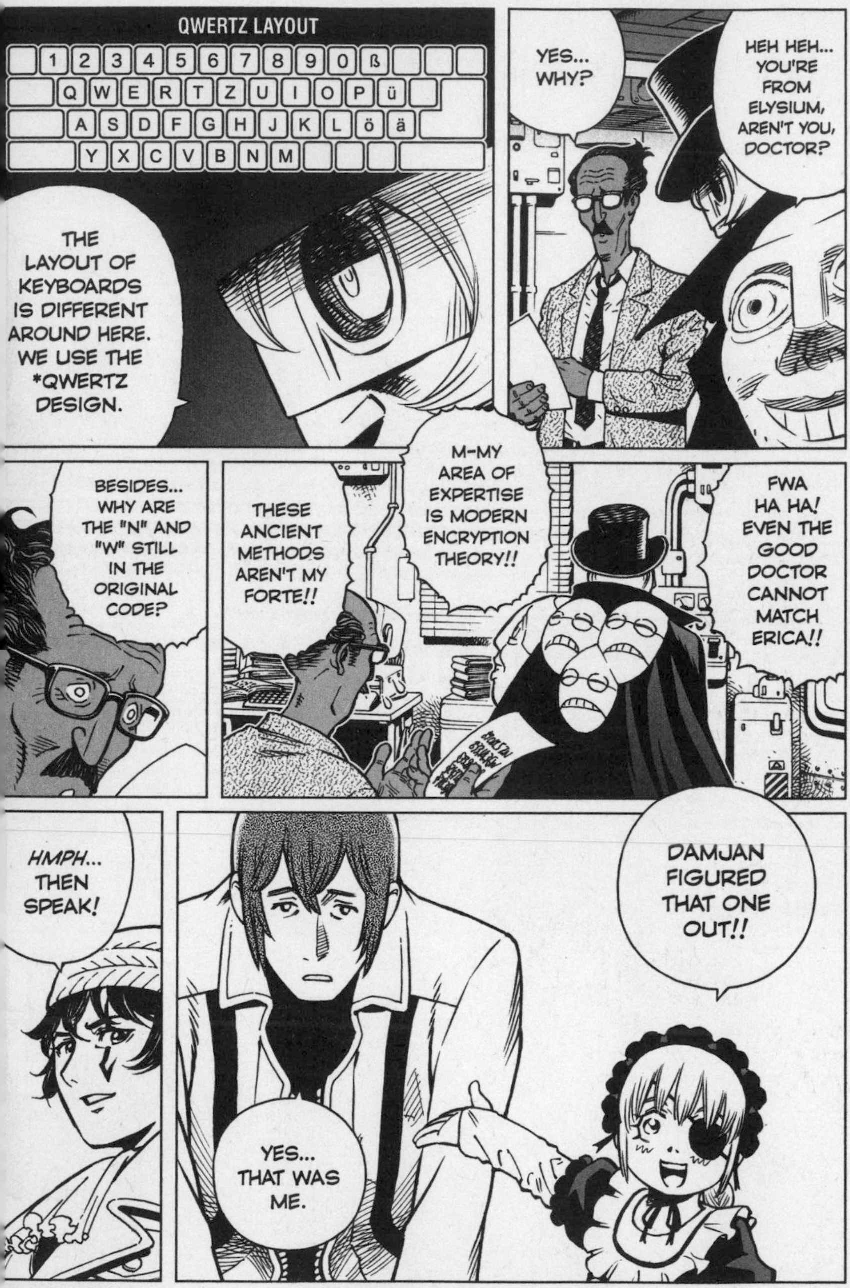
HEH HEH... YOU'RE FROM ELYSIUM, AREN'T YOU, DOCTOR?
YES... WHY?
QWERTZ LAYOUT
1 2 3 4 5 6 7 8 9 0 ß
Q W E R T Z U I O P ü
A S D F G H J K L ö ä
Y X C V B N M
THE LAYOUT OF KEYBOARDS IS DIFFERENT AROUND HERE. WE USE THE *QWERTZ DESIGN.
FWA HA HA! EVEN THE GOOD DOCTOR CANNOT MATCH ERICA!!
M-MY AREA OF EXPERTISE IS MODERN ENCRYPTION THEORY!!
THESE ANCIENT METHODS AREN'T MY FORTE!!
BESIDES... WHY ARE THE "N" AND "W" STILL IN THE ORIGINAL CODE?
DAMJAN FIGURED THAT ONE OUT!!
YES... THAT WAS ME.
HMPH... THEN SPEAK!

QWERTZ LAYOUT: A keyboard layout used widely in German-speaking areas. Because German uses "Z" so often, it switches places with the "Y" key.

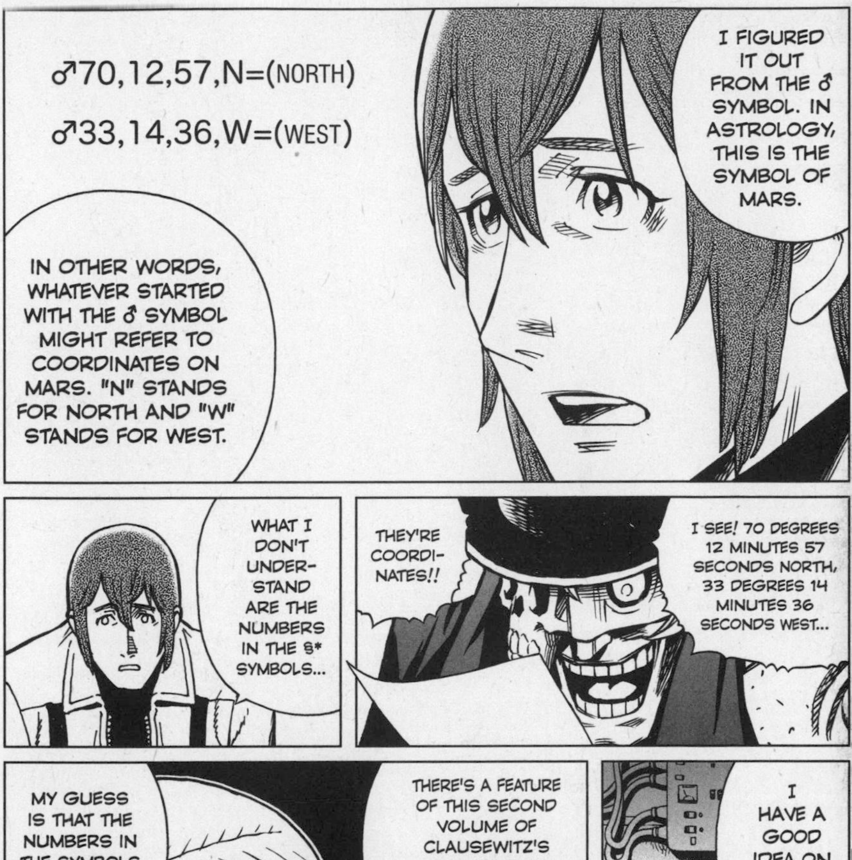
I FIGURED IT OUT FROM THE ♂ SYMBOL. IN ASTROLOGY, THIS IS THE SYMBOL OF MARS.
♂70,12,57,N=(NORTH)
♂33,14,36,W=(WEST)
IN OTHER WORDS, WHATEVER STARTED WITH THE ♂ SYMBOL MIGHT REFER TO COORDINATES ON MARS. "N" STANDS FOR NORTH AND "W" STANDS FOR WEST.
I SEE! 70 DEGREES 12 MINUTES 57 SECONDS NORTH, 33 DEGREES 14 MINUTES 36 SECONDS WEST...
THEY'RE COORDINATES!!
WHAT I DON'T UNDERSTAND ARE THE NUMBERS IN THE §* SYMBOLS...
I HAVE A GOOD IDEA ON THAT ONE.
THERE'S A FEATURE OF THIS SECOND VOLUME OF CLAUSEWITZ'S *ON WAR* THAT OTHER EDITIONS DON'T HAVE... THE LIBERAL USE OF § SYMBOLS.
MY GUESS IS THAT THE NUMBERS IN THE SYMBOLS REFER TO SOMETHING IN THIS BOOK.
Vom Kriege.
Zwei

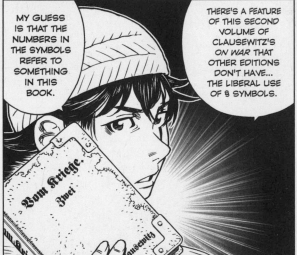

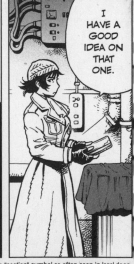

***§**: This is the "section" symbol as often seen in legal docs.

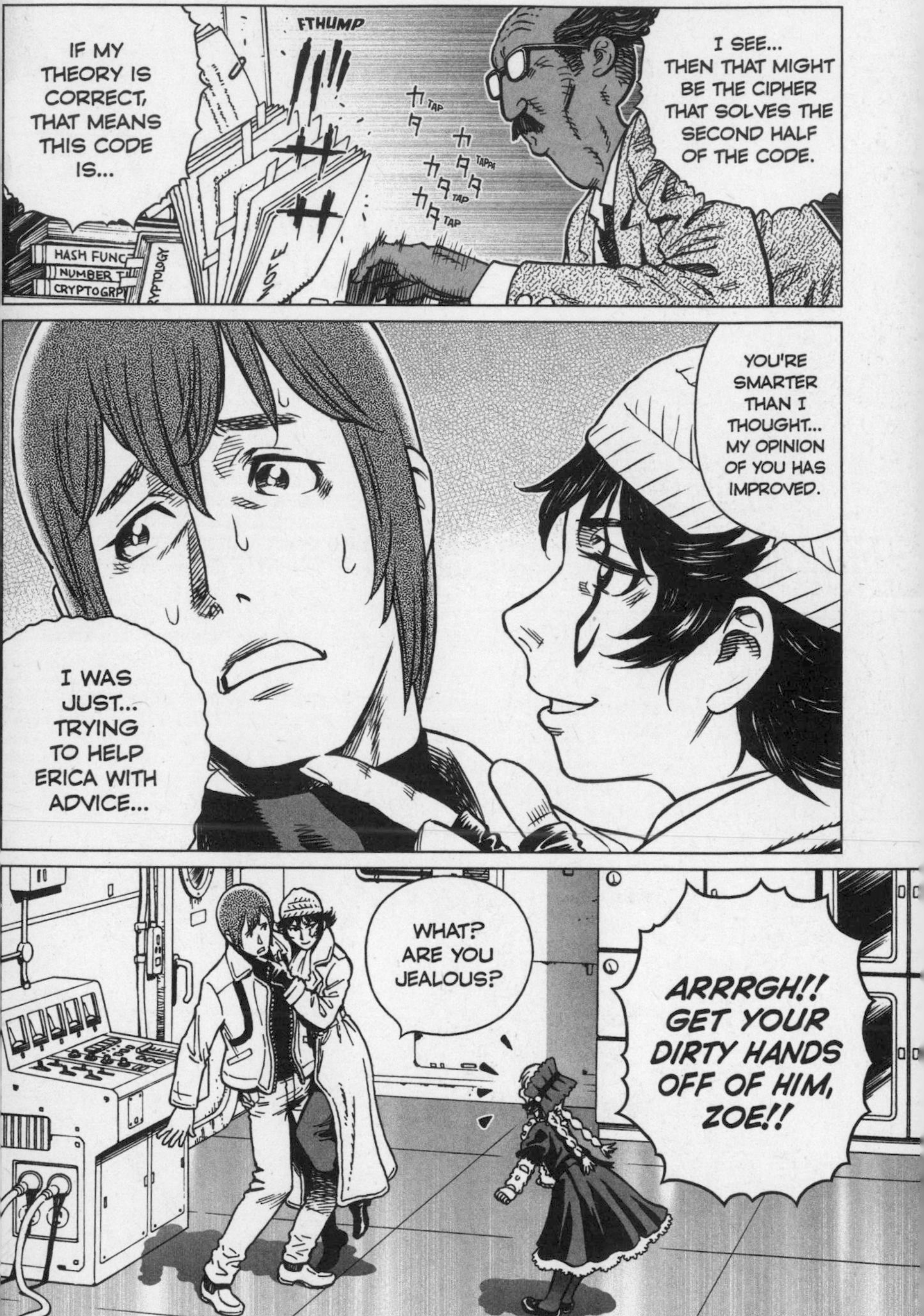
I SEE... THEN THAT MIGHT BE THE CIPHER THAT SOLVES THE SECOND HALF OF THE CODE.
FTHUMP
TAP
TAPPA
TAP
TAP
IF MY THEORY IS CORRECT, THAT MEANS THIS CODE IS...
HASH FUNC
NUMBER T
CRYPTOGRPY
YOU'RE SMARTER THAN I THOUGHT... MY OPINION OF YOU HAS IMPROVED.
I WAS JUST... TRYING TO HELP ERICA WITH ADVICE...
ARRRGH!! GET YOUR DIRTY HANDS OFF OF HIM, ZOE!!
WHAT? ARE YOU JEALOUS?

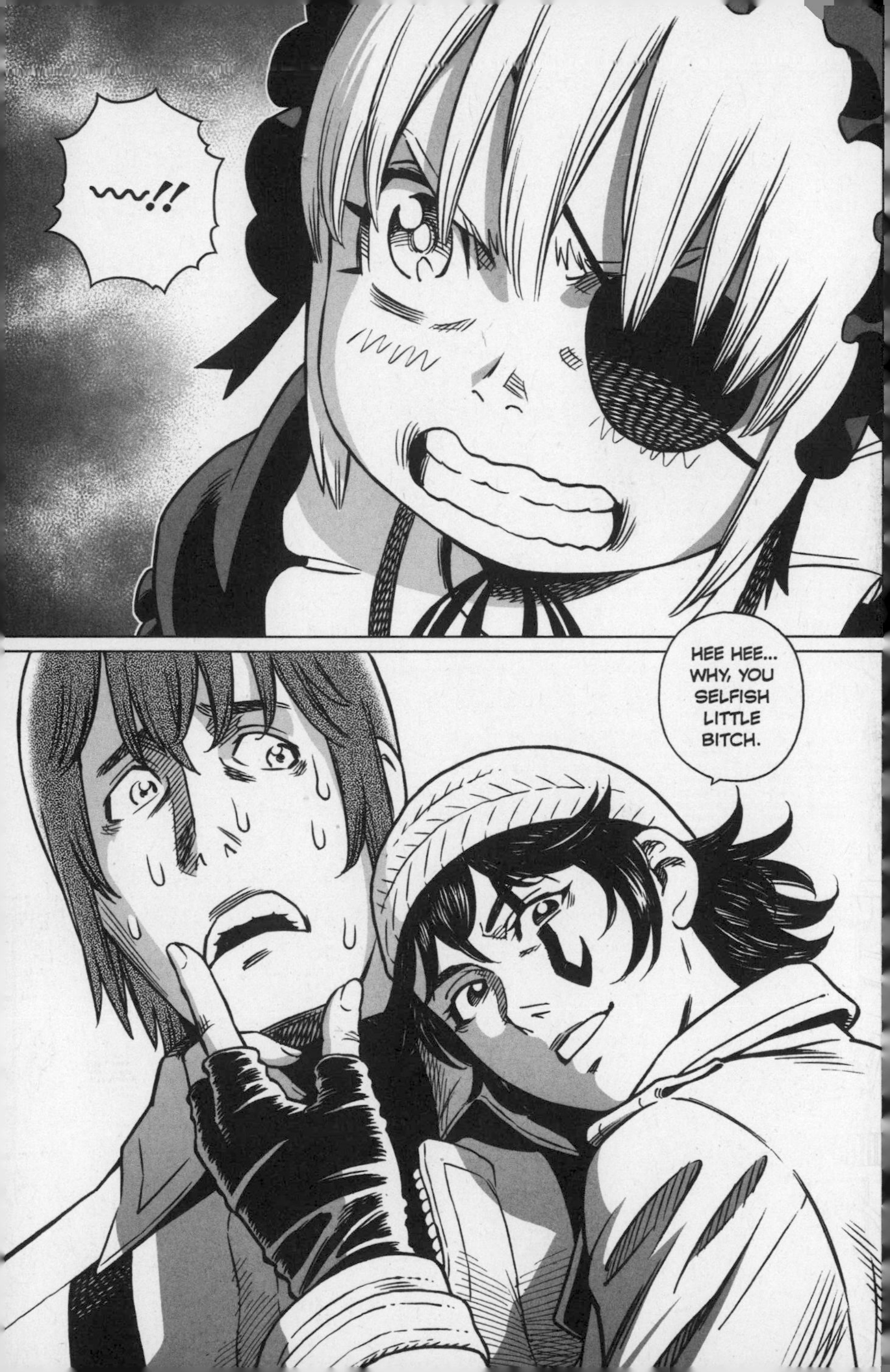
~~!!
HEE HEE... WHY, YOU SELFISH LITTLE BITCH.

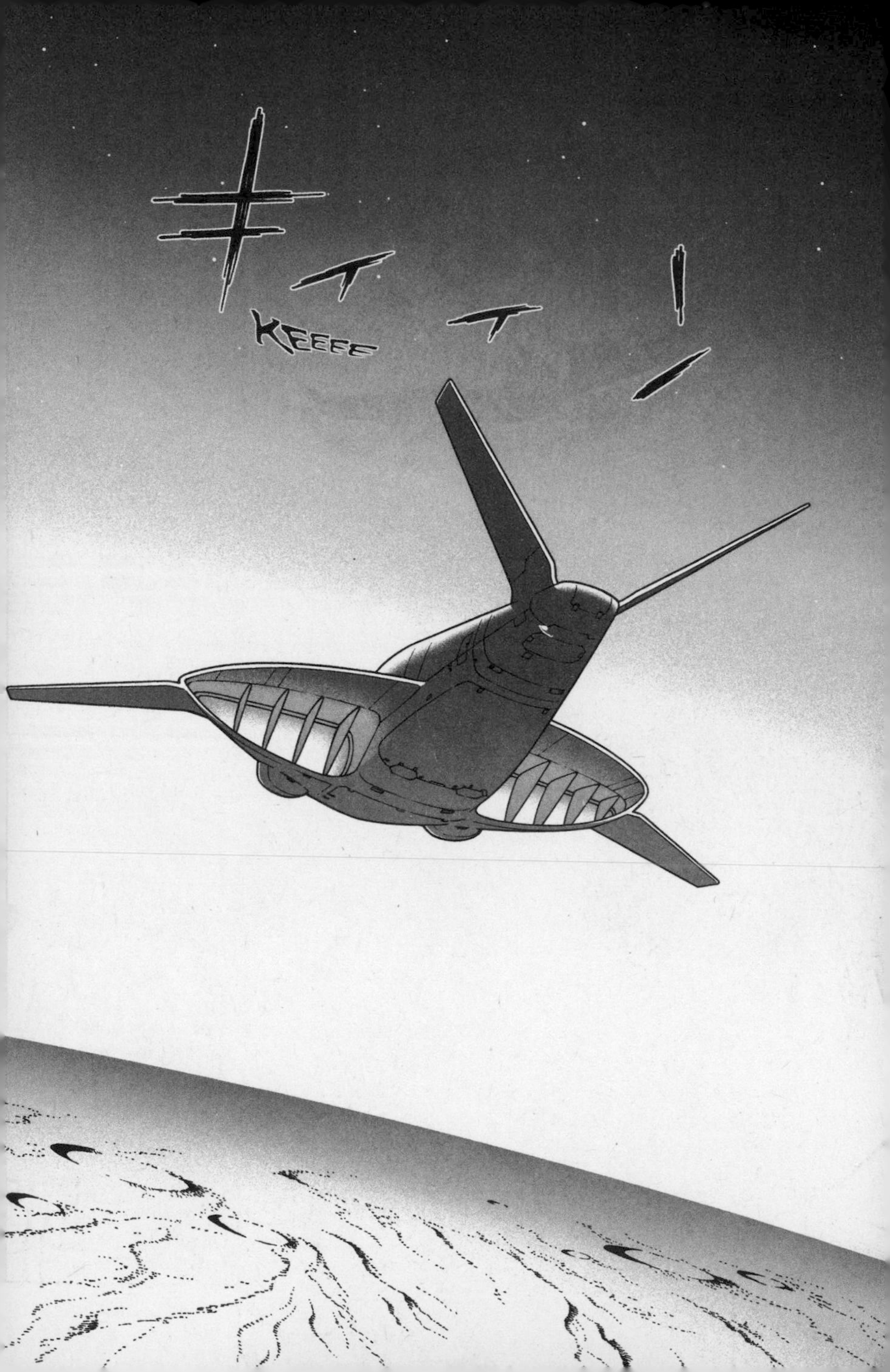
キイイ！ー
KEEEEE

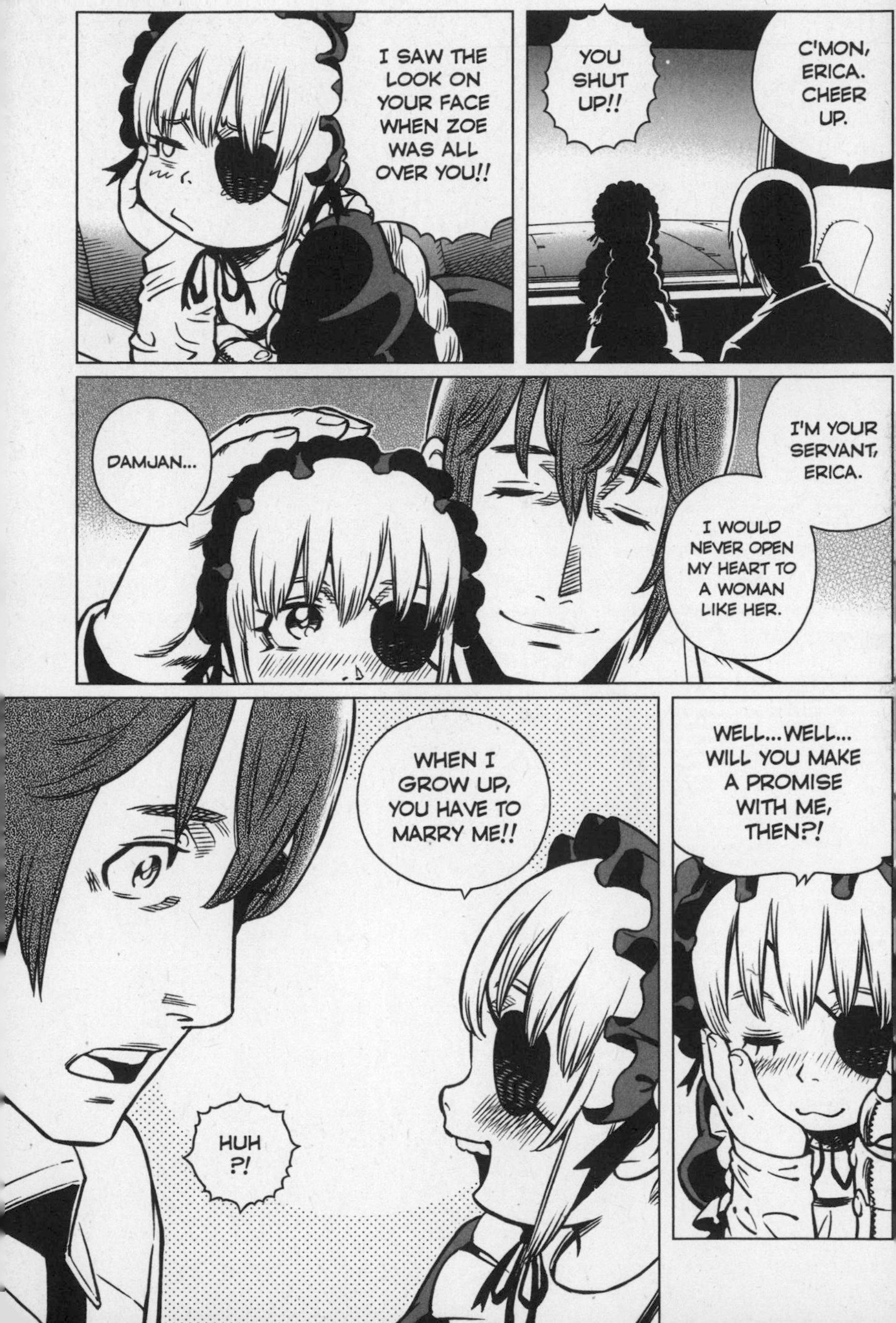
C'MON, ERICA. CHEER UP.
YOU SHUT UP!!
I SAW THE LOOK ON YOUR FACE WHEN ZOE WAS ALL OVER YOU!!
I'M YOUR SERVANT, ERICA.
I WOULD NEVER OPEN MY HEART TO A WOMAN LIKE HER.
DAMJAN...
WELL...WELL... WILL YOU MAKE A PROMISE WITH ME, THEN?!
WHEN I GROW UP, YOU HAVE TO MARRY ME!!
HUH ?!

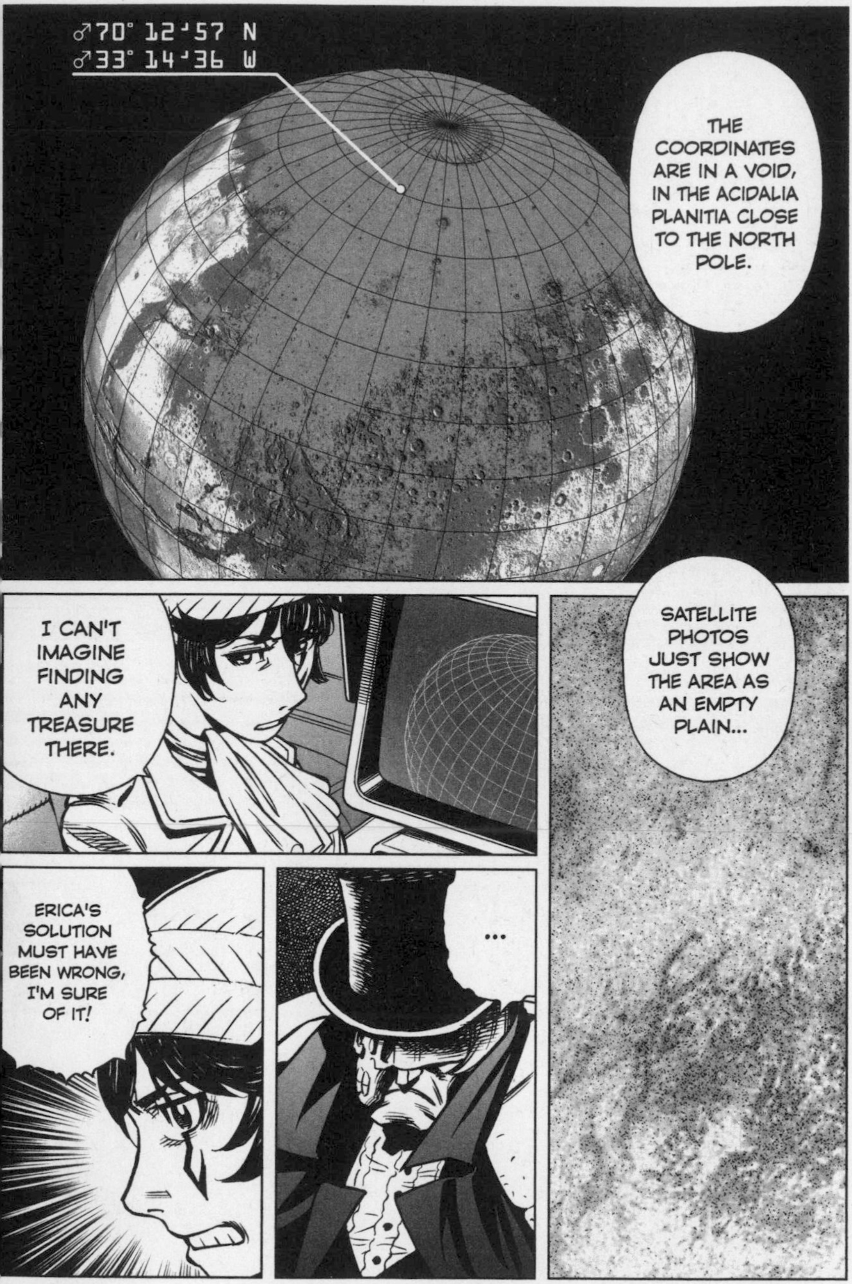

♂70° 12'57 N
♂33° 14'36 W
THE COORDINATES ARE IN A VOID, IN THE ACIDALIA PLANITIA CLOSE TO THE NORTH POLE.
SATELLITE PHOTOS JUST SHOW THE AREA AS AN EMPTY PLAIN...
I CAN'T IMAGINE FINDING ANY TREASURE THERE.
...
ERICA'S SOLUTION MUST HAVE BEEN WRONG, I'M SURE OF IT!

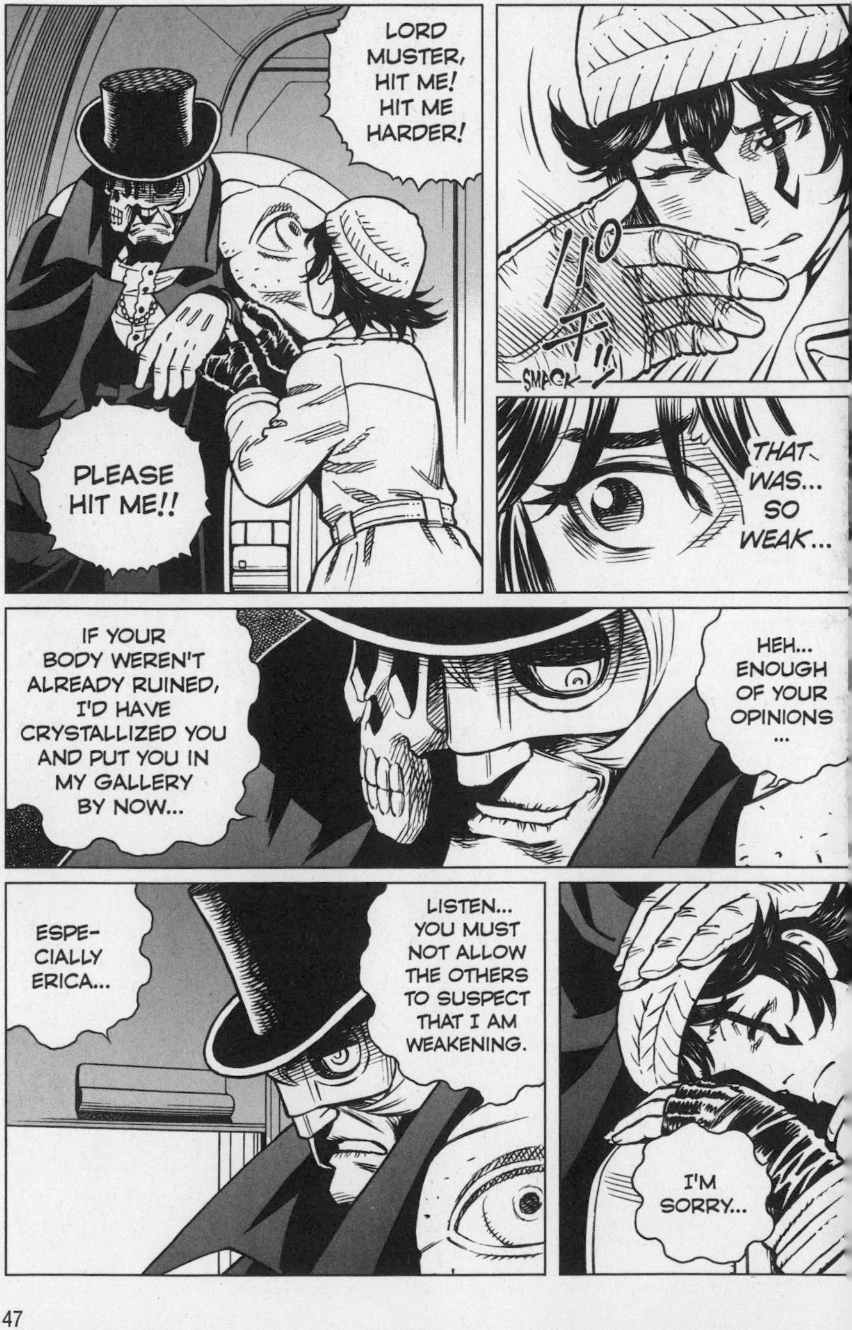
SMACK
THAT WAS... SO WEAK...
LORD MUSTER, HIT ME! HIT ME HARDER!
PLEASE HIT ME!!
HEH... ENOUGH OF YOUR OPINIONS ...
IF YOUR BODY WEREN'T ALREADY RUINED, I'D HAVE CRYSTALLIZED YOU AND PUT YOU IN MY GALLERY BY NOW...
I'M SORRY...
LISTEN... YOU MUST NOT ALLOW THE OTHERS TO SUSPECT THAT I AM WEAKENING.
ESPE-CIALLY ERICA...

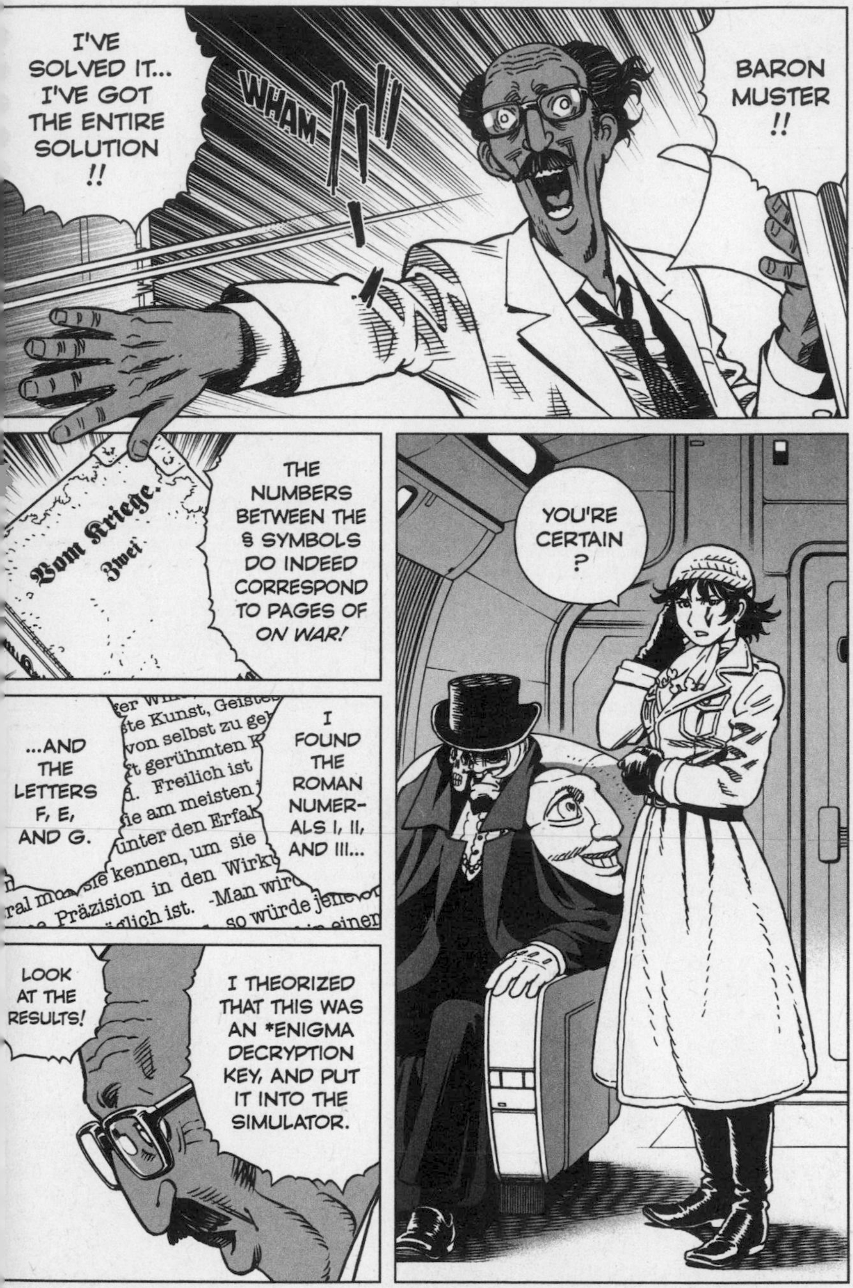
BARON MUSTER !!
WHAM
I'VE SOLVED IT... I'VE GOT THE ENTIRE SOLUTION !!
YOU'RE CERTAIN ?
THE NUMBERS BETWEEN THE § SYMBOLS DO INDEED CORRESPOND TO PAGES OF *ON WAR!*
Vom Kriege.
Zwei
I FOUND THE ROMAN NUMERALS I, II, AND III...
...AND THE LETTERS F, E, AND G.
I THEORIZED THAT THIS WAS AN *ENIGMA DECRYPTION KEY, AND PUT IT INTO THE SIMULATOR.
LOOK AT THE RESULTS!

*** ENIGMA CODE:** A rotor cipher machine used by the Nazis in WWII. Messages could be coded and decoded with a key formed from the layout and starting position of the device's three rotors.

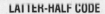

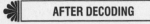

LATTER-HALF CODE

BKTTDGEAJNTQRGPVVVPRSRZKIXAWGH
HBYBVLTEHBSBZRLFCLHPHTMXRTAPVM

AFTER DECODING

WO DER ADLER AM AUGAPFEL DES SKELETTS
PICKT BIETE DEN TANZENDEN STOCK AN

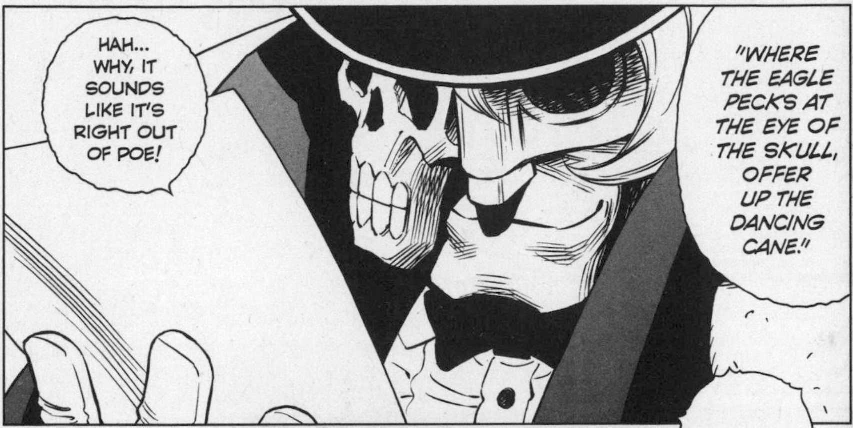
"WHERE THE EAGLE PECKS AT THE EYE OF THE SKULL, OFFER UP THE DANCING CANE."
HAH... WHY, IT SOUNDS LIKE IT'S RIGHT OUT OF POE!

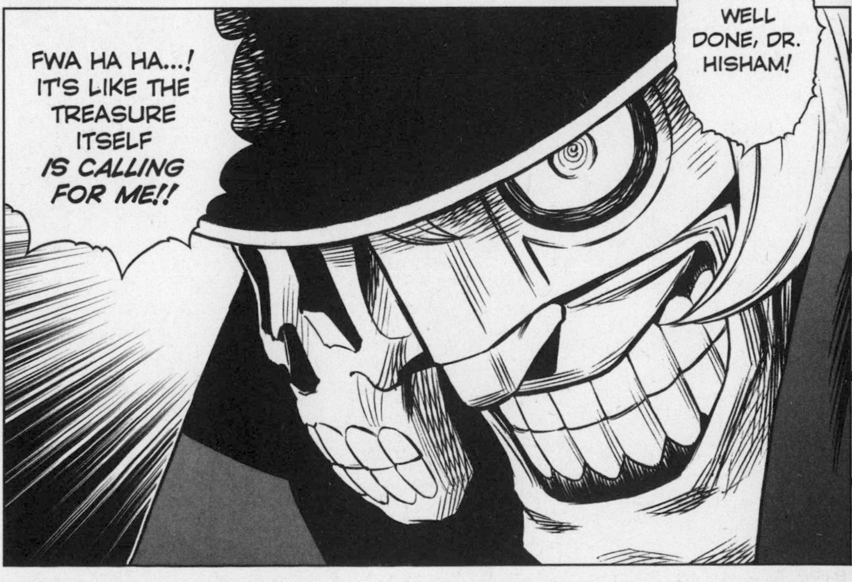
WELL DONE, DR. HISHAM!
FWA HA HA...! IT'S LIKE THE TREASURE ITSELF *IS CALLING FOR ME!!*

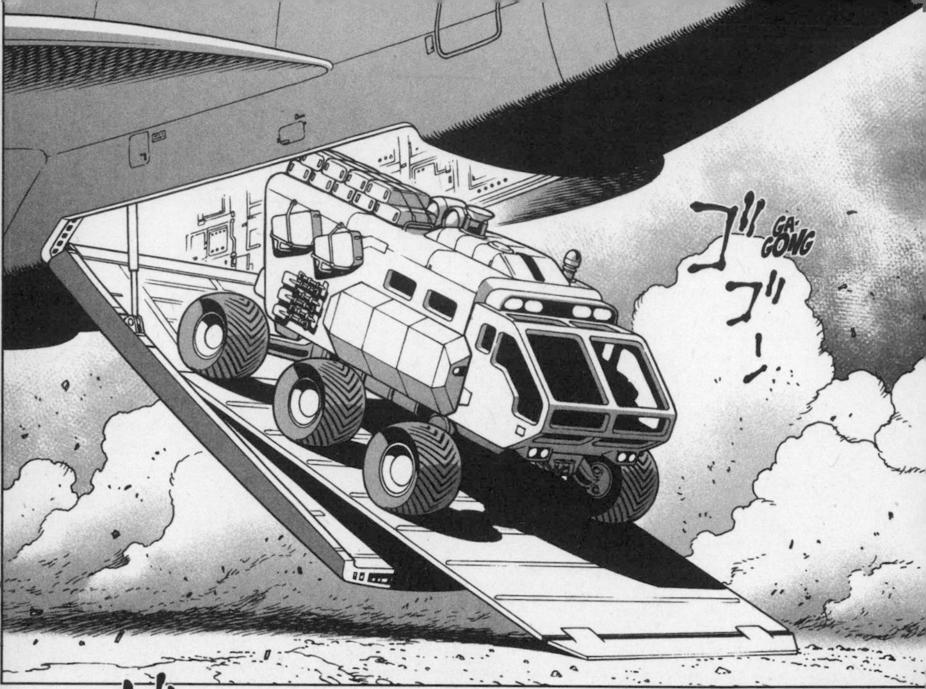
GA-GONG
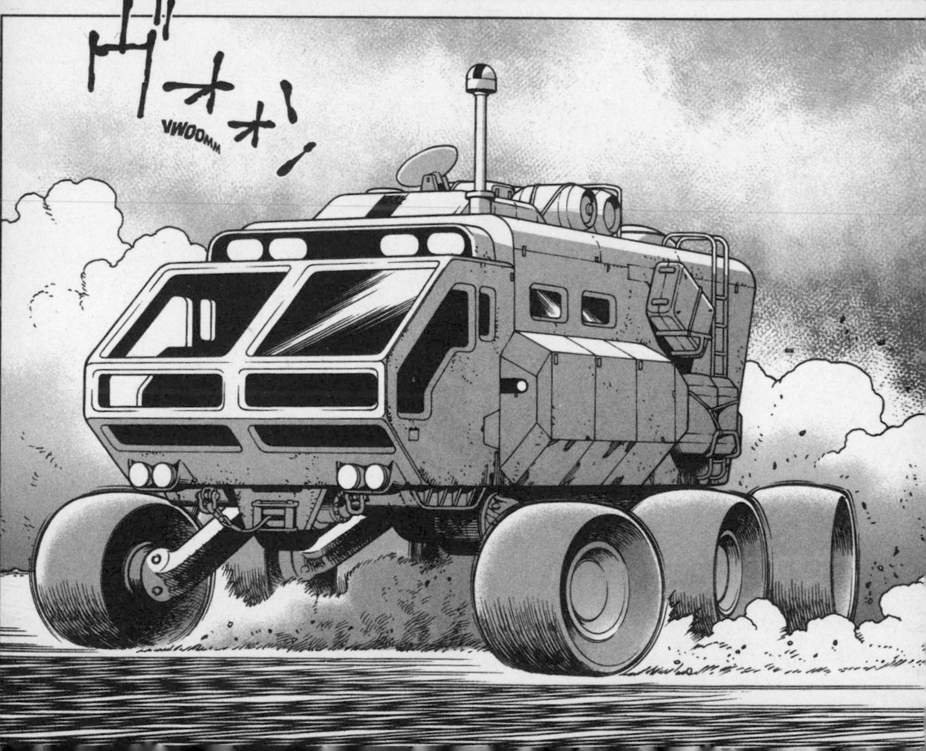
VWOOMM

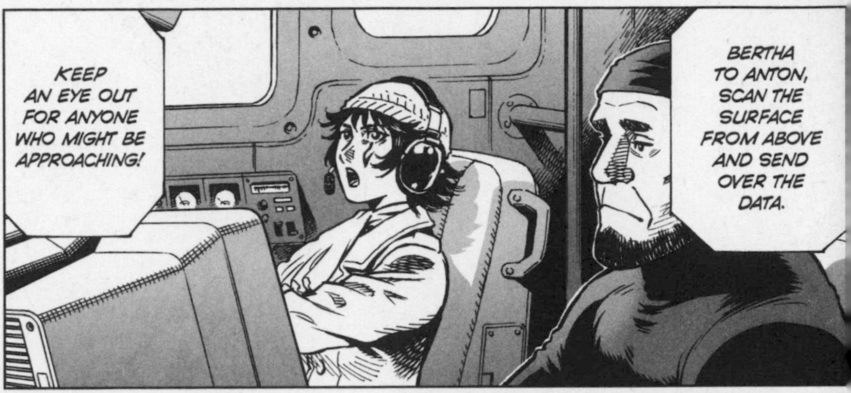
BERTHA TO ANTON, SCAN THE SURFACE FROM ABOVE AND SEND OVER THE DATA.
KEEP AN EYE OUT FOR ANYONE WHO MIGHT BE APPROACHING!

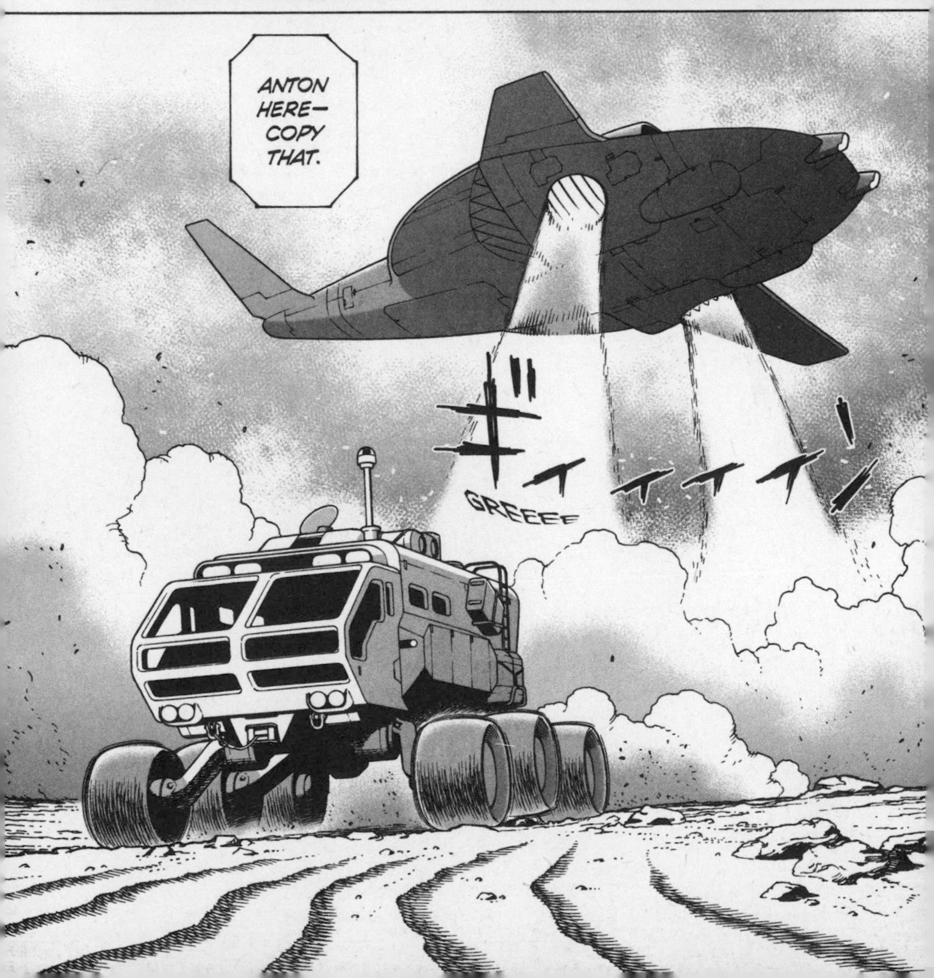
ANTON HERE—COPY THAT.
GREEEEE

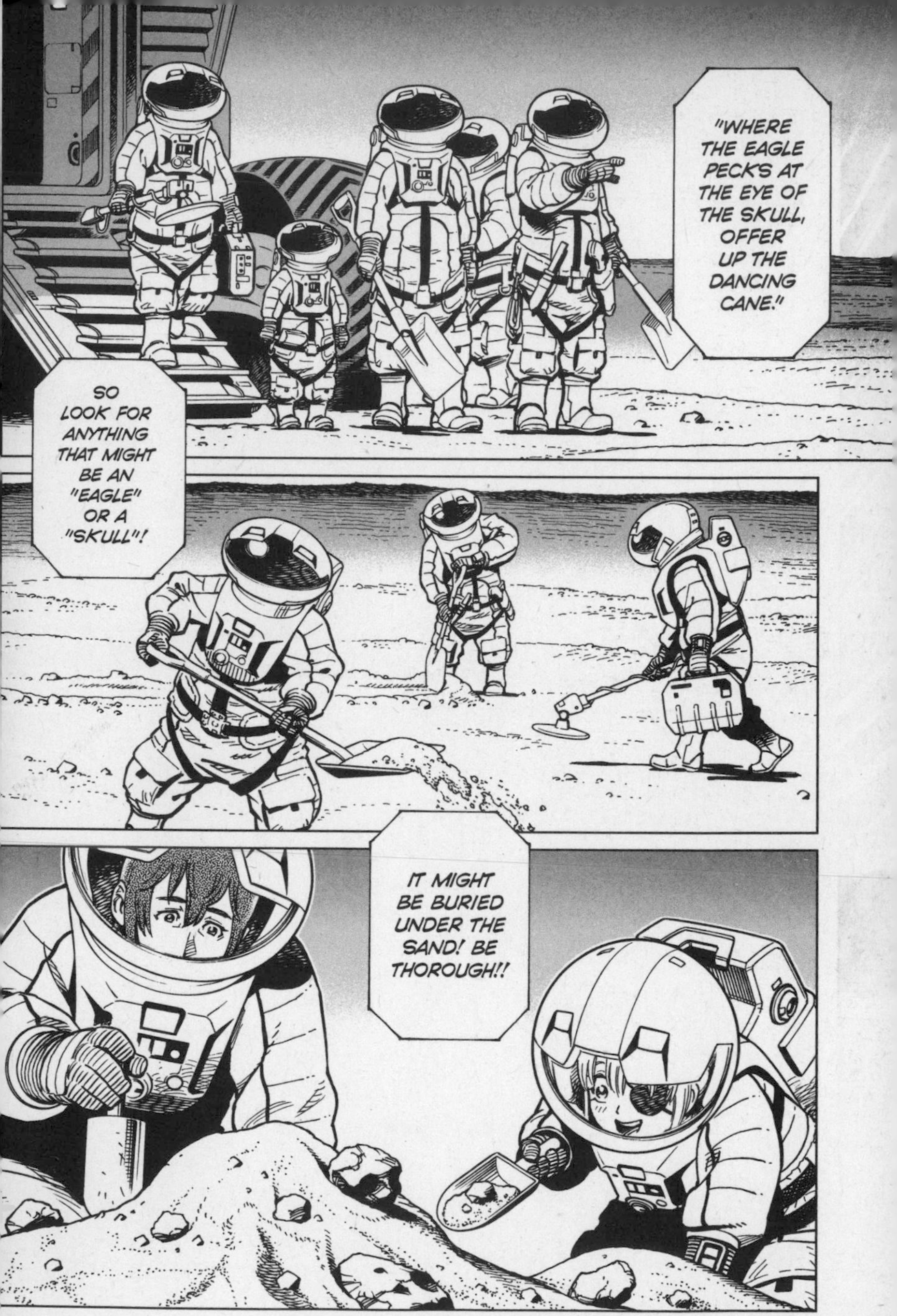
"WHERE THE EAGLE PECK'S AT THE EYE OF THE SKULL, OFFER UP THE DANCING CANE."
SO LOOK FOR ANYTHING THAT MIGHT BE AN "EAGLE" OR A "SKULL"!
IT MIGHT BE BURIED UNDER THE SAND! BE THOROUGH!!

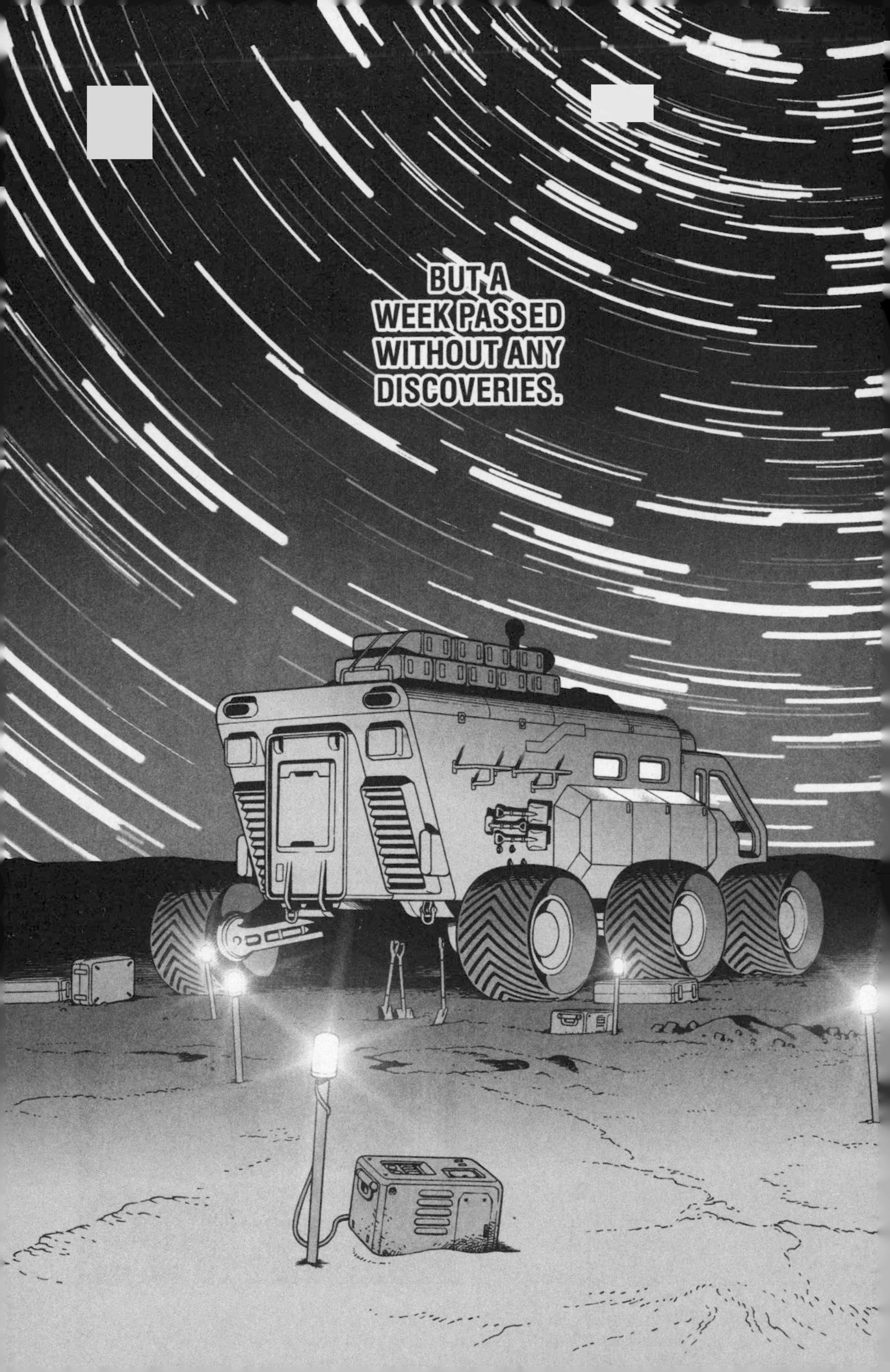
BUT A WEEK PASSED WITHOUT ANY DISCOVERIES.

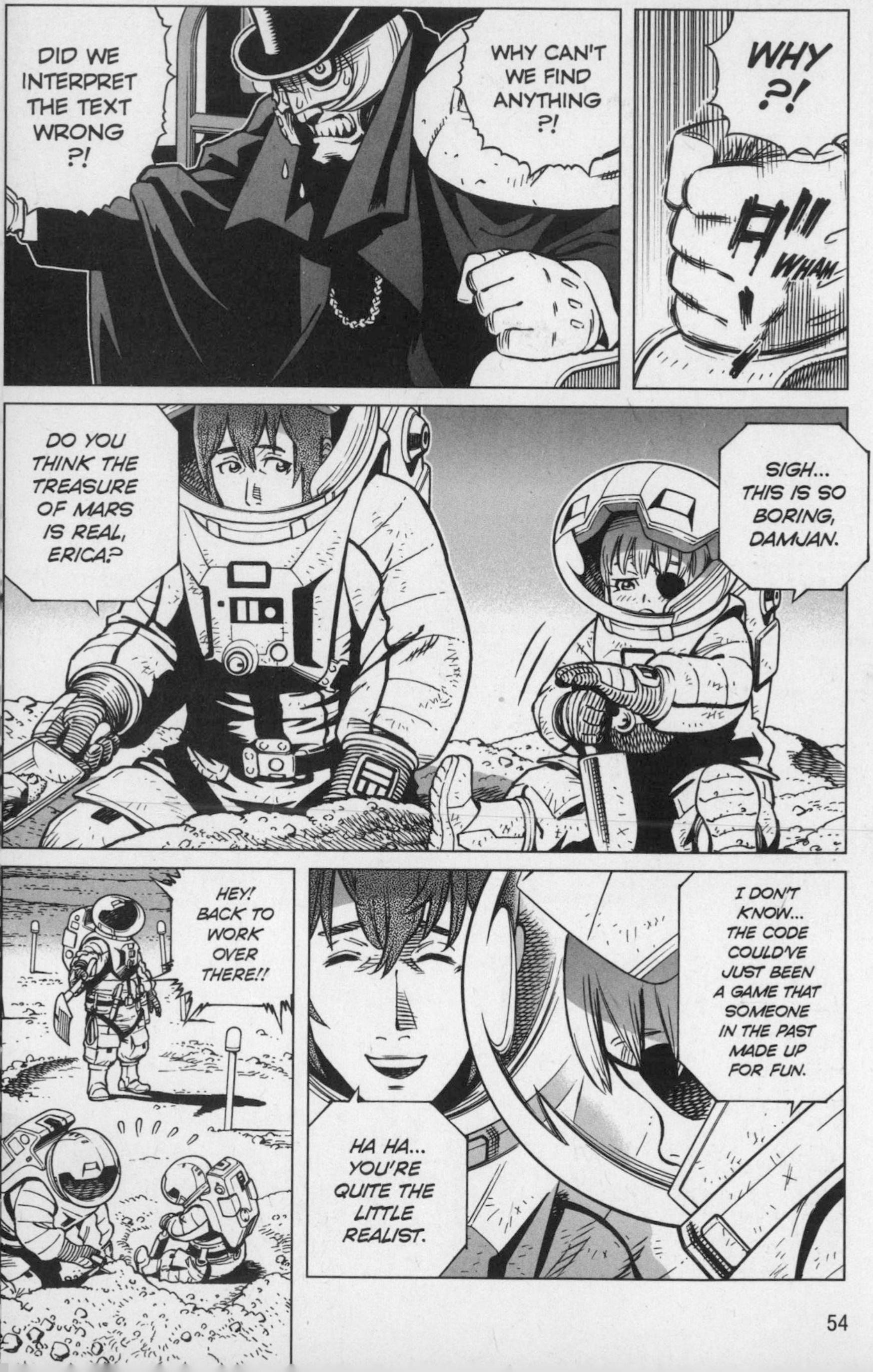
WHY ?!
WHAM
WHY CAN'T WE FIND ANYTHING ?!
DID WE INTERPRET THE TEXT WRONG ?!
SIGH... THIS IS SO BORING, DAMJAN.
DO YOU THINK THE TREASURE OF MARS IS REAL, ERICA?
I DON'T KNOW... THE CODE COULD'VE JUST BEEN A GAME THAT SOMEONE IN THE PAST MADE UP FOR FUN.
HA HA... YOU'RE QUITE THE LITTLE REALIST.
HEY! BACK TO WORK OVER THERE!!

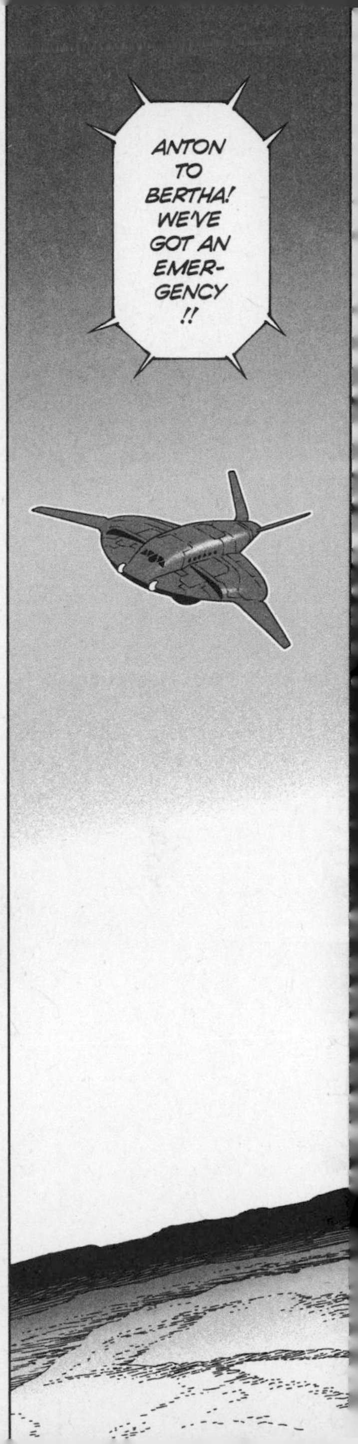
ANTON TO BERTHA! WE'VE GOT AN EMER-GENCY !!

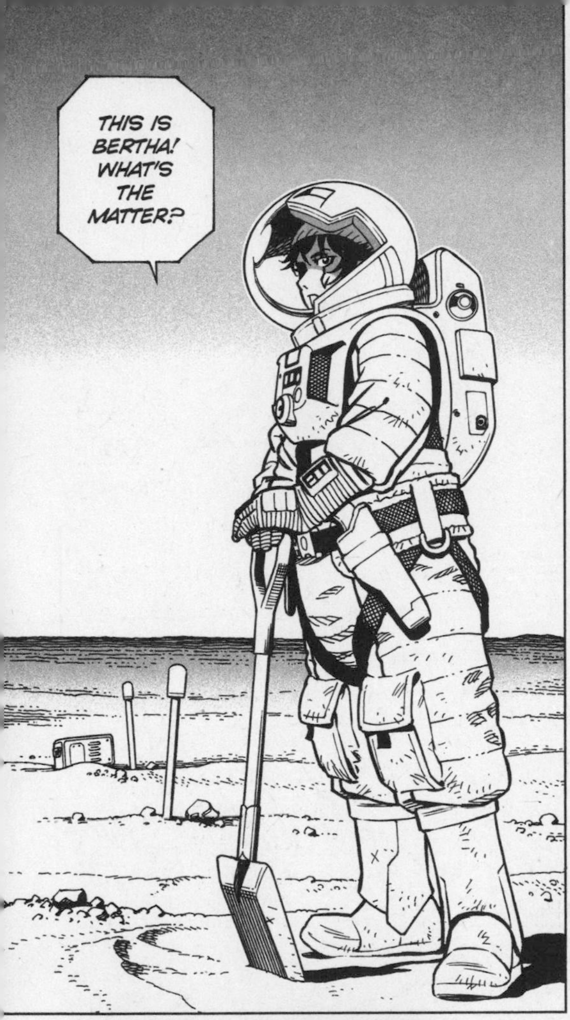
THIS IS BERTHA! WHAT'S THE MATTER?

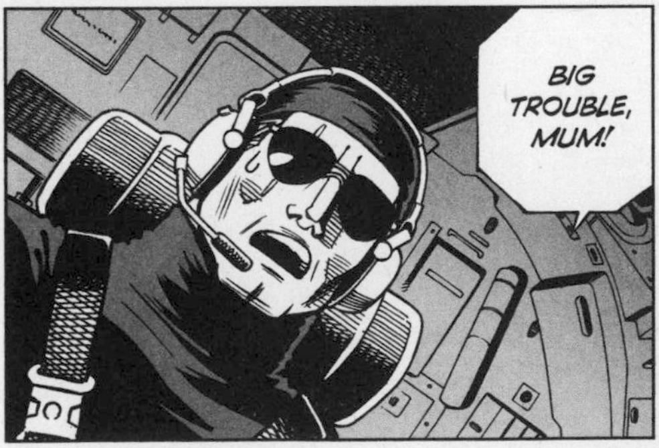
BIG TROUBLE, MUM!

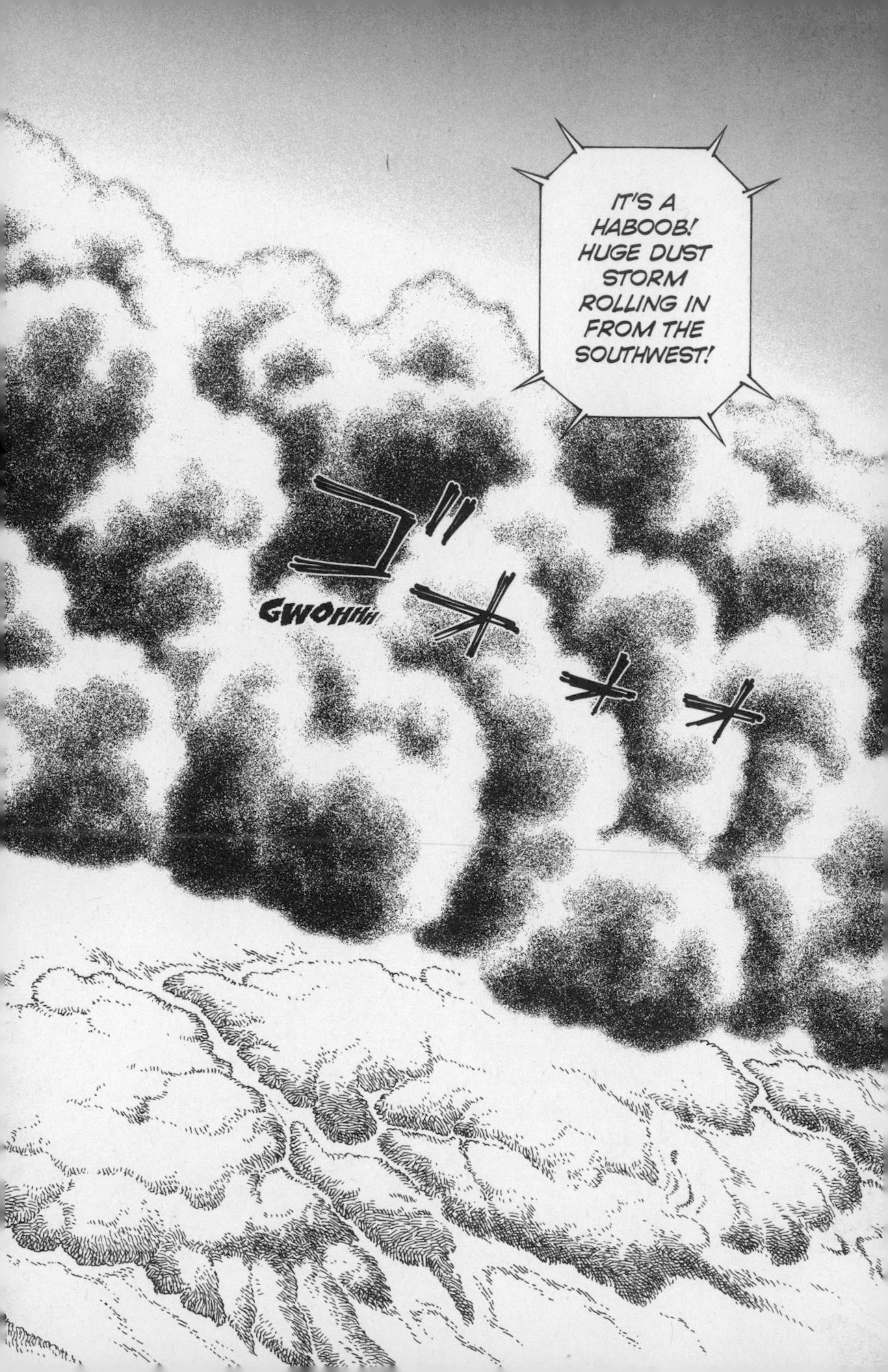
IT'S A HABOOB! HUGE DUST STORM ROLLING IN FROM THE SOUTHWEST!
GWOHHH

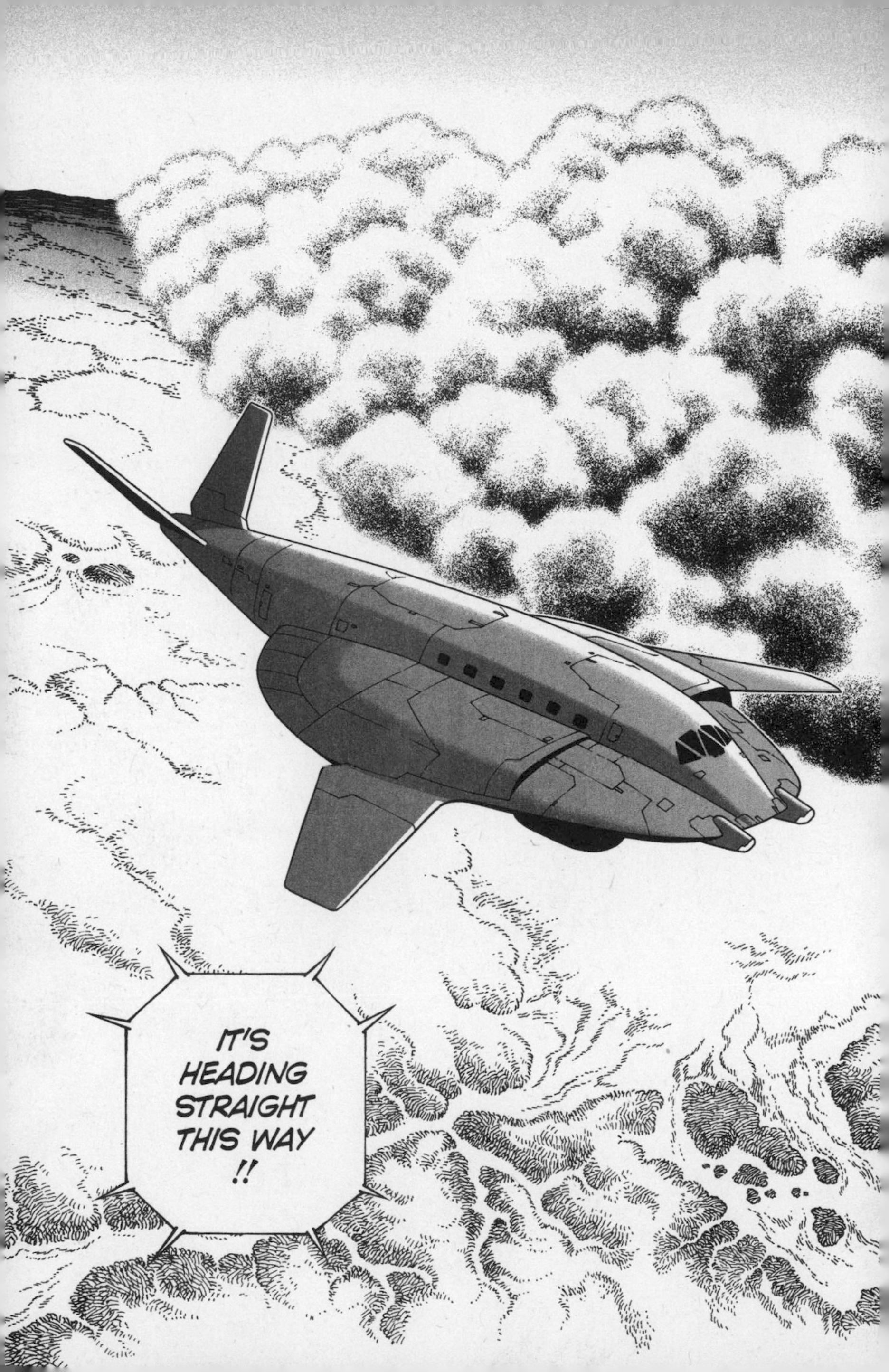
IT'S HEADING STRAIGHT THIS WAY !!

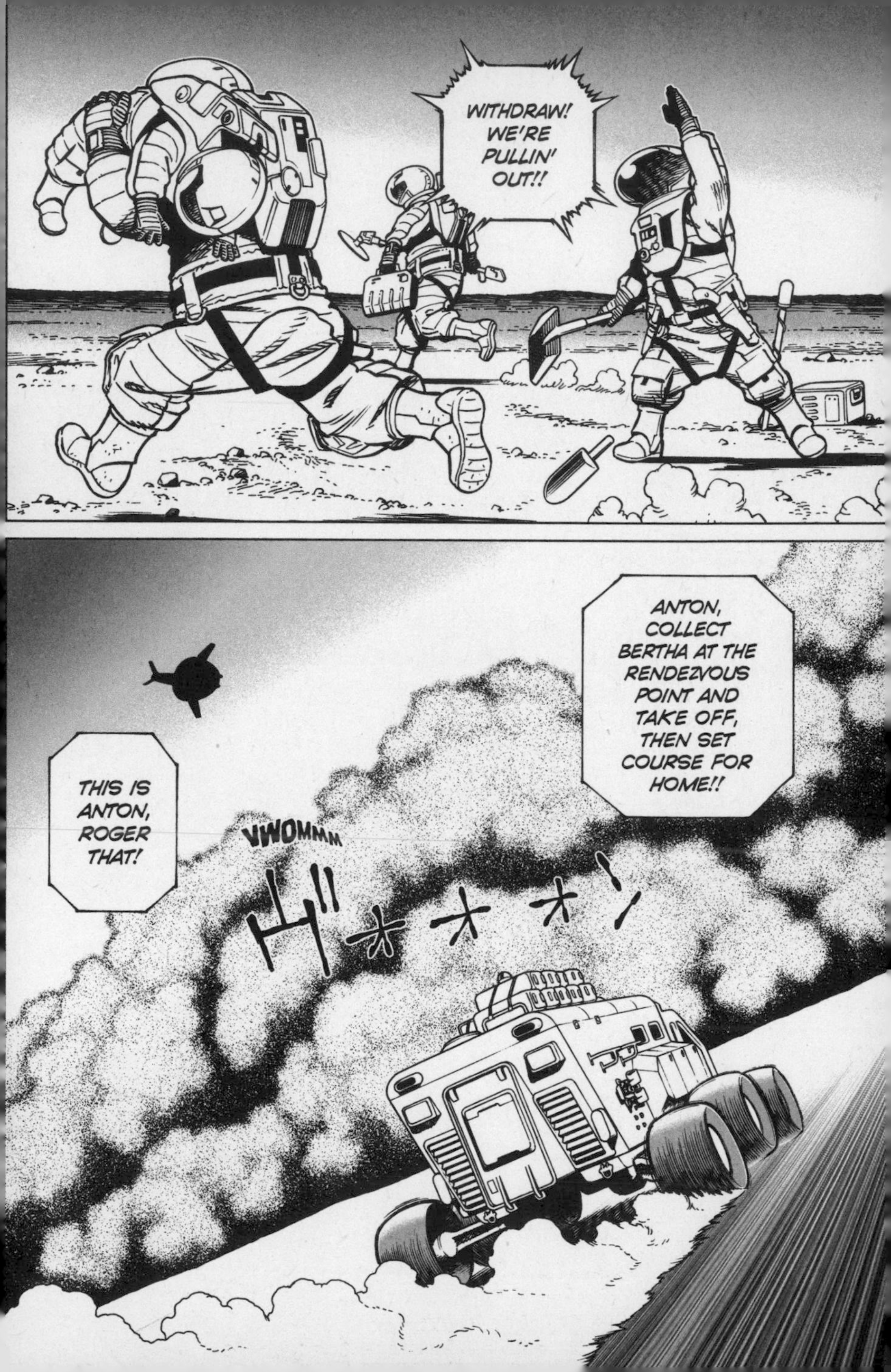
WITHDRAW! WE'RE PULLIN' OUT!!
ANTON, COLLECT BERTHA AT THE RENDEZVOUS POINT AND TAKE OFF, THEN SET COURSE FOR HOME!!
THIS IS ANTON, ROGER THAT!
VWOMMM

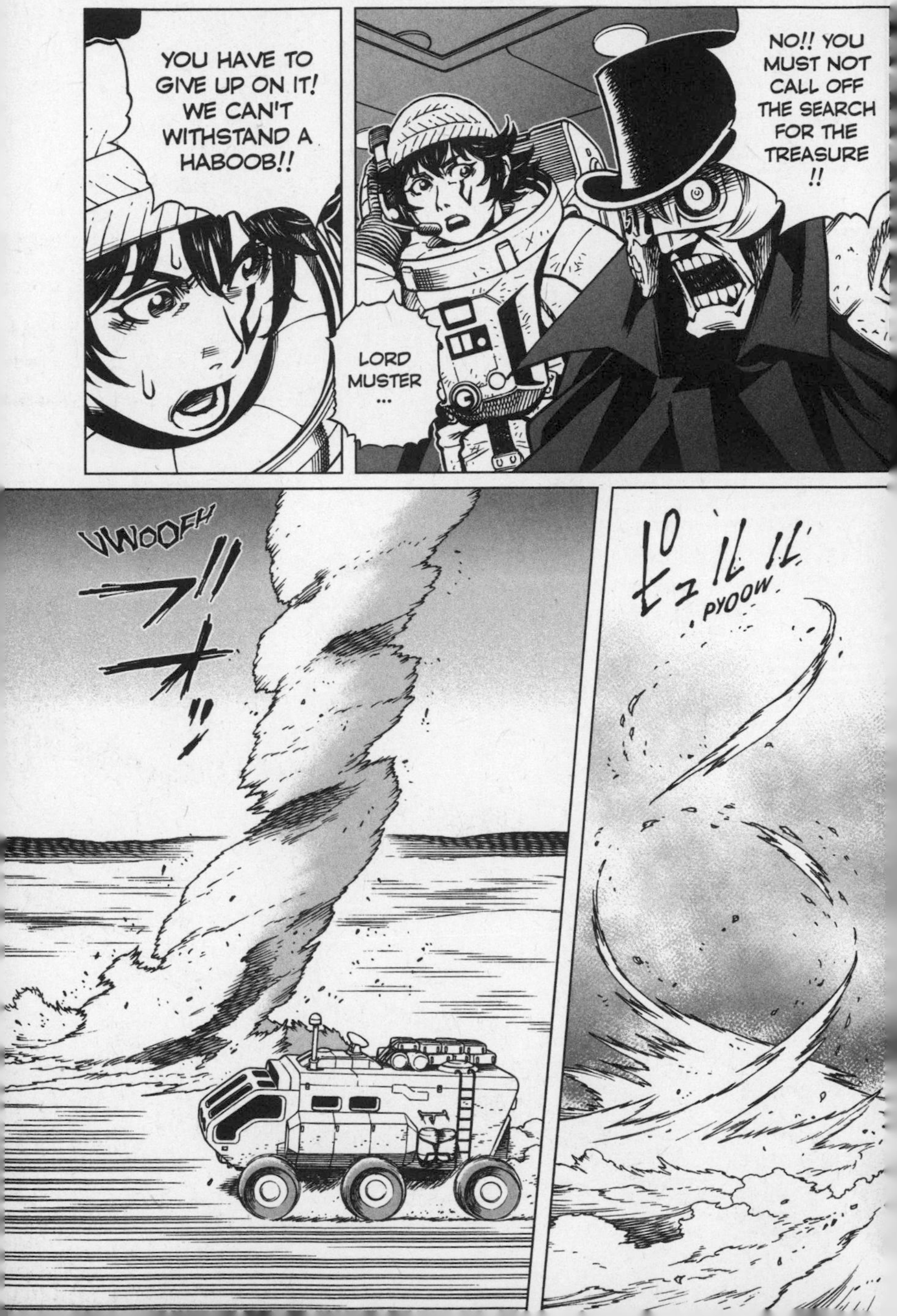
NO!! YOU MUST NOT CALL OFF THE SEARCH FOR THE TREASURE !!
LORD MUSTER ...
YOU HAVE TO GIVE UP ON IT! WE CAN'T WITHSTAND A HABOOB!!
ピュルル
PYOOW
VWOOFH
ブオッ!!

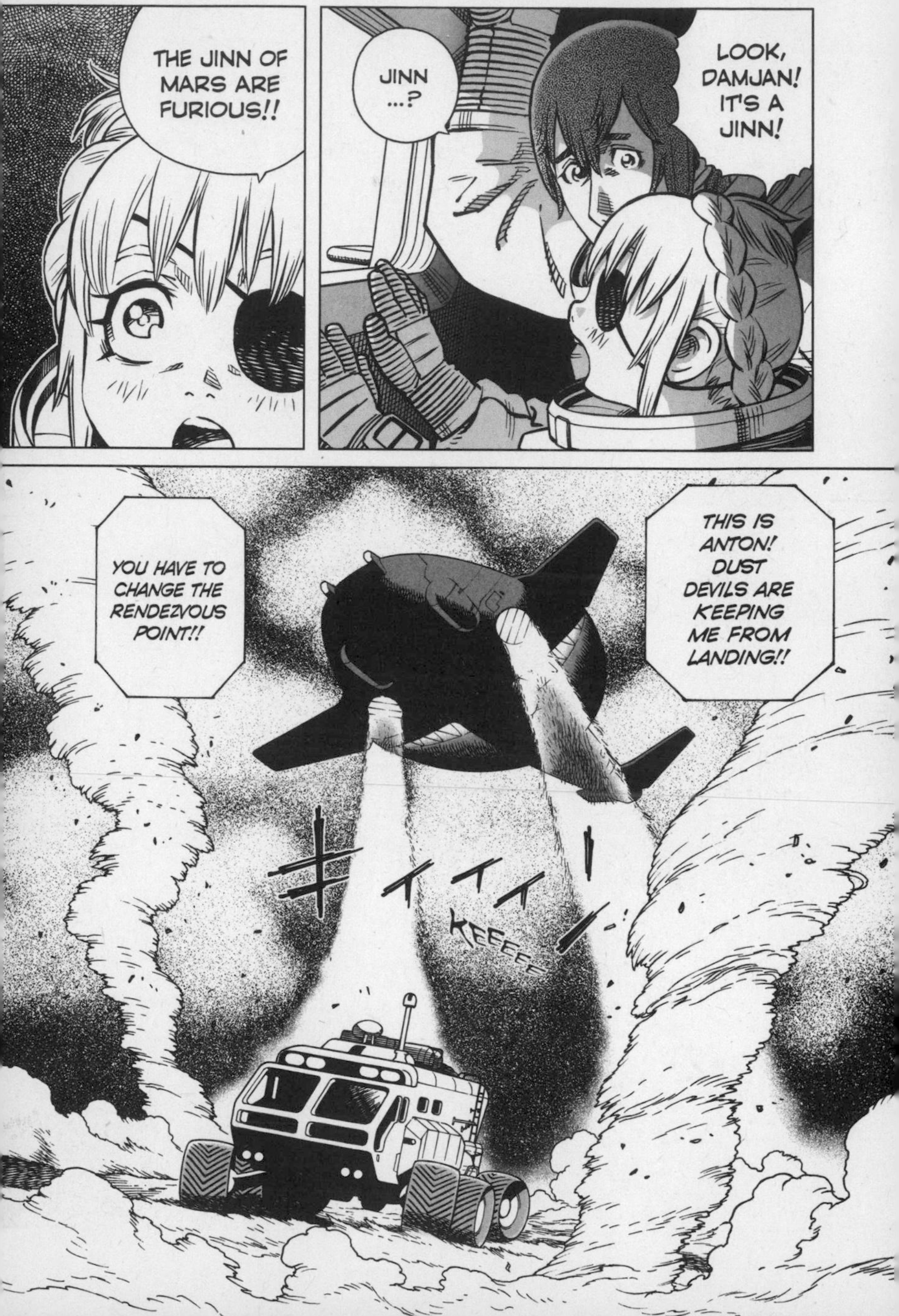
LOOK, DAMJAN! IT'S A JINN!
JINN ...?
THE JINN OF MARS ARE FURIOUS!!
THIS IS ANTON! DUST DEVILS ARE KEEPING ME FROM LANDING!!
YOU HAVE TO CHANGE THE RENDEZVOUS POINT!!
KEEEEE

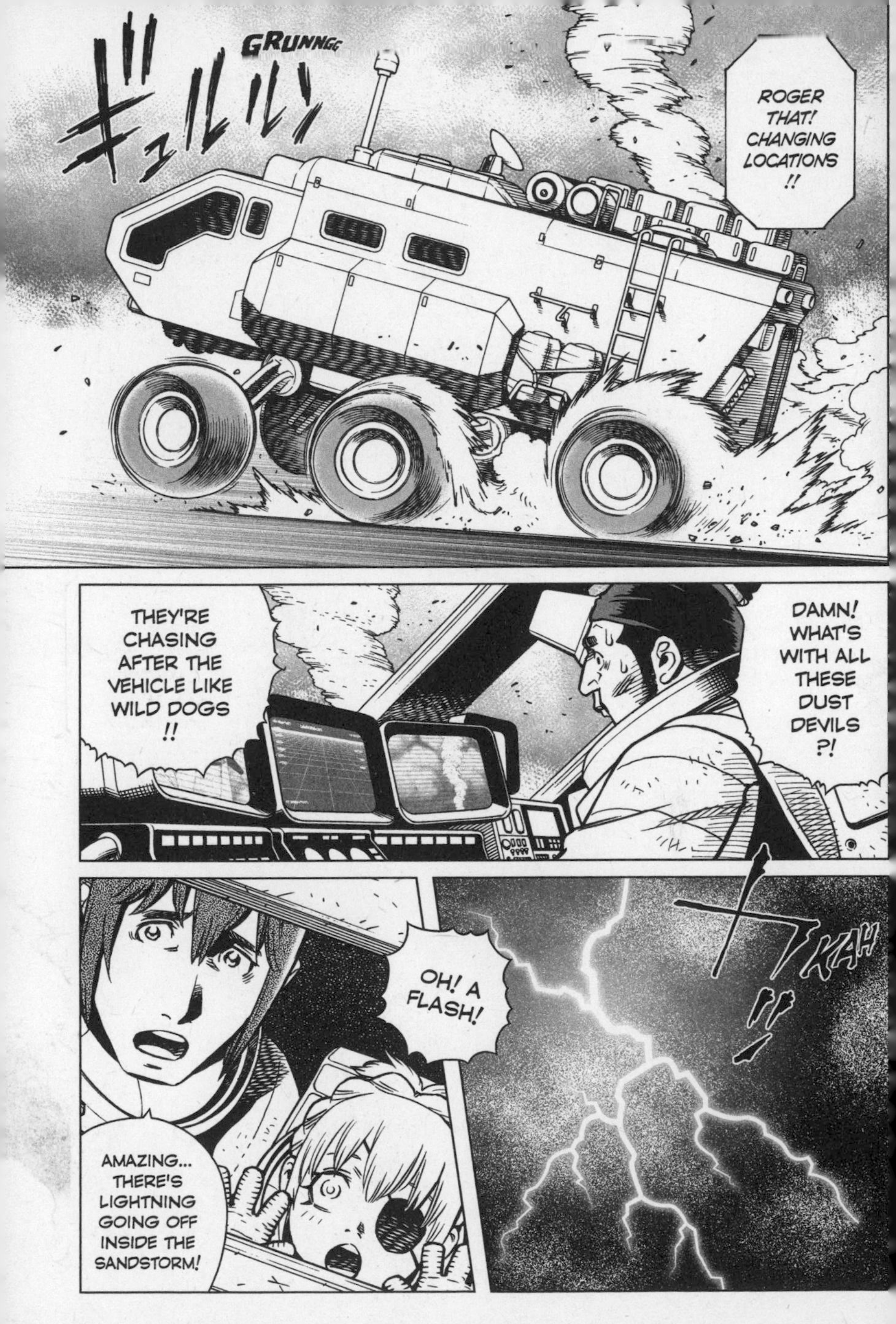
ROGER THAT! CHANGING LOCATIONS !!
ギュルルン
GRUNNGG
DAMN! WHAT'S WITH ALL THESE DUST DEVILS ?!
THEY'RE CHASING AFTER THE VEHICLE LIKE WILD DOGS !!
KAH
OH! A FLASH!
AMAZING... THERE'S LIGHTNING GOING OFF INSIDE THE SANDSTORM!

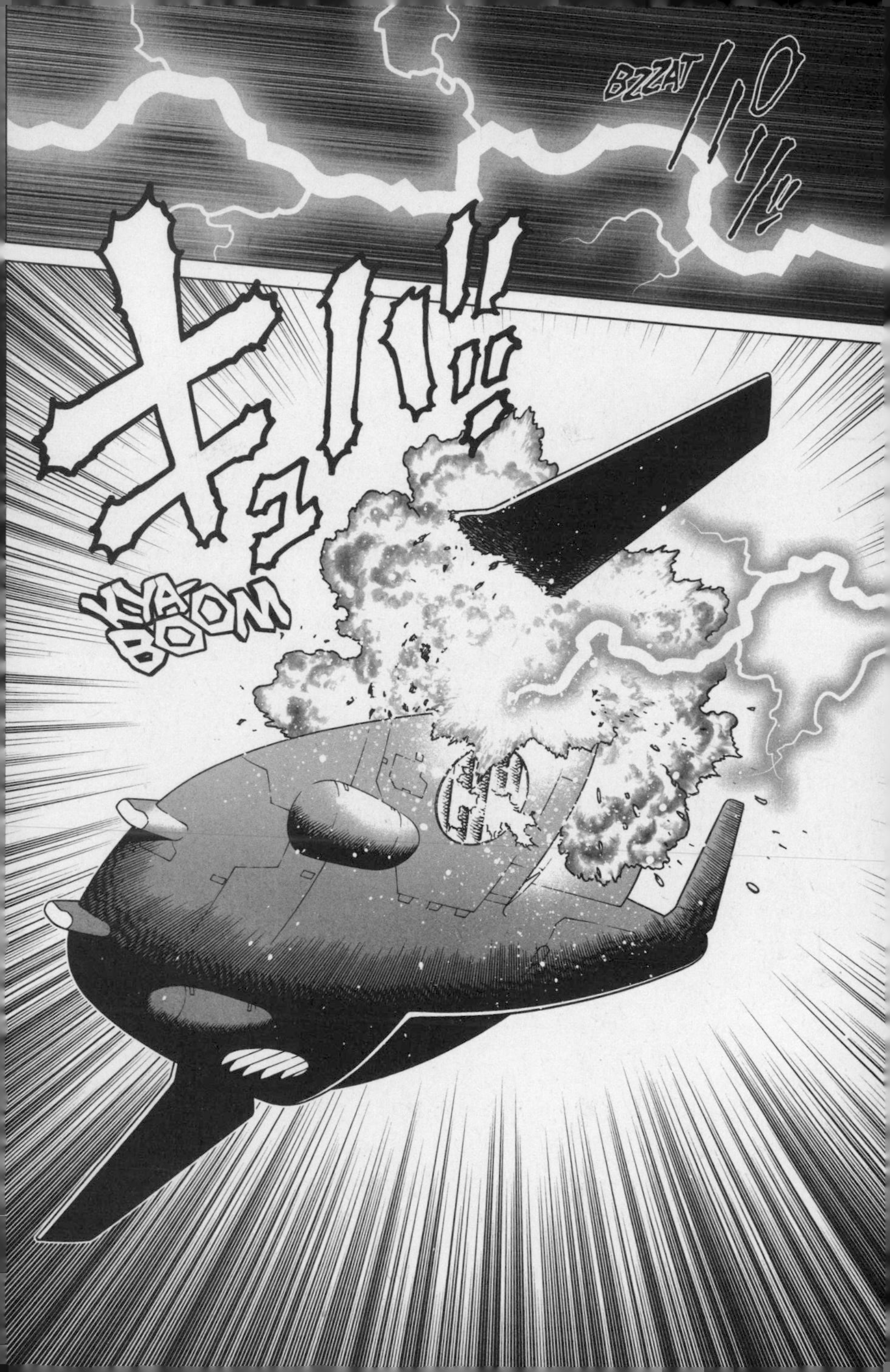
BZZAT
KA-BOOM

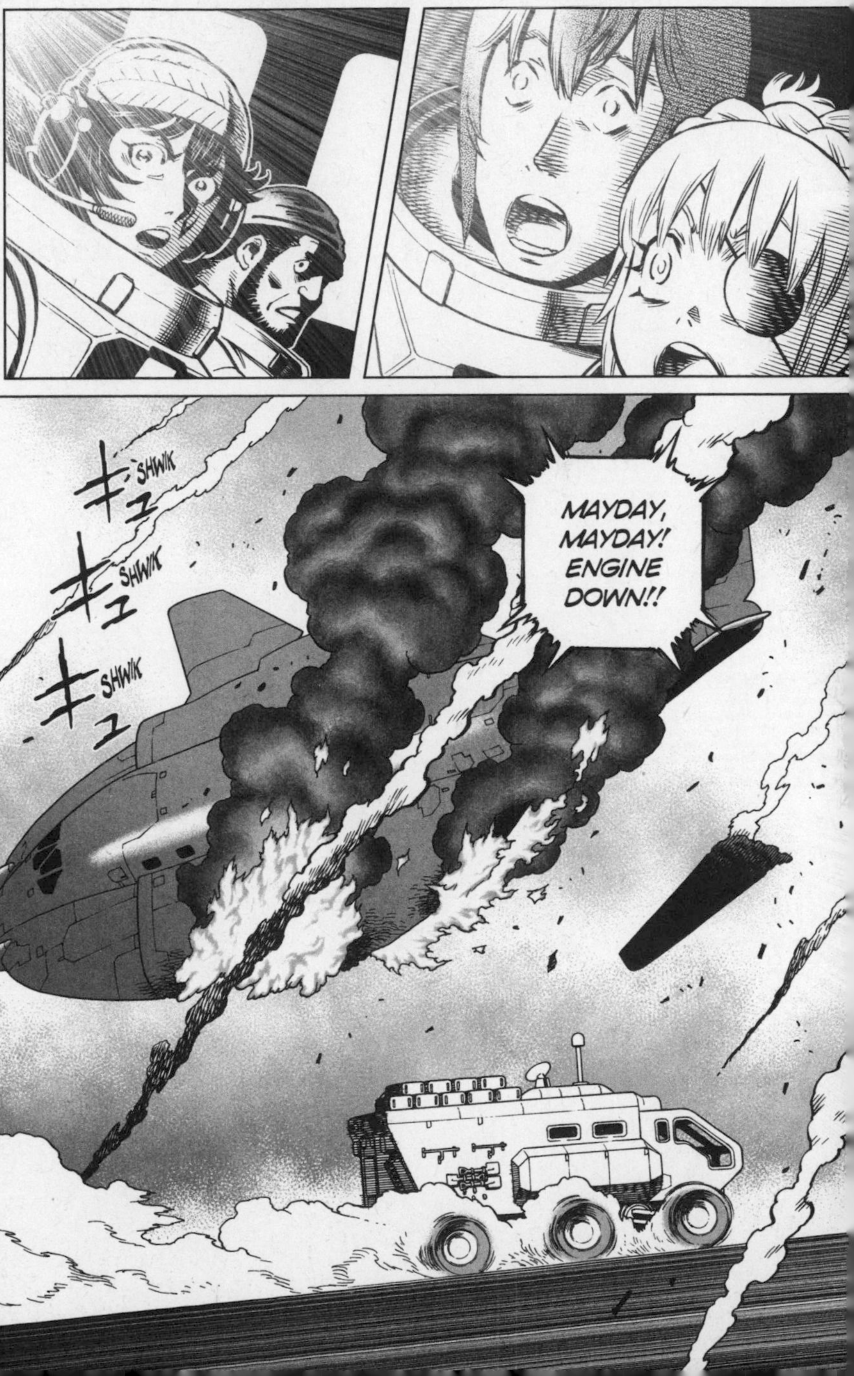
MAYDAY, MAYDAY! ENGINE DOWN!!
SHWIK
SHWIK
SHWIK

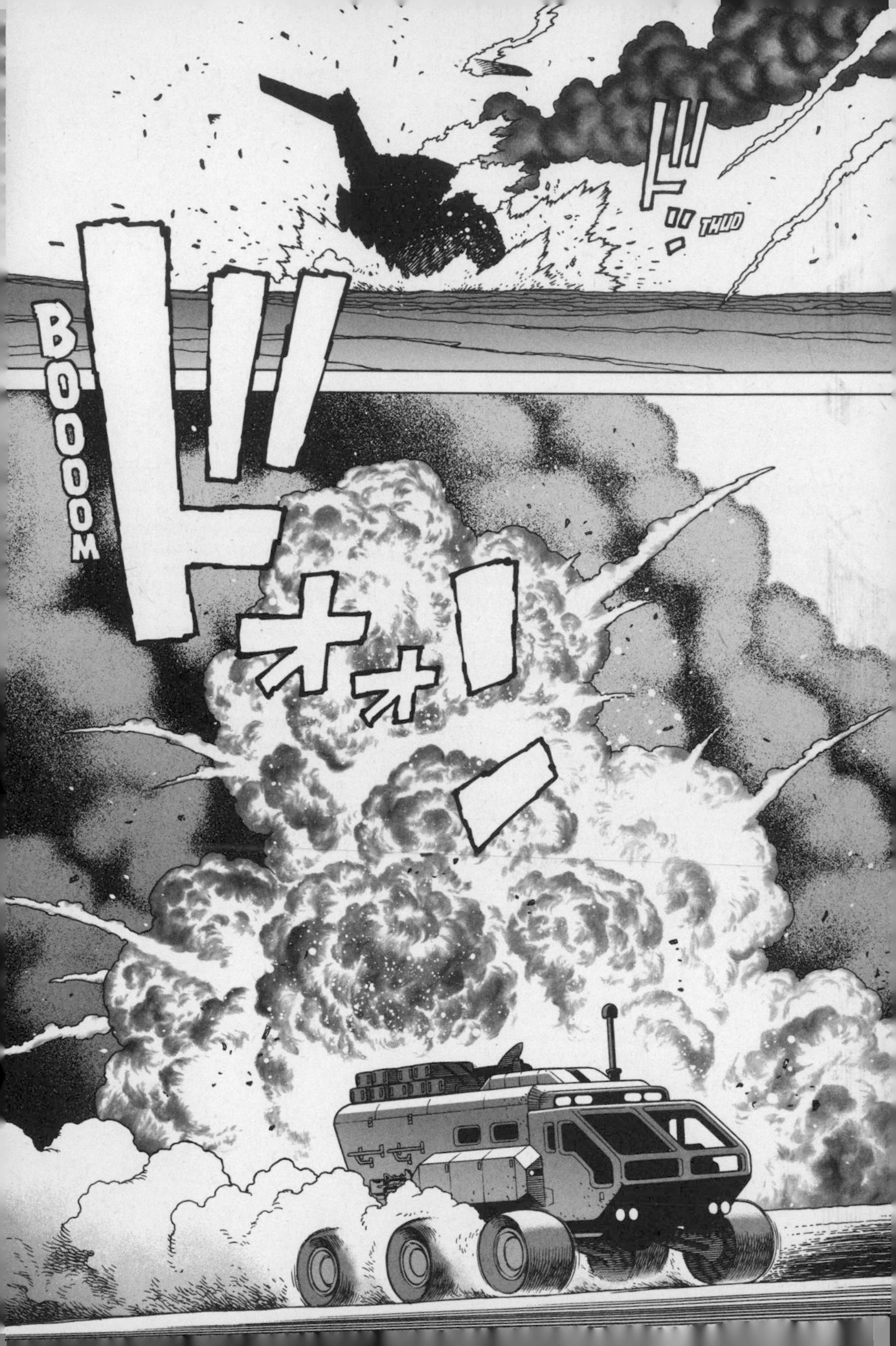

ドッ
THUD
ドォォーン
BOOOOOM

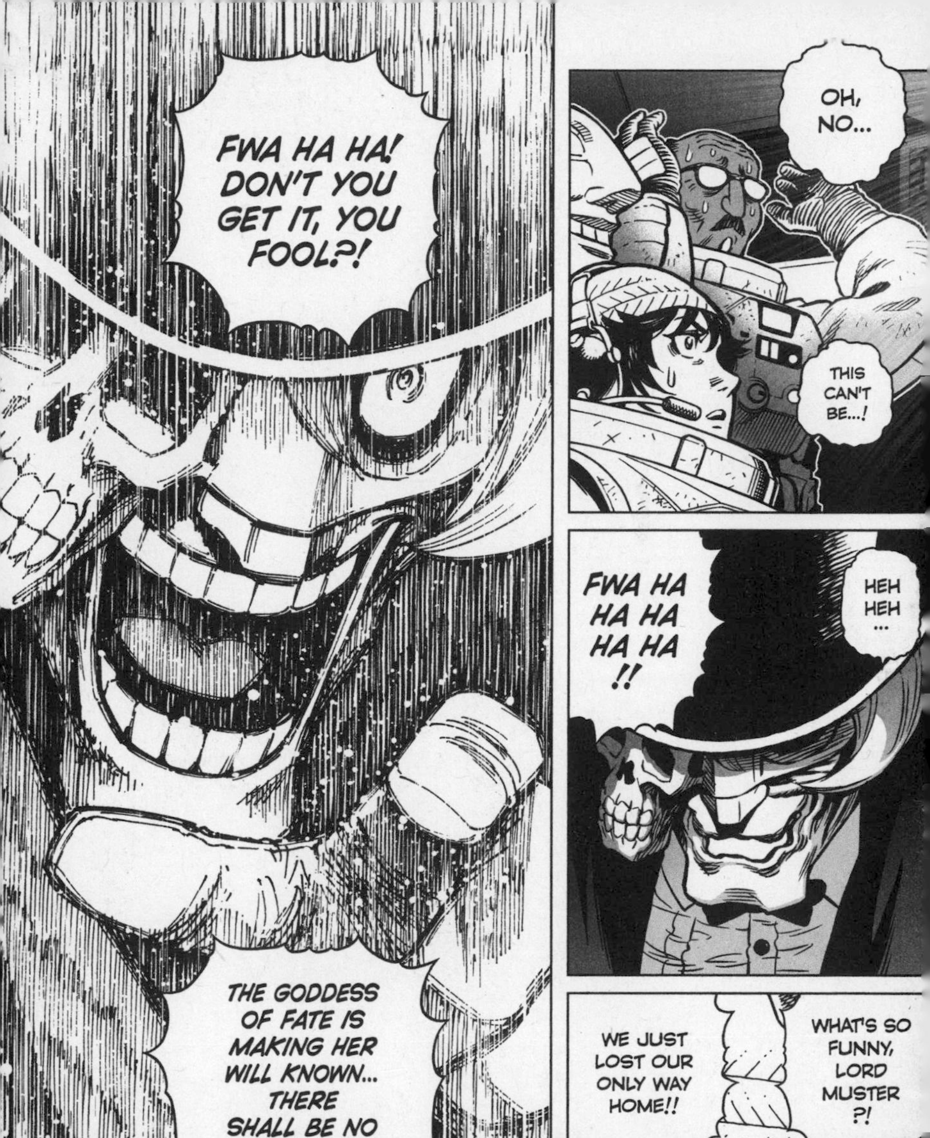
OH, NO...
THIS CAN'T BE...!
HEH HEH ...
FWA HA HA HA HA HA !!
WHAT'S SO FUNNY, LORD MUSTER ?!
WE JUST LOST OUR ONLY WAY HOME!!
FWA HA HA! DON'T YOU GET IT, YOU FOOL?!
THE GODDESS OF FATE IS MAKING HER WILL KNOWN... THERE SHALL BE NO RETREAT FROM HER CLUTCHES UNTIL WE FIND THE TREASURE!!

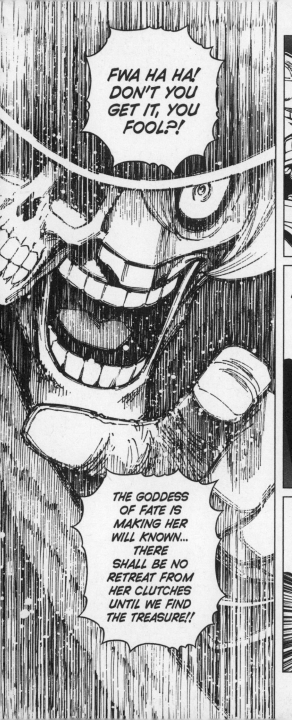

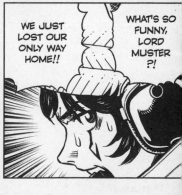

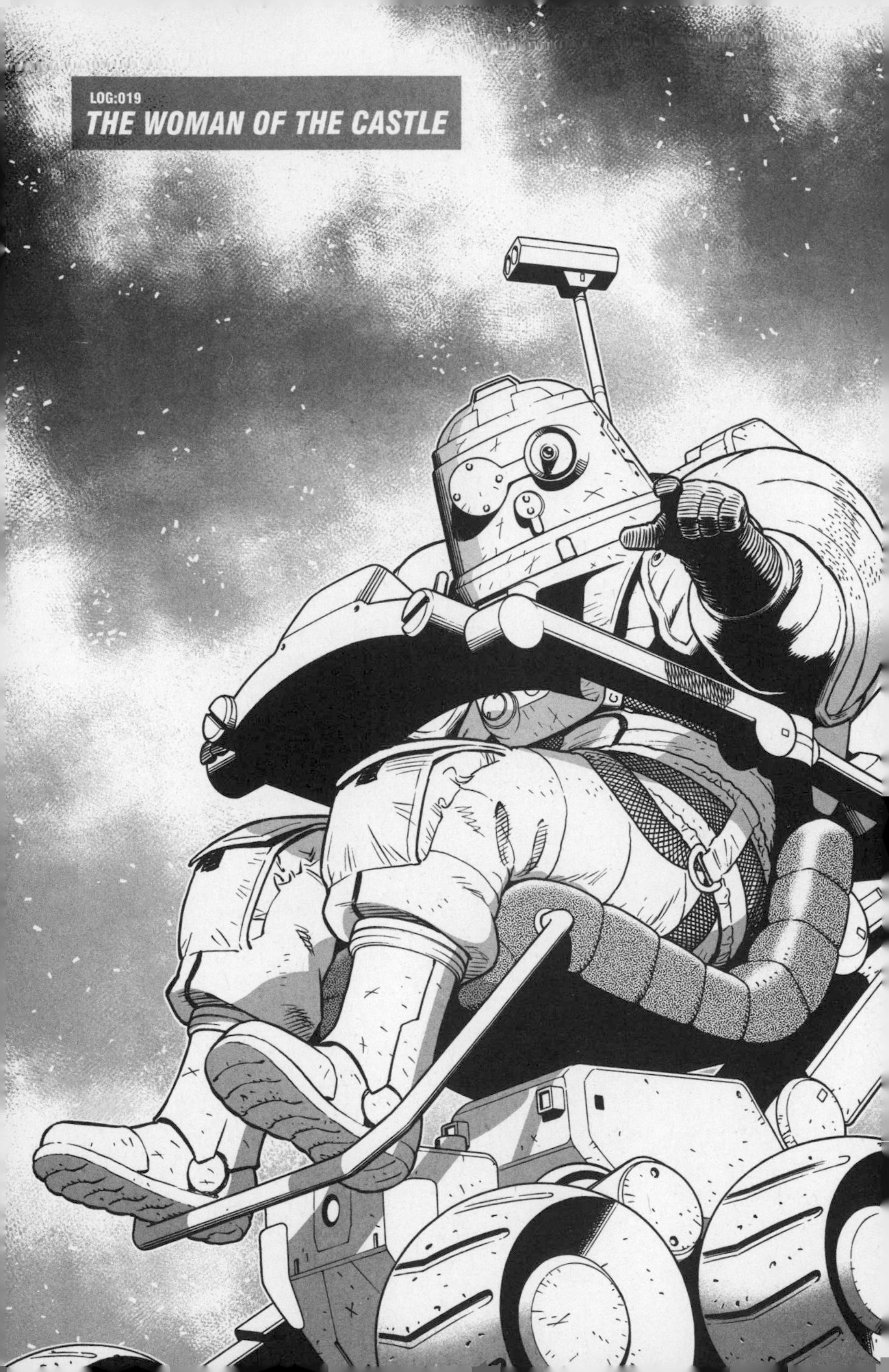
LOG:019
THE WOMAN OF THE CASTLE

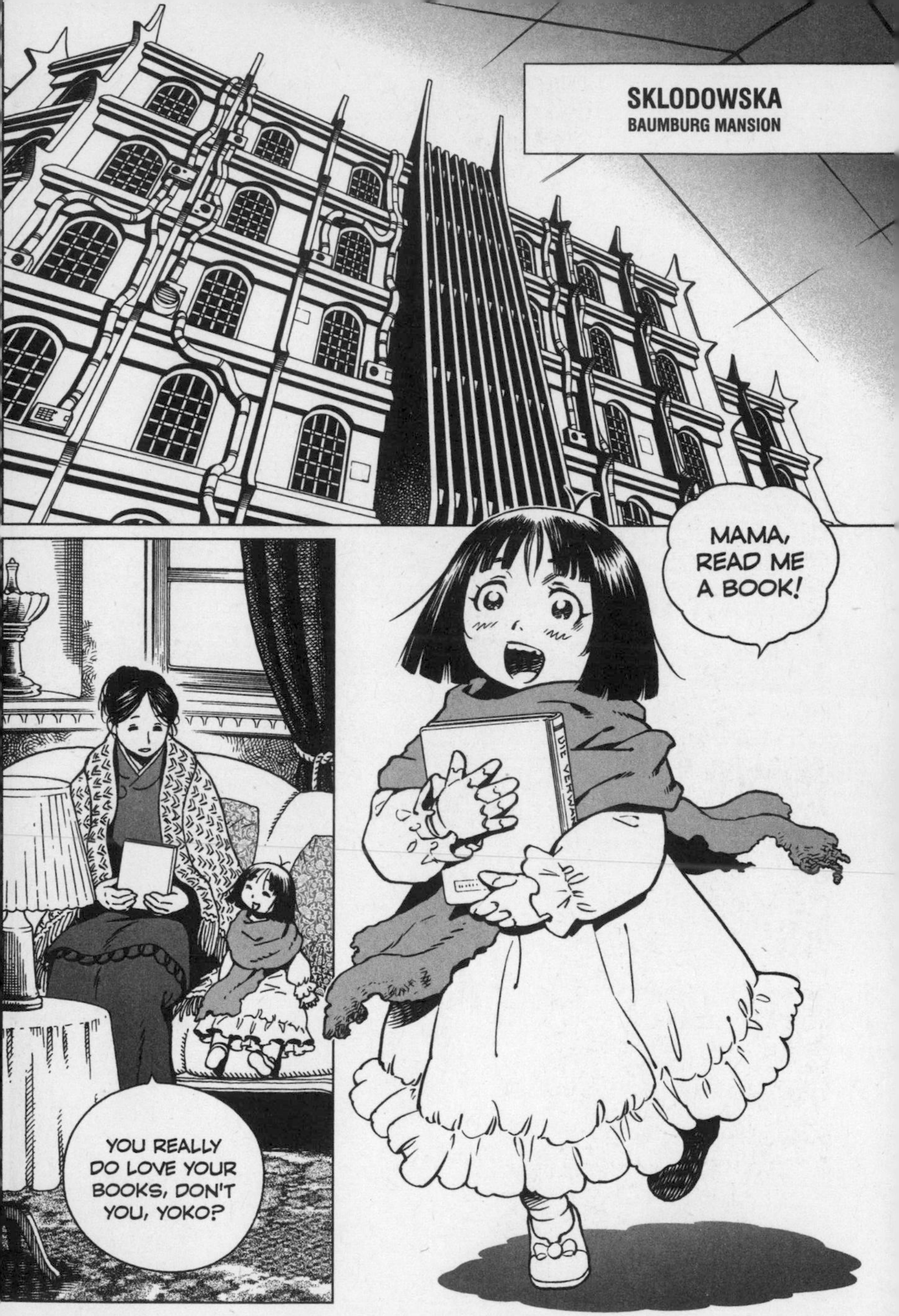
SKLODOWSKA
BAUMBURG MANSION
MAMA, READ ME A BOOK!
YOU REALLY DO LOVE YOUR BOOKS, DON'T YOU, YOKO?

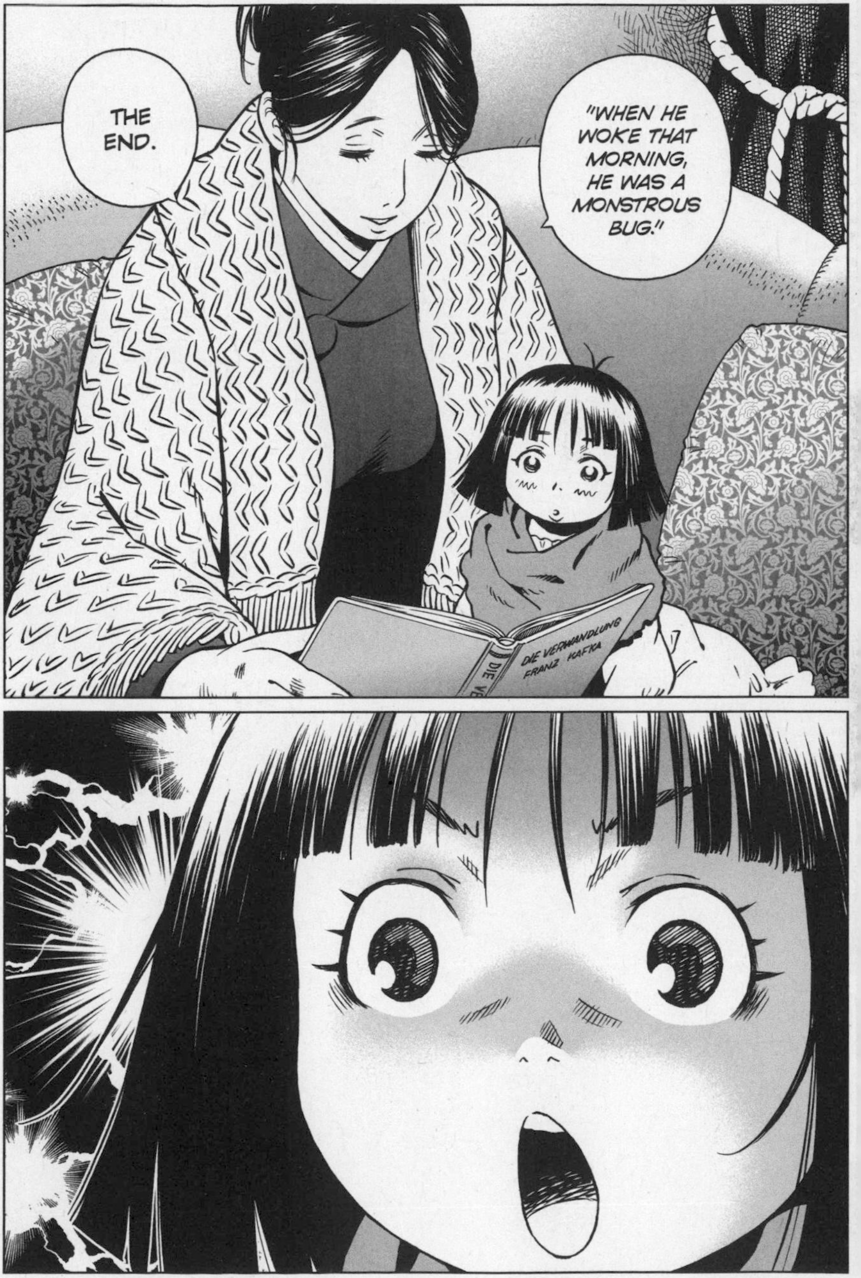
"WHEN HE WOKE THAT MORNING, HE WAS A MONSTROUS BUG."
THE END.
DIE VERWANDLUNG FRANZ KAFKA

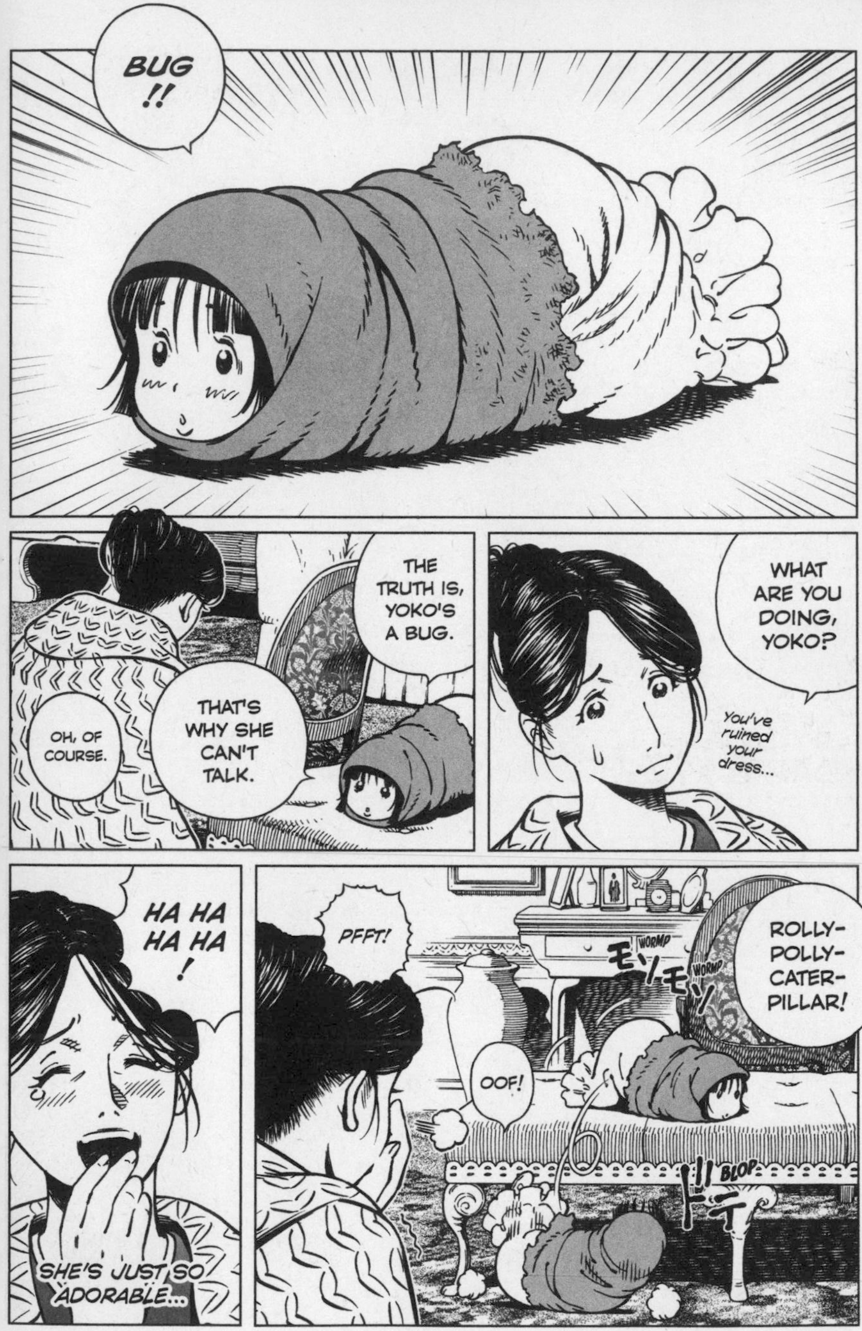
BUG !!
WHAT ARE YOU DOING, YOKO?
You've ruined your dress...
THE TRUTH IS, YOKO'S A BUG.
THAT'S WHY SHE CAN'T TALK.
OH, OF COURSE.
ROLLY-POLLY-CATER-PILLAR!
モソ WORMP
モソ WORMP
PFFT!
OOF!
!! BLOP
ドテ
HA HA HA HA !
SHE'S JUST SO ADORABLE...

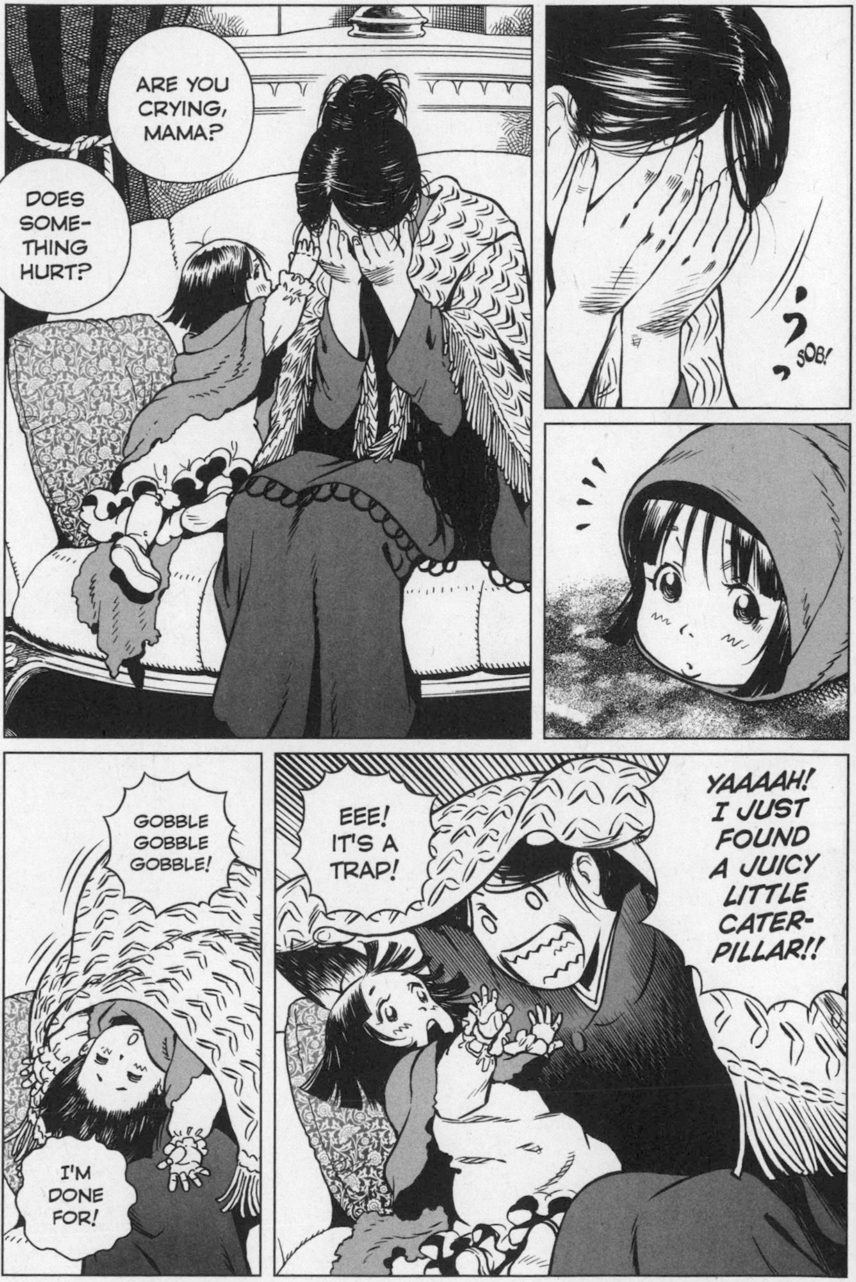
SOB!
ARE YOU CRYING, MAMA?
DOES SOME-THING HURT?
YAAAAH! I JUST FOUND A JUICY LITTLE CATER-PILLAR!!
EEE! IT'S A TRAP!
GOBBLE GOBBLE GOBBLE!
I'M DONE FOR!

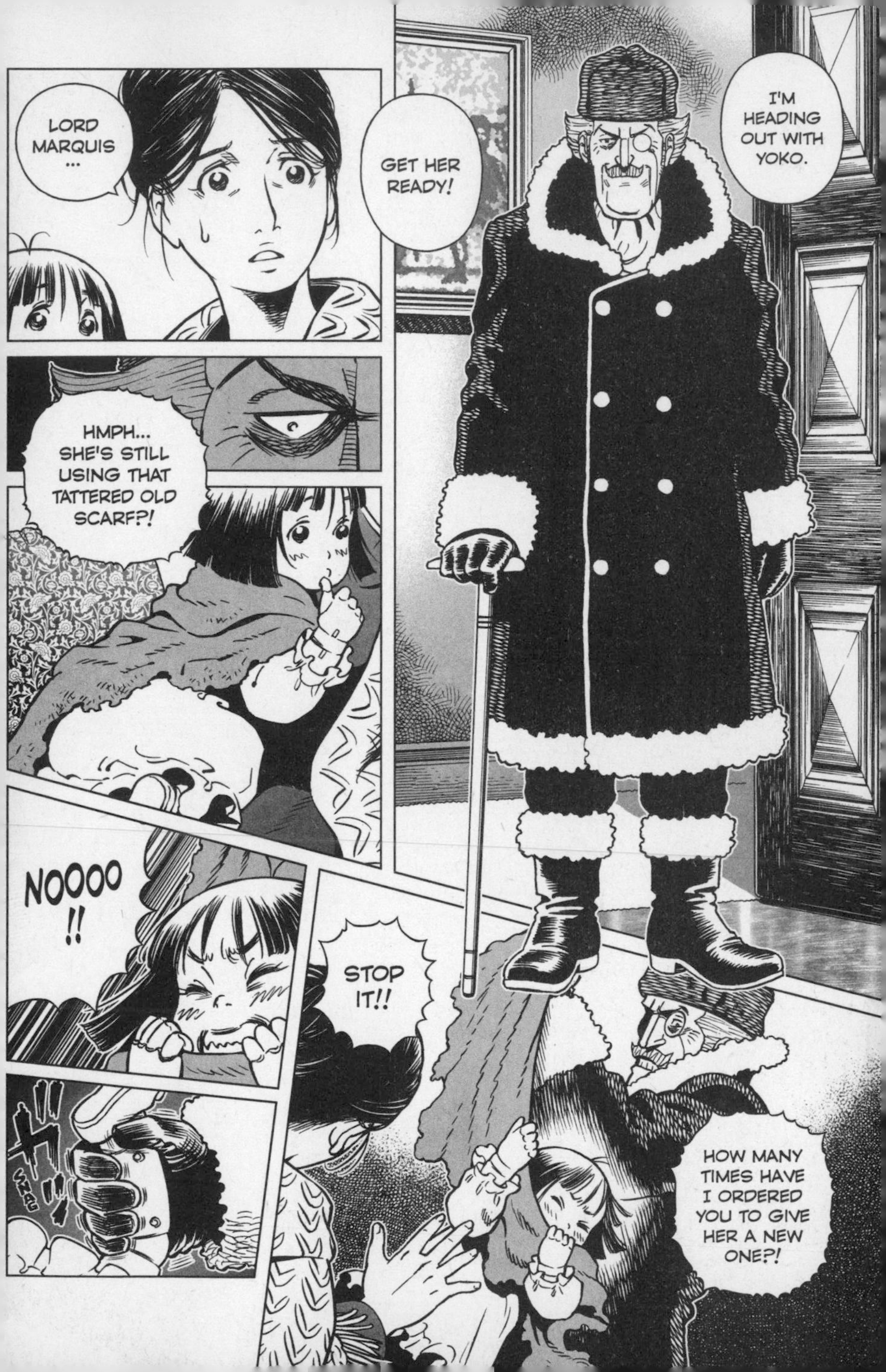
I'M HEADING OUT WITH YOKO.
GET HER READY!
LORD MARQUIS ...
HMPH... SHE'S STILL USING THAT TATTERED OLD SCARF?!
HOW MANY TIMES HAVE I ORDERED YOU TO GIVE HER A NEW ONE?!
STOP IT!!
NOOOO !!
SNAG

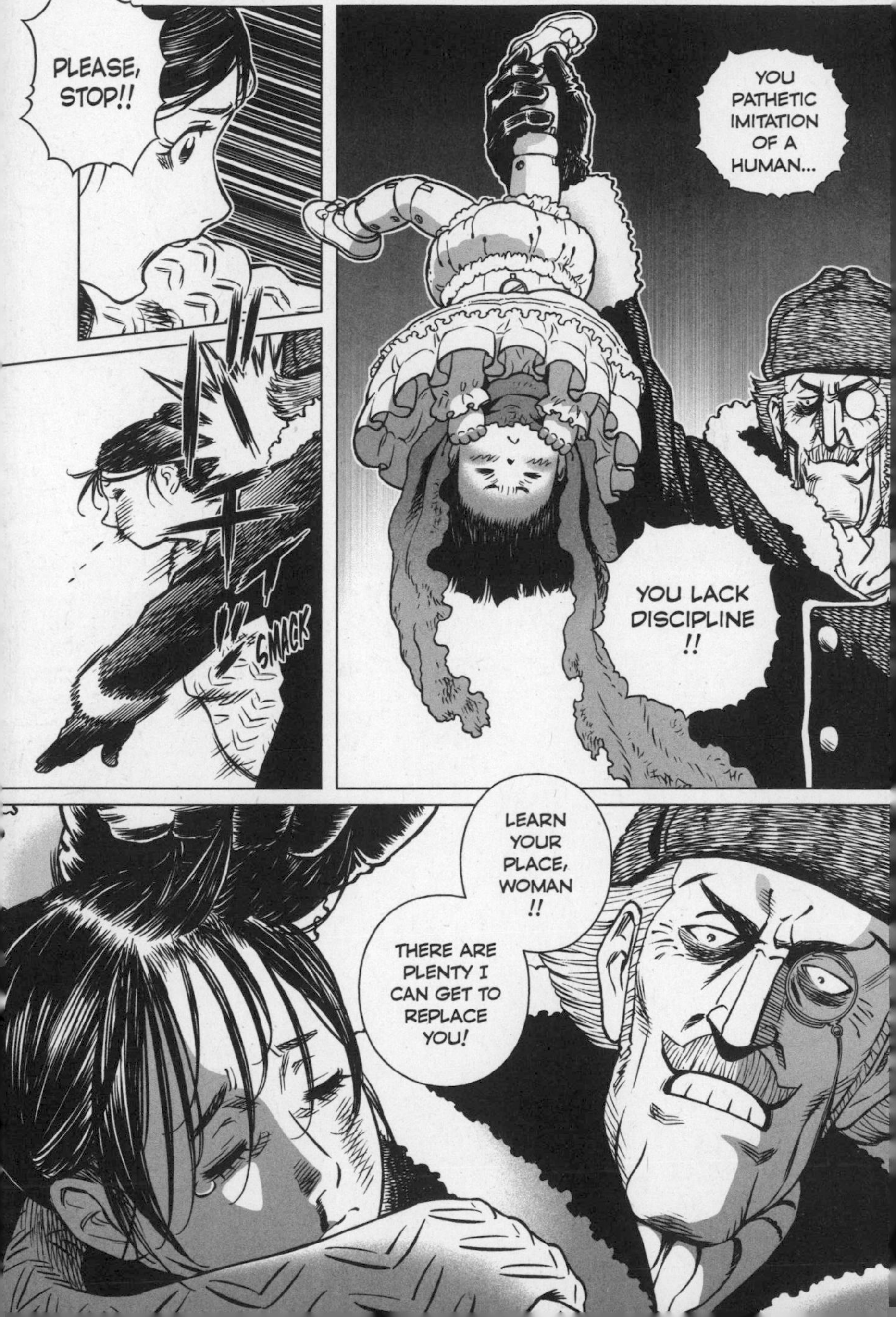
YOU PATHETIC IMITATION OF A HUMAN...
YOU LACK DISCIPLINE !!
PLEASE, STOP!!
SMACK
LEARN YOUR PLACE, WOMAN !!
THERE ARE PLENTY I CAN GET TO REPLACE YOU!

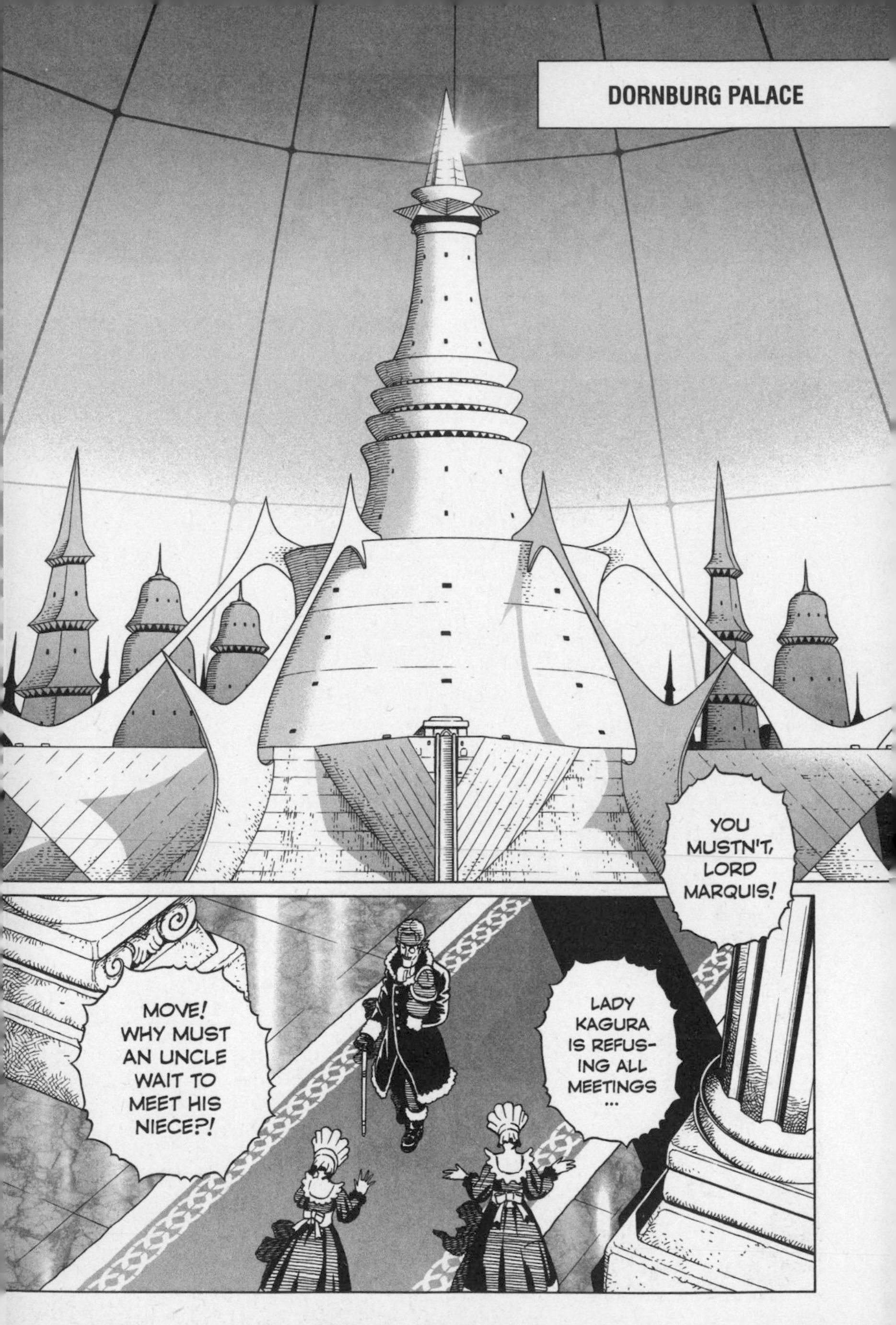
DORNBURG PALACE
YOU MUSTN'T, LORD MARQUIS!
LADY KAGURA IS REFUSING ALL MEETINGS ...
MOVE! WHY MUST AN UNCLE WAIT TO MEET HIS NIECE?!

HOW ARE YOU FEELING, KAGURA ?!

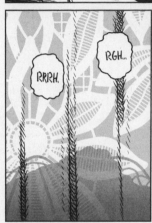

RRRH.

RGH...

シュー、コー
SHHHK KOH

シュー、コー
SHHHK KOH

シュー、コー
SHHHK KOH

I'VE BROUGHT YOU SOMETHING I'D LIKE YOU TO SEE.

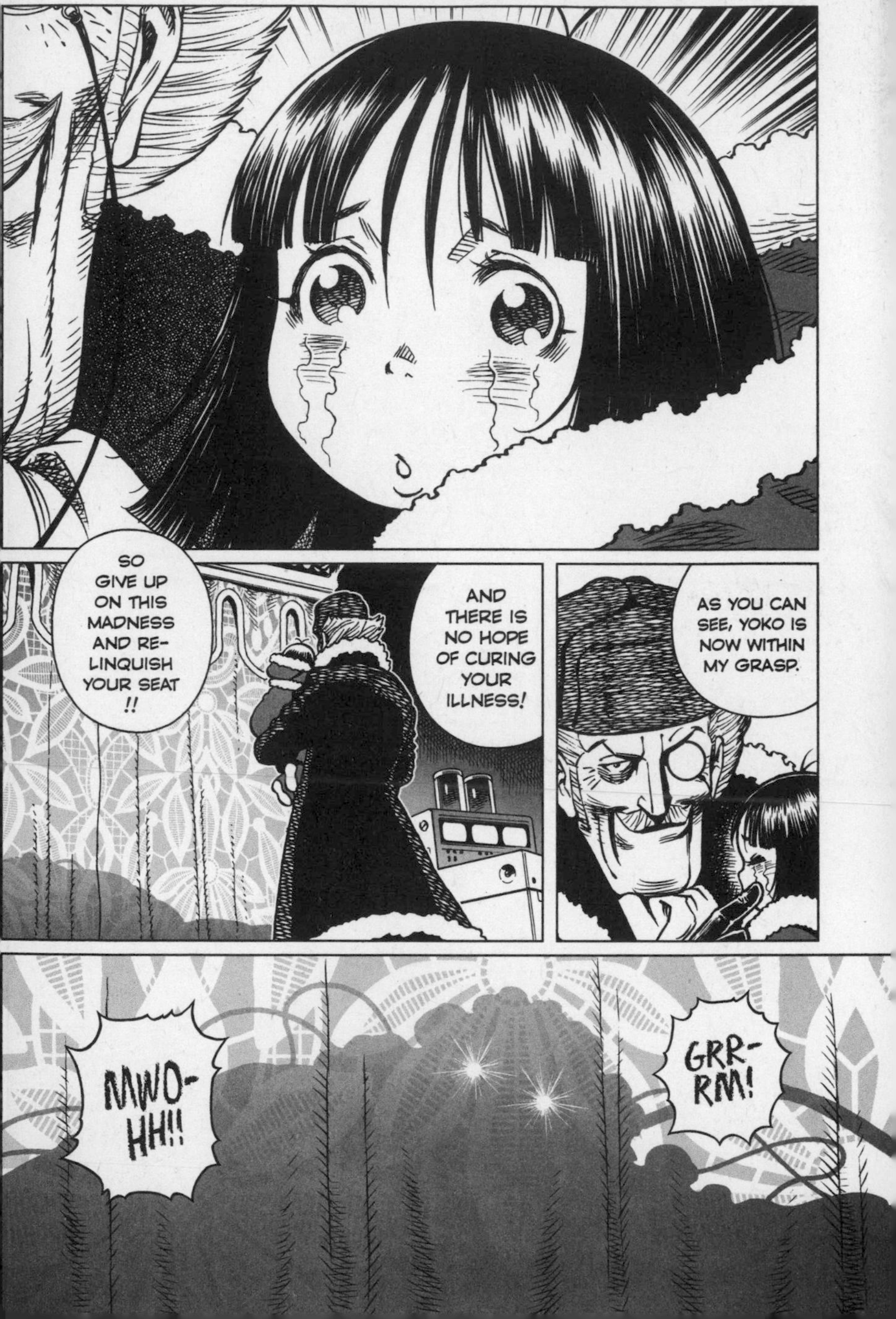
AS YOU CAN SEE, YOKO IS NOW WITHIN MY GRASP.
AND THERE IS NO HOPE OF CURING YOUR ILLNESS!
SO GIVE UP ON THIS MADNESS AND RE-LINQUISH YOUR SEAT !!
GRR-RM!
MWO-HH!!

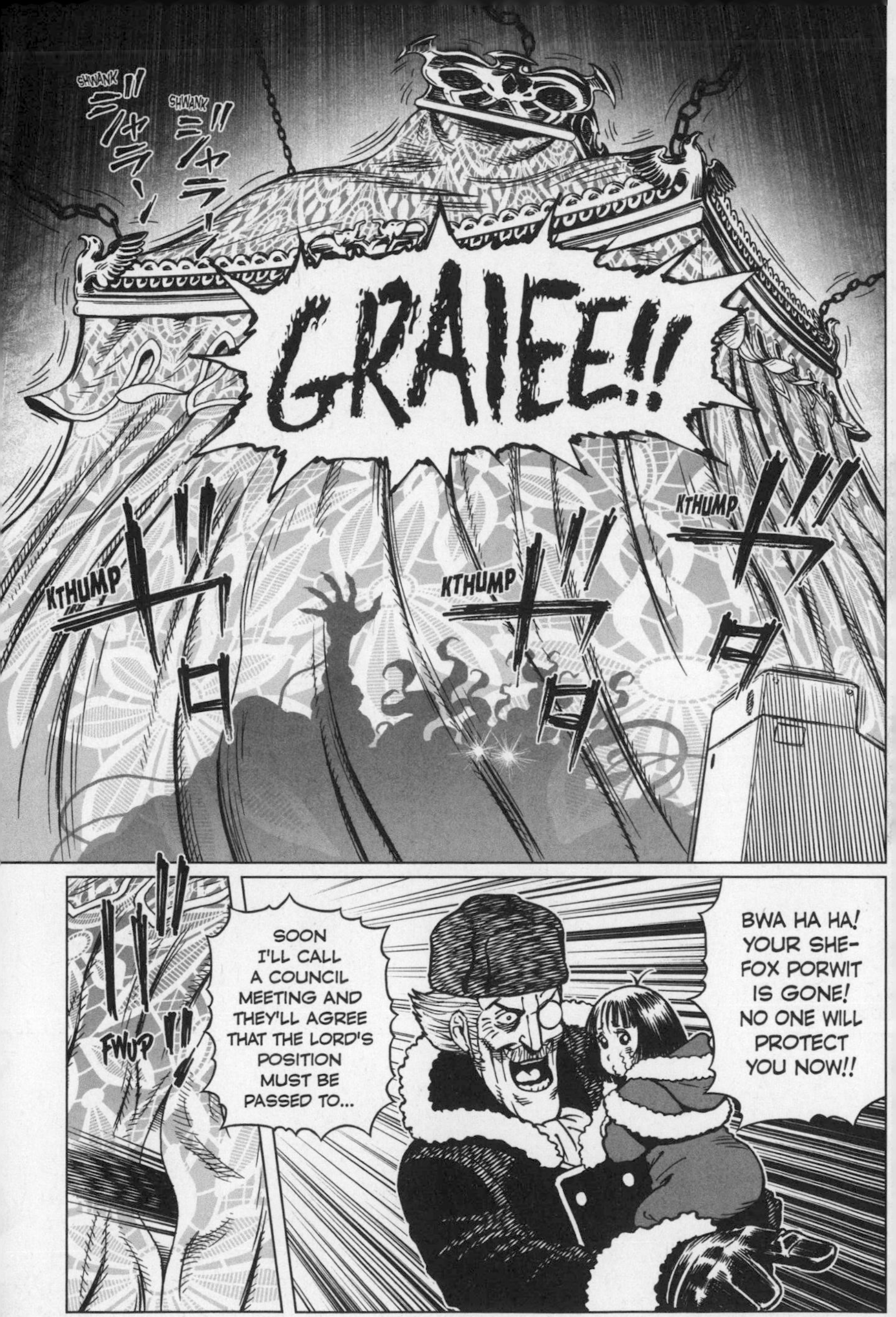
SHWANK
SHWANK
GRAIEE!!
KTHUMP
KTHUMP
KTHUMP
BWA HA HA! YOUR SHE-FOX PORWIT IS GONE! NO ONE WILL PROTECT YOU NOW!!
SOON I'LL CALL A COUNCIL MEETING AND THEY'LL AGREE THAT THE LORD'S POSITION MUST BE PASSED TO...
FWUP

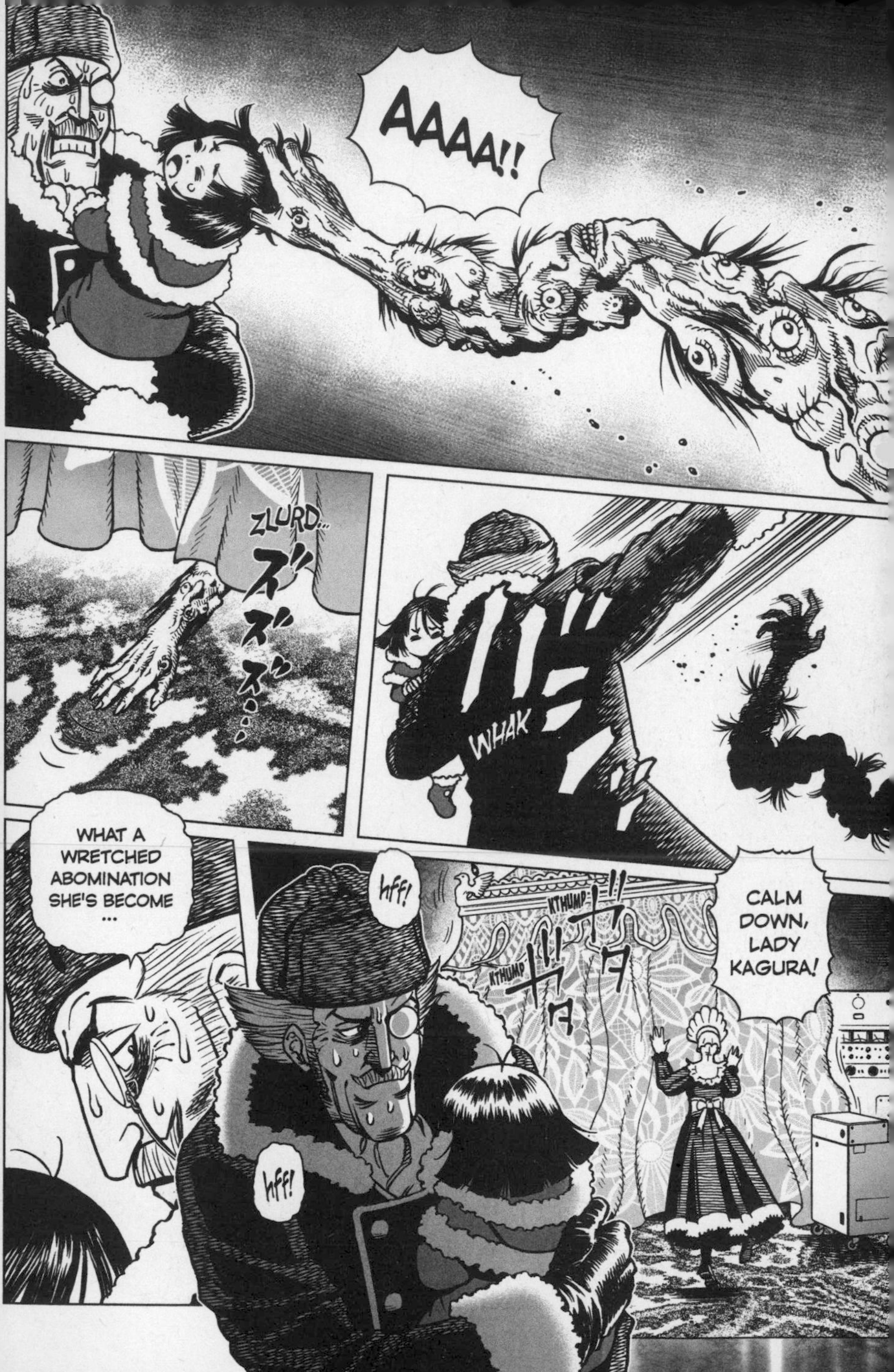
AAAA!!
WHAK
ZLURD...
ズズズズ...
CALM DOWN, LADY KAGURA!
KTHUMP
ガタ!!
KTHUMP
ガタ!!
hff!
hff!
WHAT A WRETCHED ABOMINATION SHE'S BECOME ...

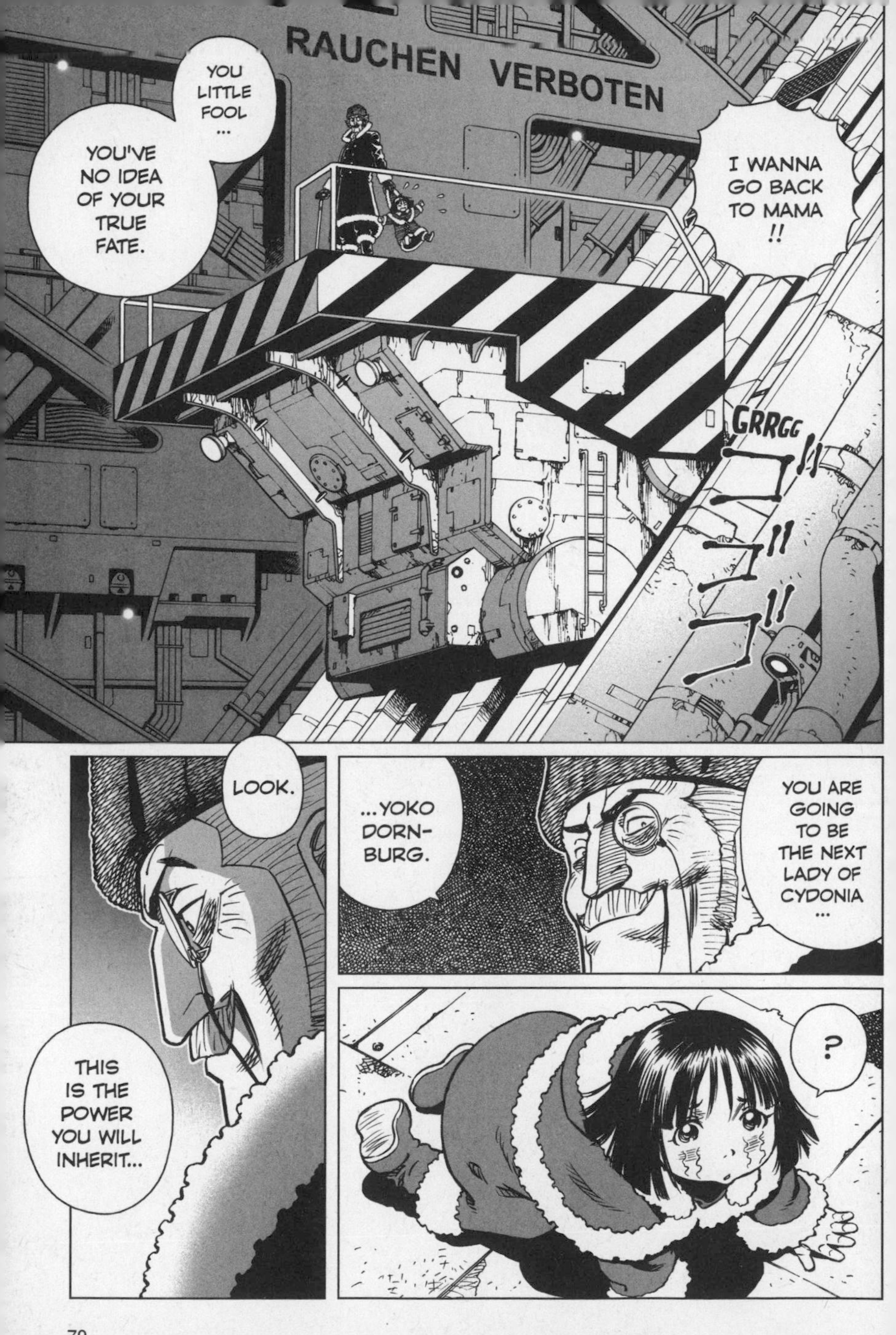
RAUCHEN VERBOTEN
I WANNA GO BACK TO MAMA !!
YOU LITTLE FOOL ...
YOU'VE NO IDEA OF YOUR TRUE FATE.
GRRGG
YOU ARE GOING TO BE THE NEXT LADY OF CYDONIA ...
...YOKO DORNBURG.
?
LOOK.
THIS IS THE POWER YOU WILL INHERIT...

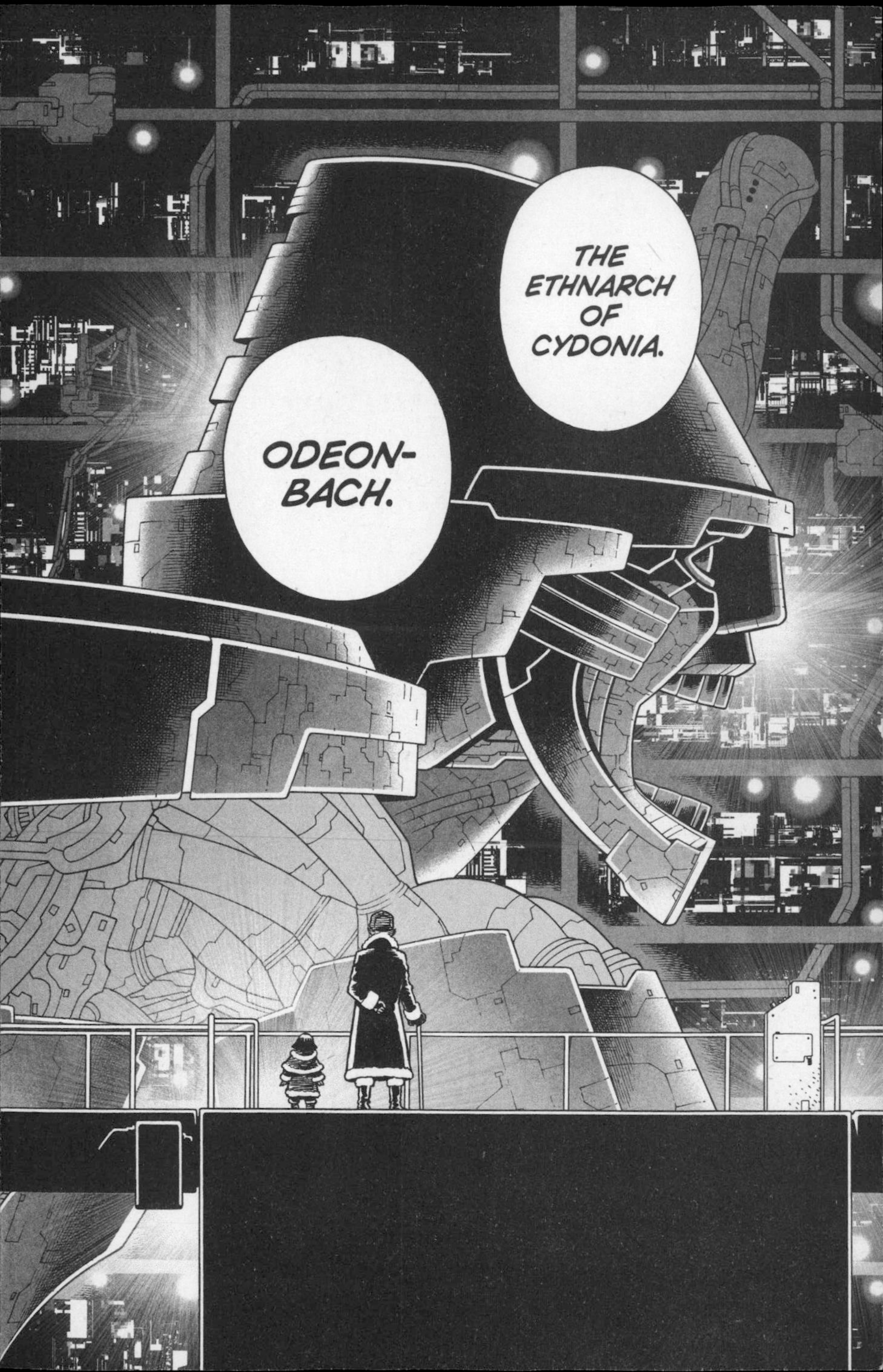
THE ETHNARCH OF CYDONIA.
ODEON-BACH.

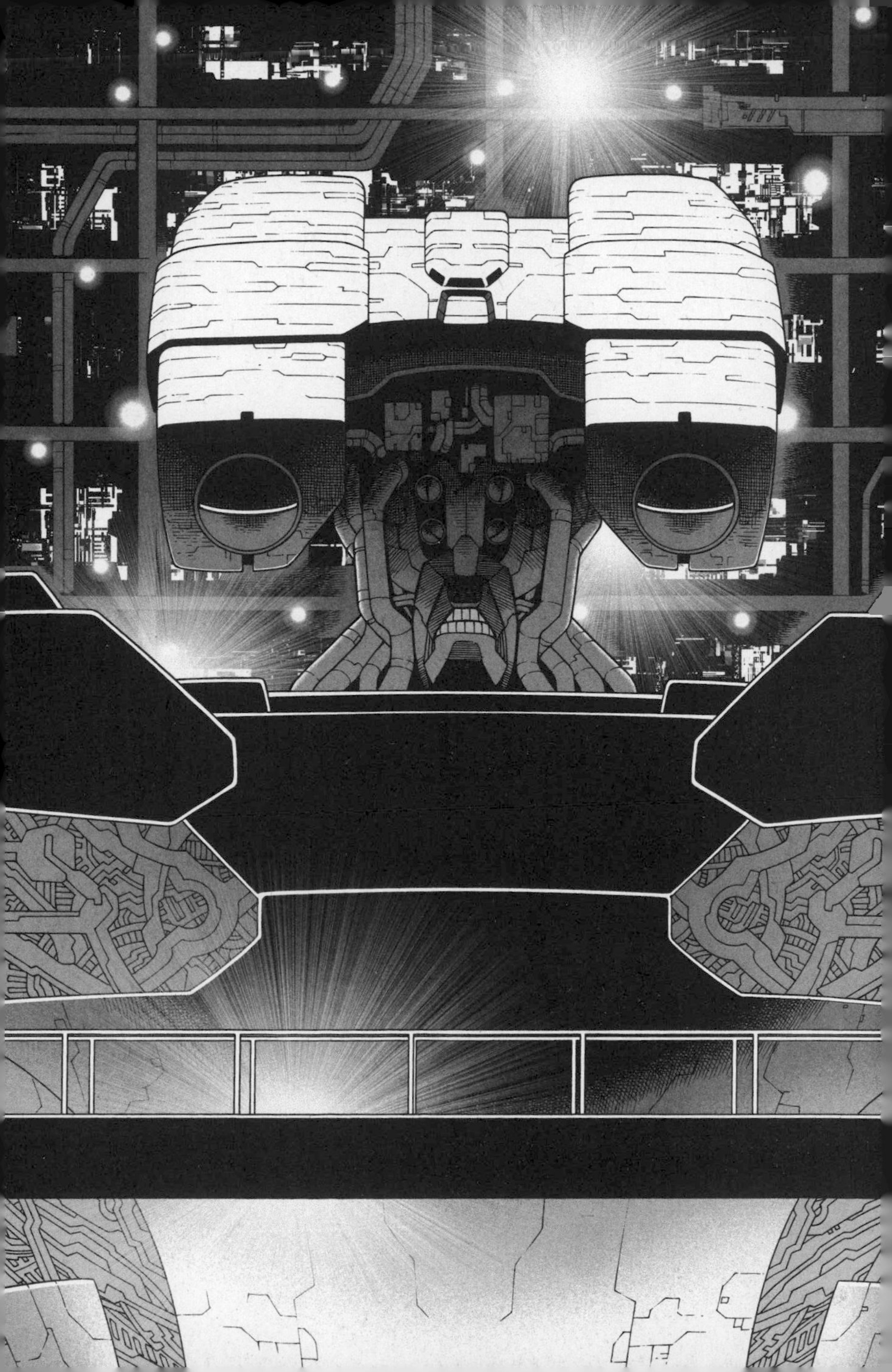

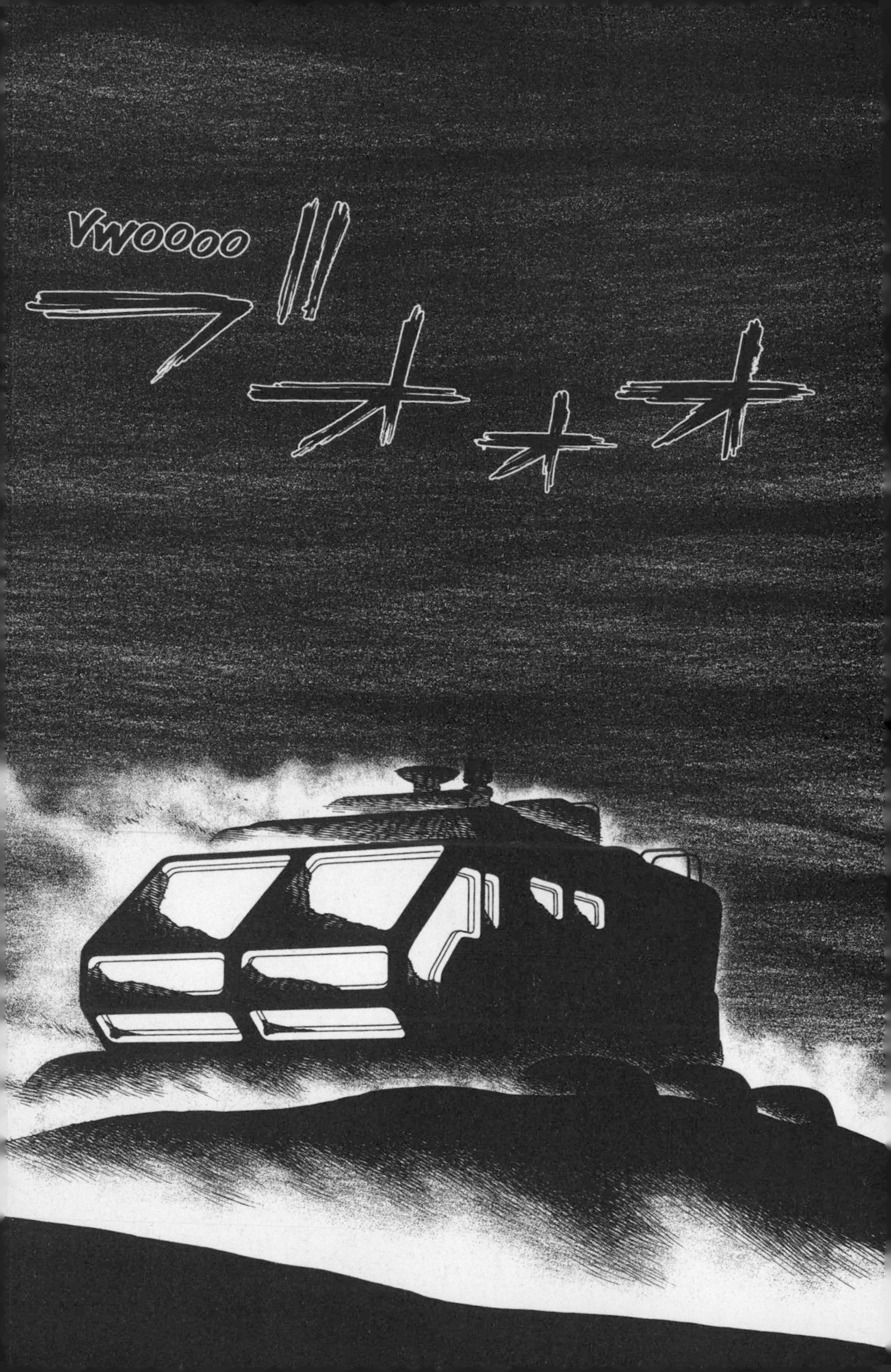
VWOOOO
ブォォォ

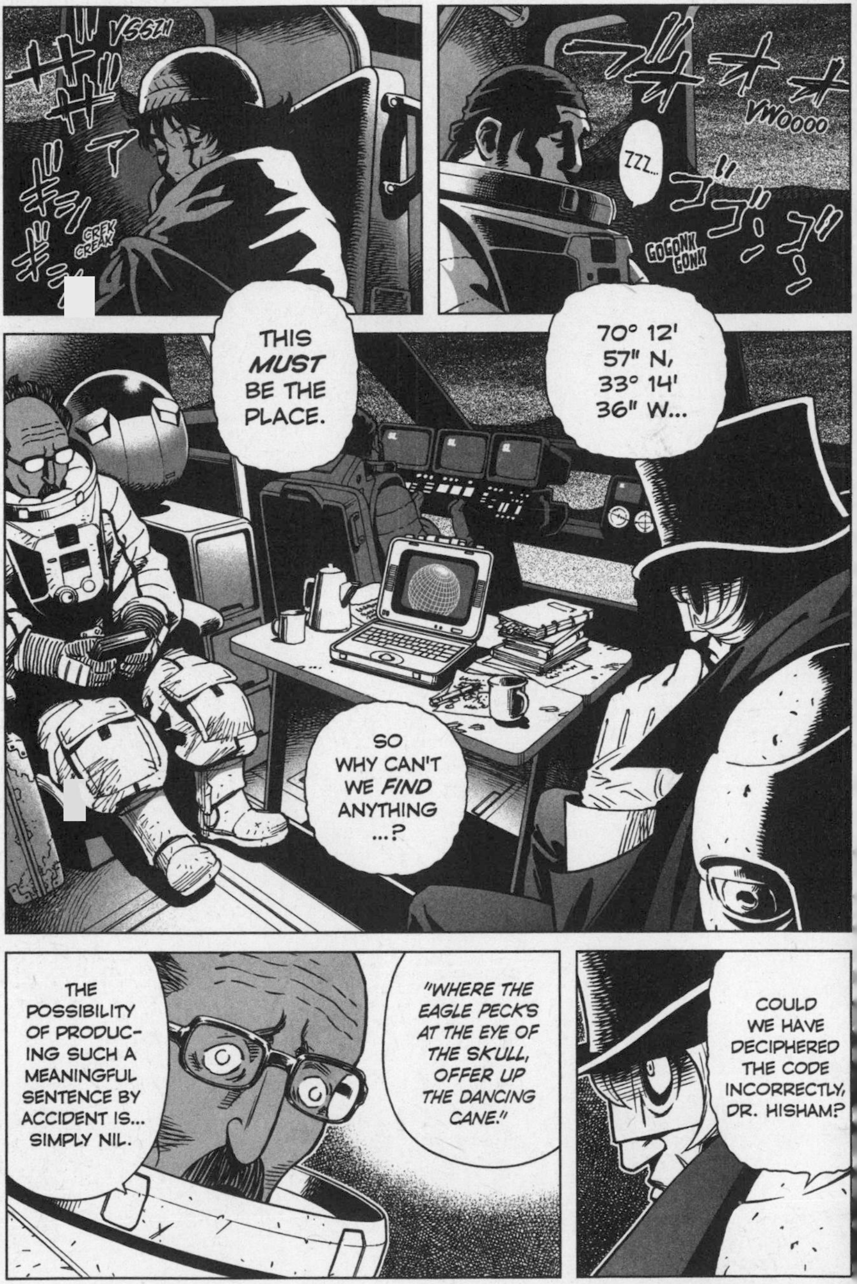

VWOOOO
ZZZ...
GOGONK GONK
VSSZH
GREK GREAK
70° 12' 57" N, 33° 14' 36" W...
THIS *MUST* BE THE PLACE.
SO WHY CAN'T WE *FIND* ANYTHING ...?
COULD WE HAVE DECIPHERED THE CODE INCORRECTLY, DR. HISHAM?
"WHERE THE EAGLE PECKS AT THE EYE OF THE SKULL, OFFER UP THE DANCING CANE."
THE POSSIBILITY OF PRODUCING SUCH A MEANINGFUL SENTENCE BY ACCIDENT IS... SIMPLY NIL.

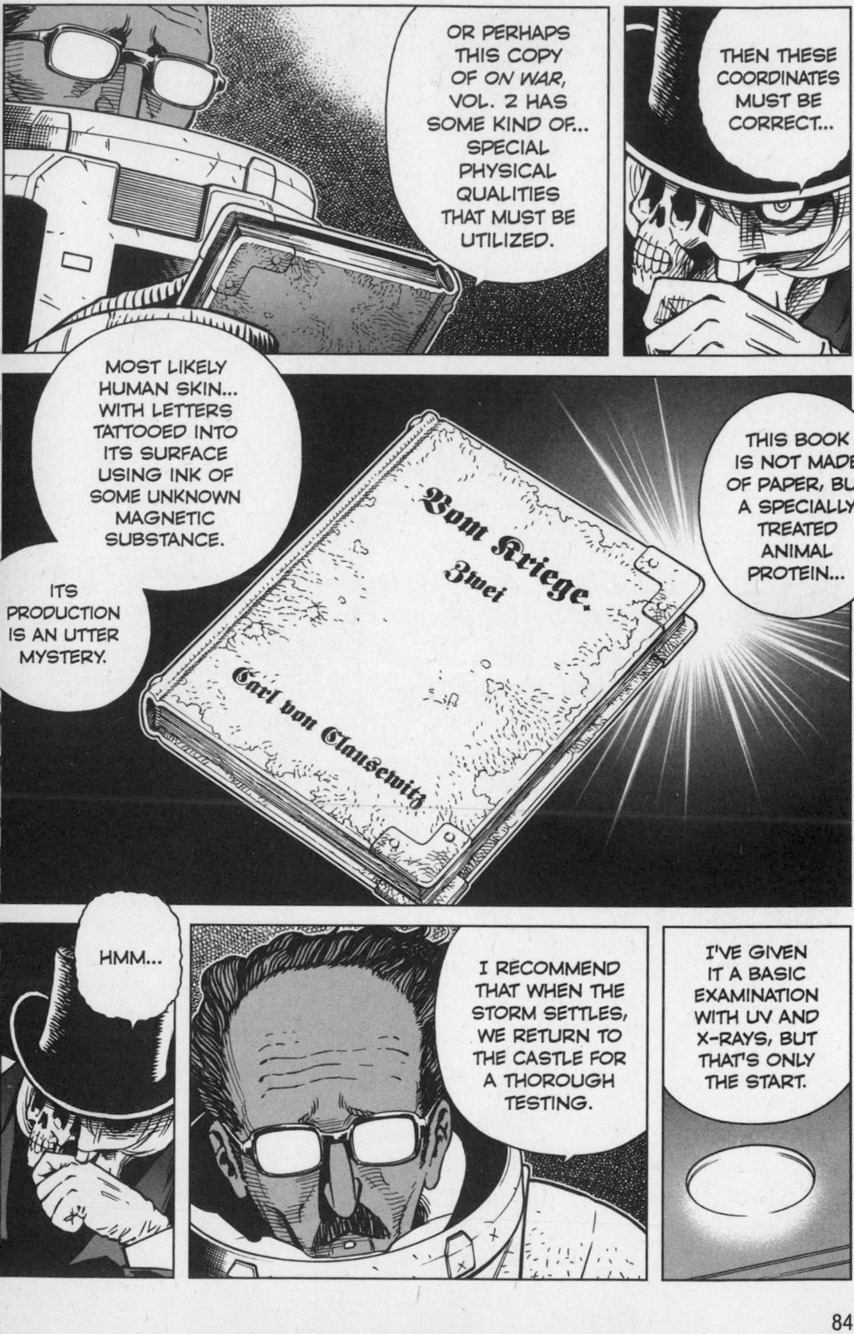
THEN THESE COORDINATES MUST BE CORRECT...
OR PERHAPS THIS COPY OF *ON WAR*, VOL. 2 HAS SOME KIND OF... SPECIAL PHYSICAL QUALITIES THAT MUST BE UTILIZED.
THIS BOOK IS NOT MADE OF PAPER, BUT A SPECIALLY TREATED ANIMAL PROTEIN...
Vom Kriege. Zwei
Carl von Clausewitz
MOST LIKELY HUMAN SKIN... WITH LETTERS TATTOOED INTO ITS SURFACE USING INK OF SOME UNKNOWN MAGNETIC SUBSTANCE.
ITS PRODUCTION IS AN UTTER MYSTERY.
I'VE GIVEN IT A BASIC EXAMINATION WITH UV AND X-RAYS, BUT THAT'S ONLY THE START.
I RECOMMEND THAT WHEN THE STORM SETTLES, WE RETURN TO THE CASTLE FOR A THOROUGH TESTING.
HMM...

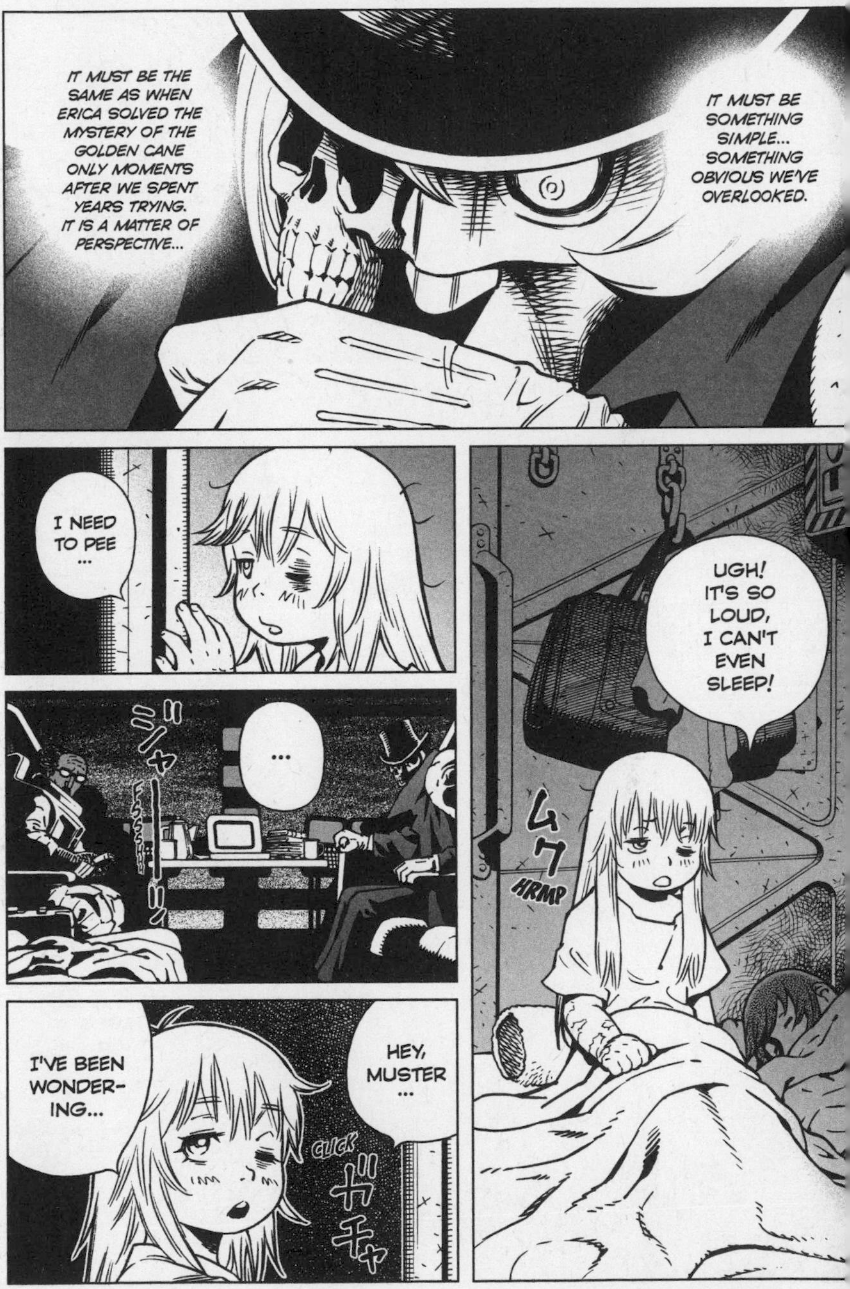

IT MUST BE SOMETHING SIMPLE... SOMETHING OBVIOUS WE'VE OVERLOOKED.
IT MUST BE THE SAME AS WHEN ERICA SOLVED THE MYSTERY OF THE GOLDEN CANE ONLY MOMENTS AFTER WE SPENT YEARS TRYING. IT IS A MATTER OF PERSPECTIVE...
UGH! IT'S SO LOUD, I CAN'T EVEN SLEEP!
ムク
HRMP
I NEED TO PEE ...
ジャーッ
FSSSHHH
...
HEY, MUSTER ...
I'VE BEEN WONDER-ING...
CLICK
ガチャ

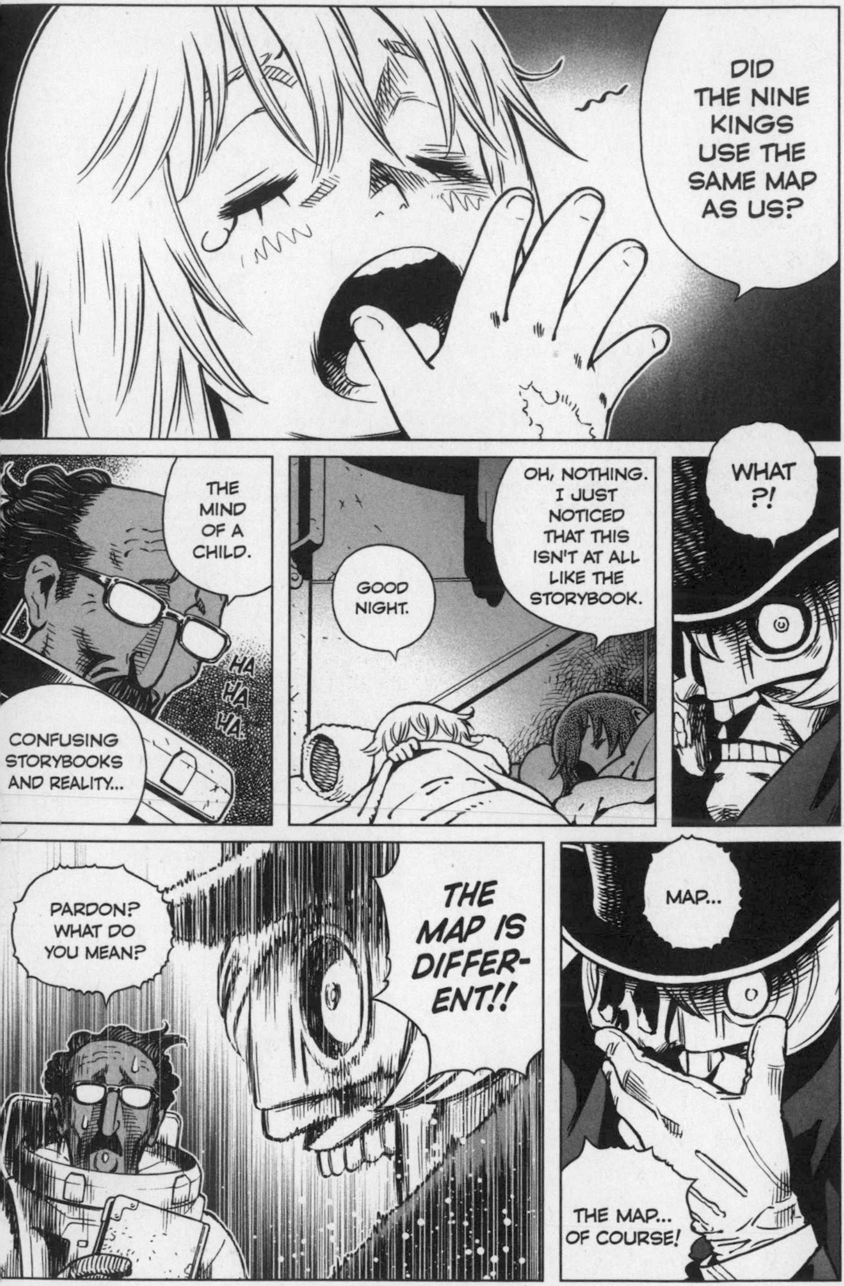
DID THE NINE KINGS USE THE SAME MAP AS US?
WHAT ?!
OH, NOTHING. I JUST NOTICED THAT THIS ISN'T AT ALL LIKE THE STORYBOOK.
GOOD NIGHT.
THE MIND OF A CHILD.
HA HA HA.
CONFUSING STORYBOOKS AND REALITY...
MAP...
THE MAP... OF COURSE!
THE MAP IS DIFFER-ENT!!
PARDON? WHAT DO YOU MEAN?

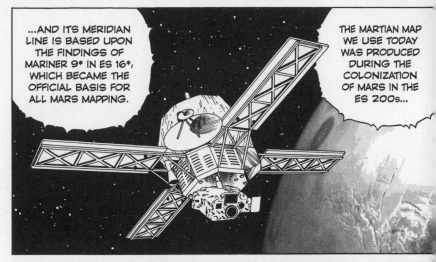

THE MARTIAN MAP WE USE TODAY WAS PRODUCED DURING THE COLONIZATION OF MARS IN THE ES 200s...
...AND ITS MERIDIAN LINE IS BASED UPON THE FINDINGS OF MARINER 9* IN ES 16*, WHICH BECAME THE OFFICIAL BASIS FOR ALL MARS MAPPING.
THAT MUST MEAN THAT THE SCHIAPARELLI* MAP THE ALT NEUN WOULD HAVE BEEN USING...
...WAS ON DIFFERENT COORDINATES!!
Argyre
MARE ERYTRAEUM
Deucalionis Regio
Edom
Arabia
SO THE PROPER DESTINATION, ONCE THE SHIFT IS ACCOUNTED FOR...
TAP
TAP
TAP
TAPPA
TAP
...IS 21.8 KM TO THE SOUTH-EAST!!
21.8km

***MARINER 9:** A Mars probe launched by NASA in 1971. It photographed over 80% of the Martian surface.
***ES 16:** Year 16 of Era Sputnik. This would be 1972 AD.
***SCHIAPARELLI:** Giovanni Virginio Schiaparelli (1835-1910), Italian astronomer, known for his study of Mars.

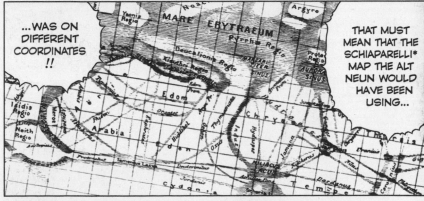

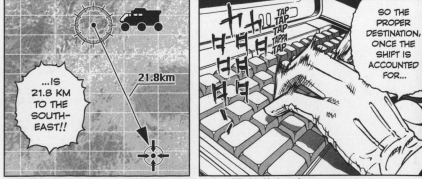

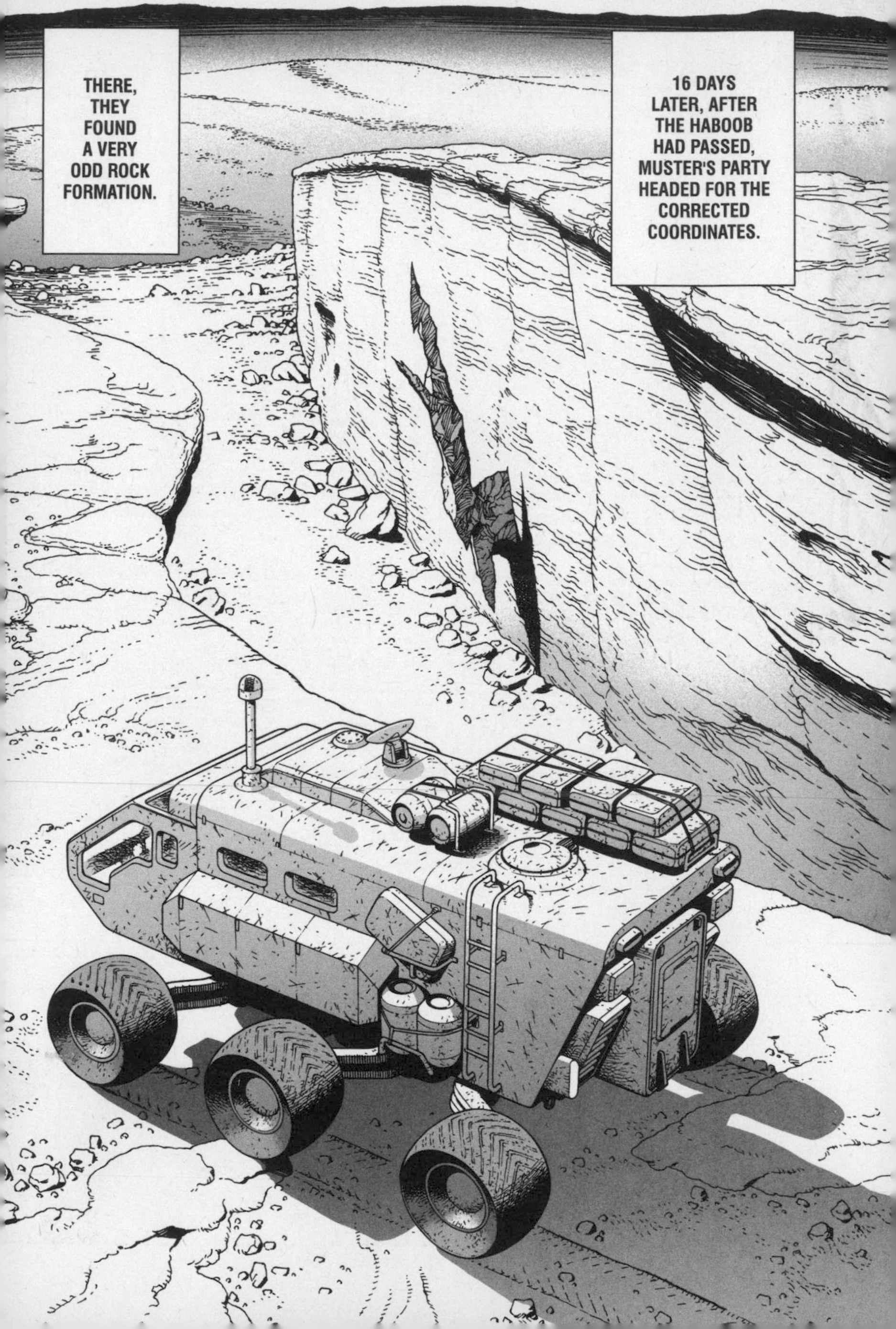
16 DAYS LATER, AFTER THE HABOOB HAD PASSED, MUSTER'S PARTY HEADED FOR THE CORRECTED COORDINATES.
THERE, THEY FOUND A VERY ODD ROCK FORMATION.

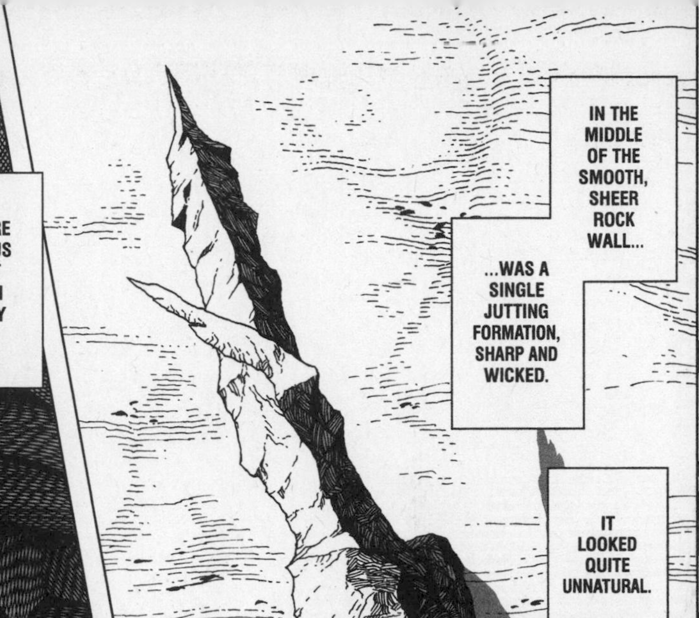
IN THE MIDDLE OF THE SMOOTH, SHEER ROCK WALL...
...WAS A SINGLE JUTTING FORMATION, SHARP AND WICKED.
IT LOOKED QUITE UNNATURAL.
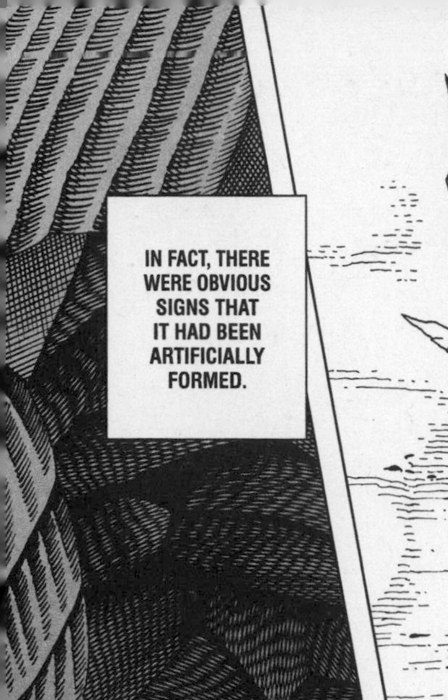
IN FACT, THERE WERE OBVIOUS SIGNS THAT IT HAD BEEN ARTIFICIALLY FORMED.
BUT NOTHING SUGGESTED AN "EAGLE" OR A "SKULL" AT FIRST GLANCE.
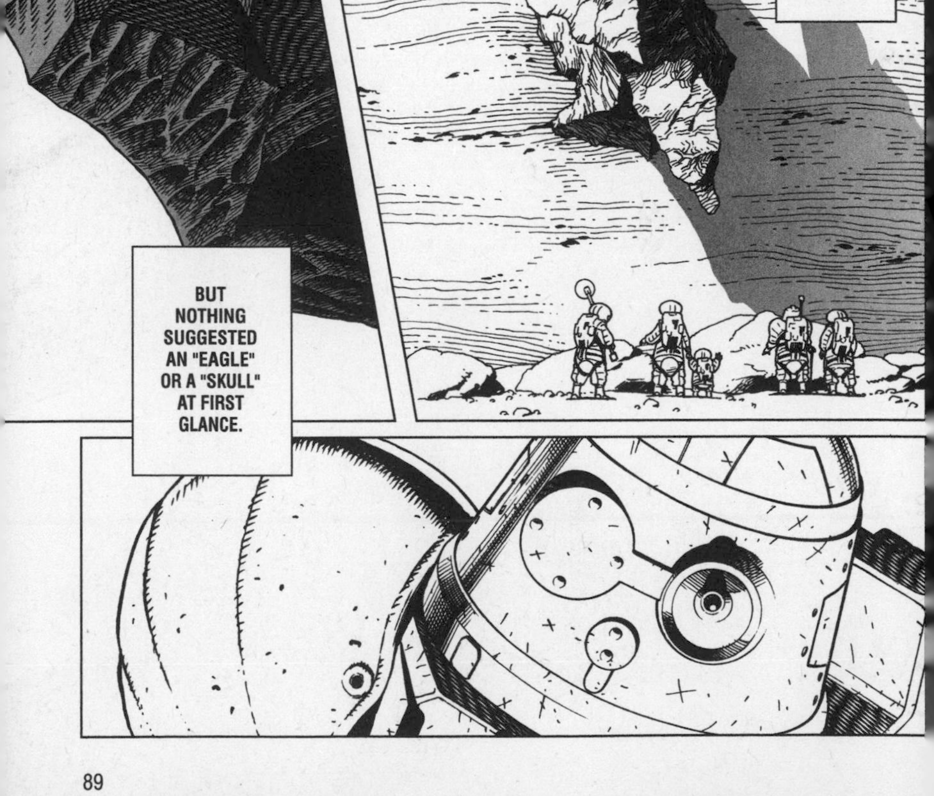

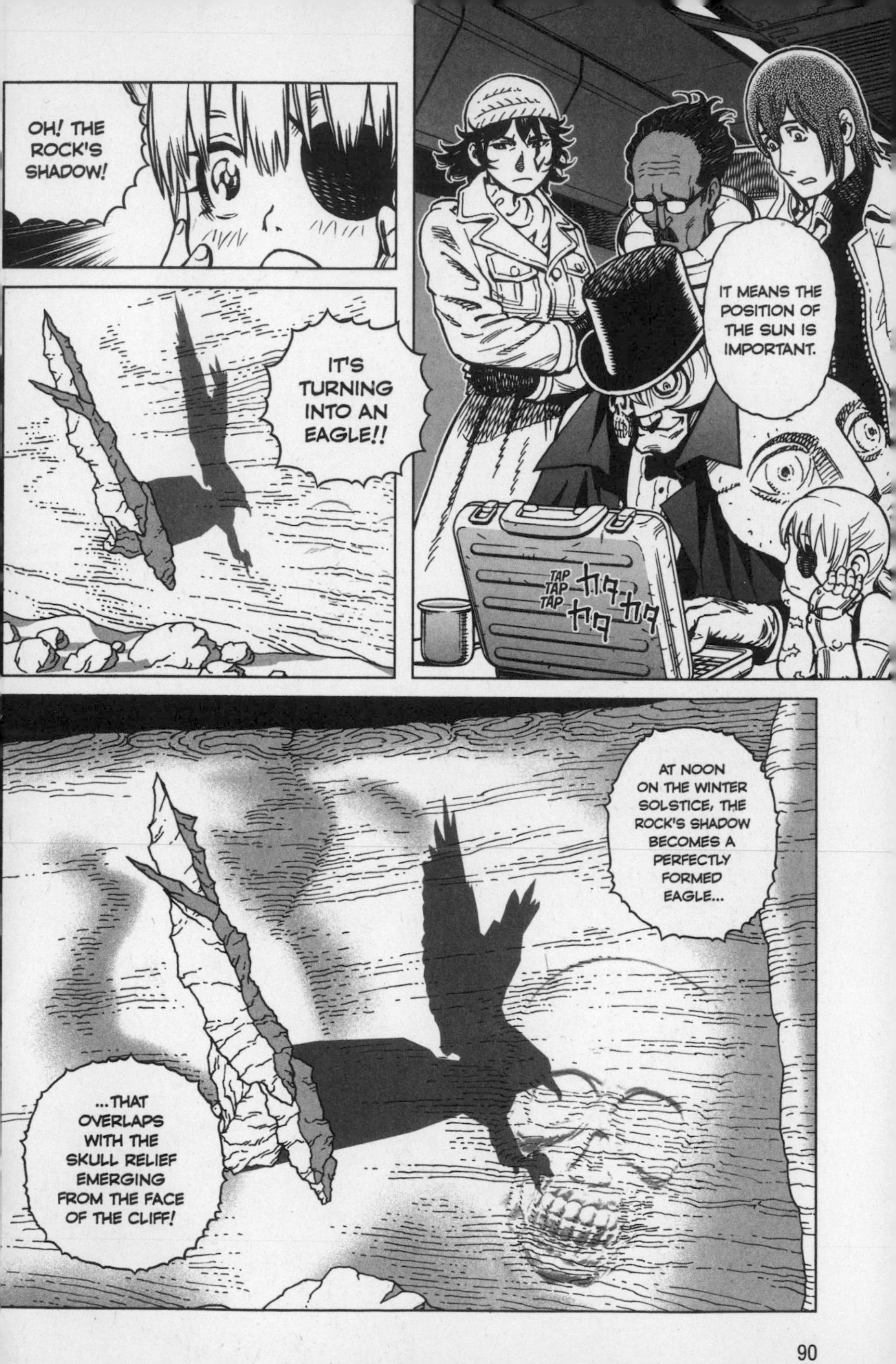
IT MEANS THE POSITION OF THE SUN IS IMPORTANT.
TAP TAP TAP
カタカタ
カタ
OH! THE ROCK'S SHADOW!
IT'S TURNING INTO AN EAGLE!!
AT NOON ON THE WINTER SOLSTICE, THE ROCK'S SHADOW BECOMES A PERFECTLY FORMED EAGLE...
...THAT OVERLAPS WITH THE SKULL RELIEF EMERGING FROM THE FACE OF THE CLIFF!

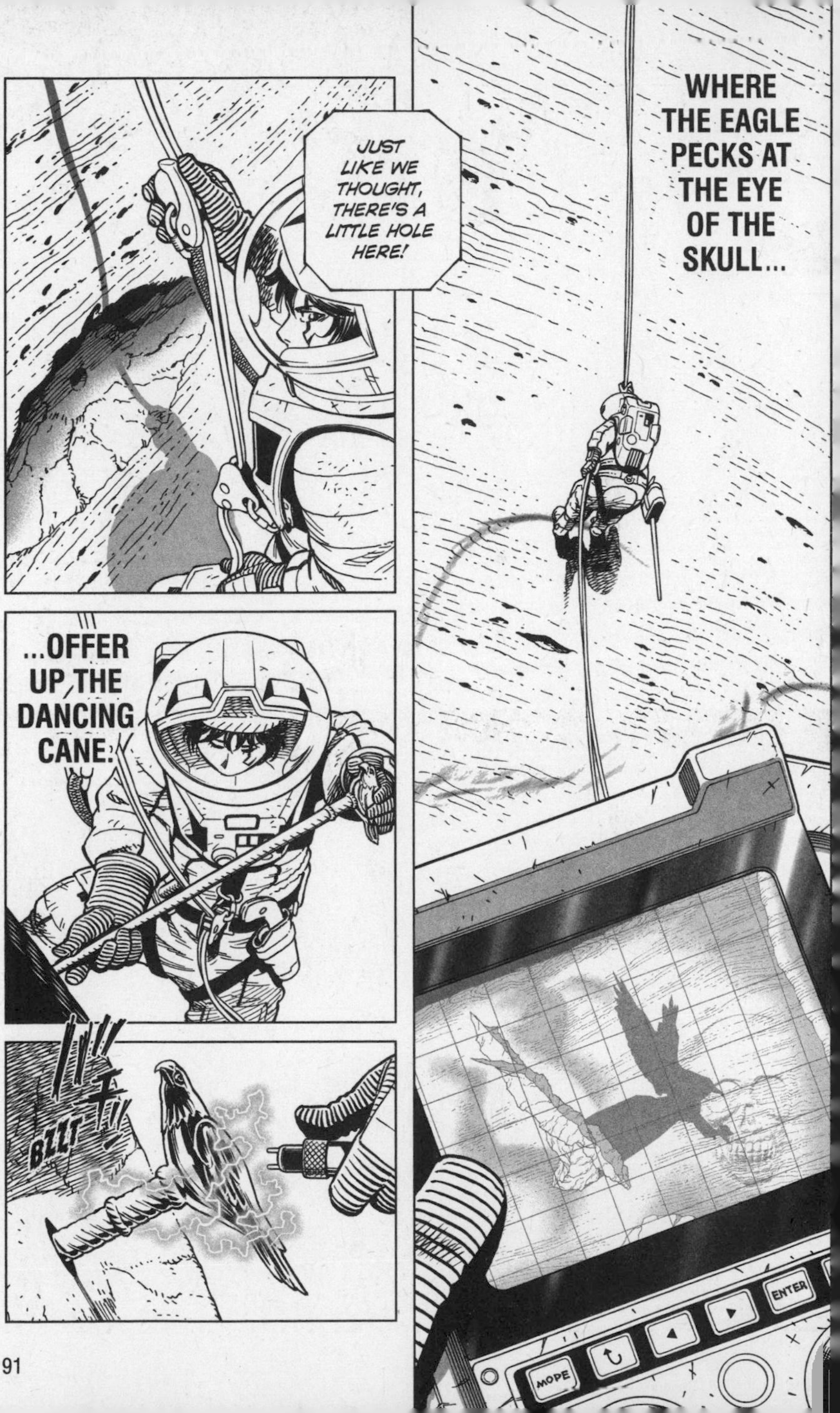
WHERE THE EAGLE PECKS AT THE EYE OF THE SKULL...
ENTER
MODE
JUST LIKE WE THOUGHT, THERE'S A LITTLE HOLE HERE!
...OFFER UP THE DANCING CANE.
BZZT

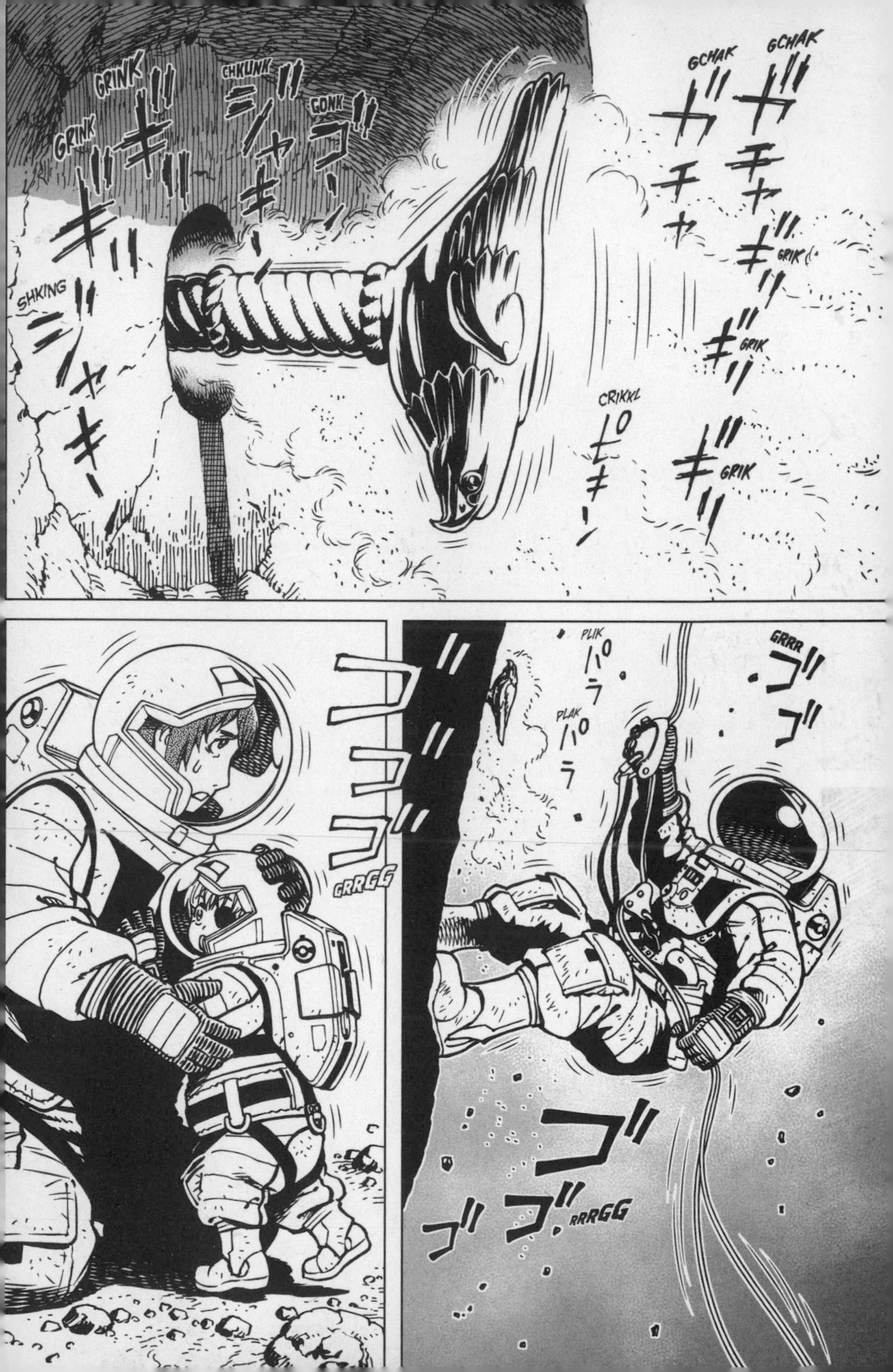

GCHAK
GCHAK
GRIK
GRIK
GRIK
CRIKKL
GONK
CHKUNK
GRINK
GRINK
SHKING
GRRR
PLIK
PLAK
RRRGG
GRRGG

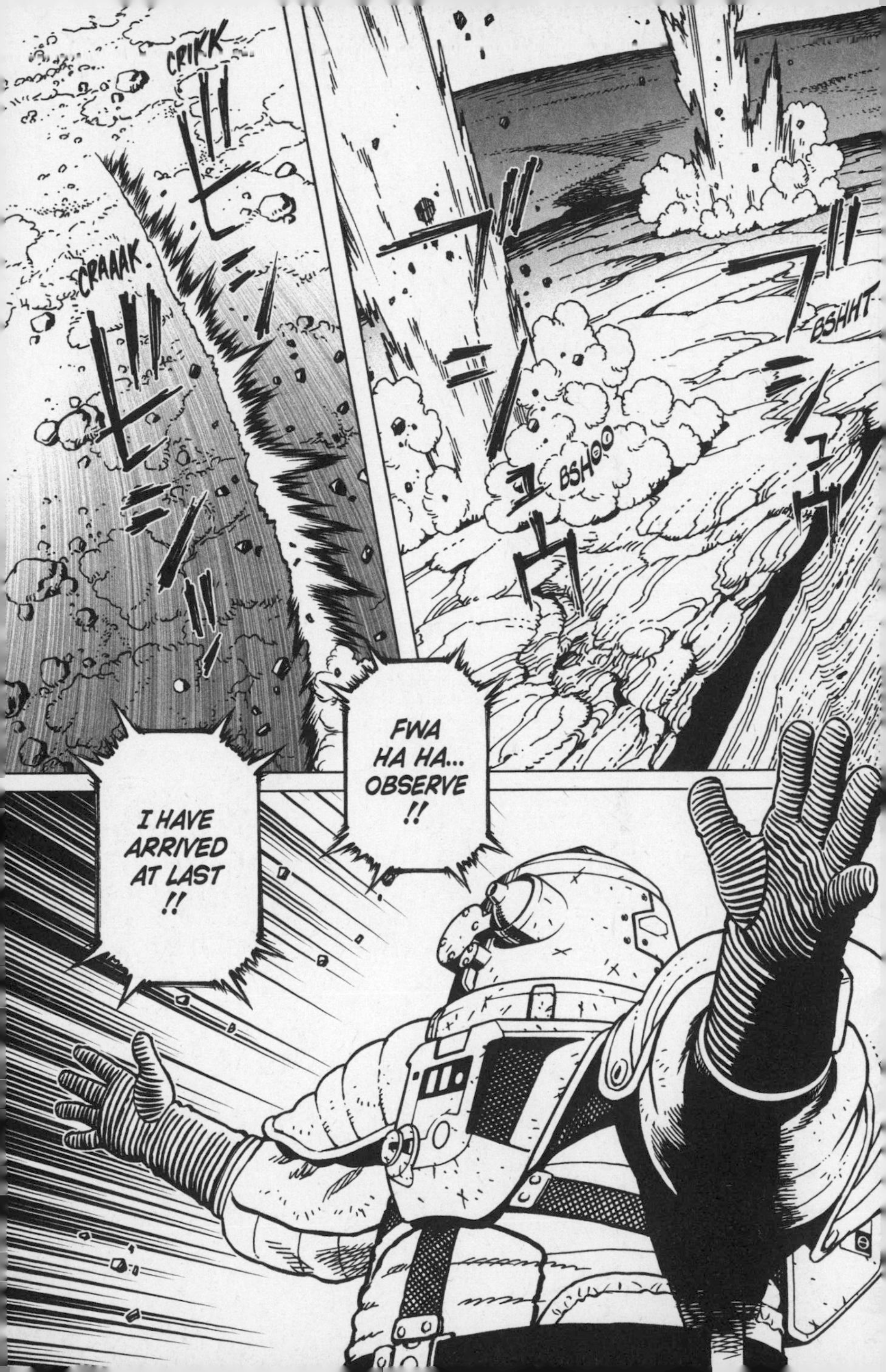
BSHHT
BSHOO
CRIKK
CRAAAK
FWA HA HA... OBSERVE !!
I HAVE ARRIVED AT LAST !!

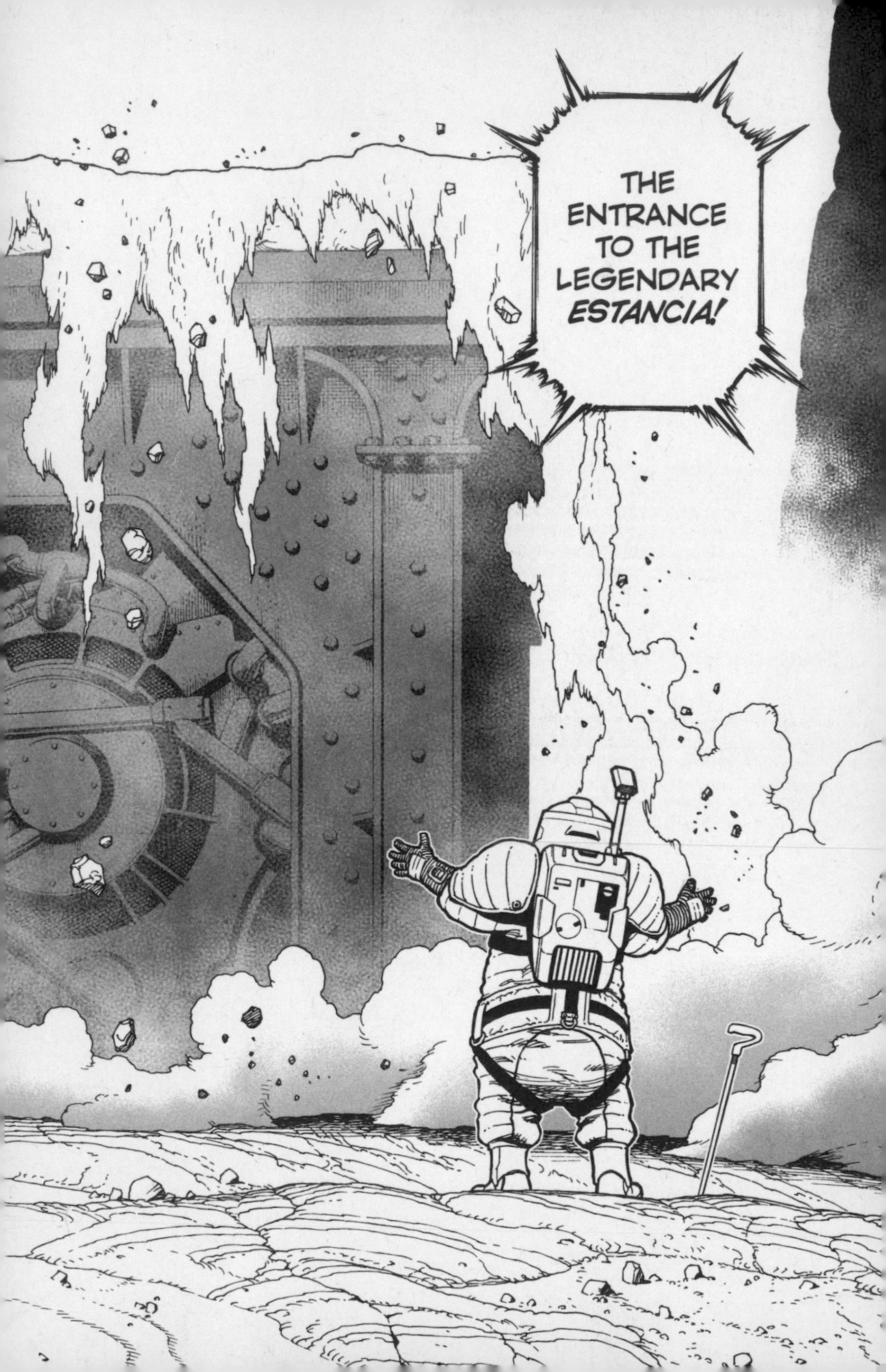
THE ENTRANCE TO THE LEGENDARY *ESTANCIA!*

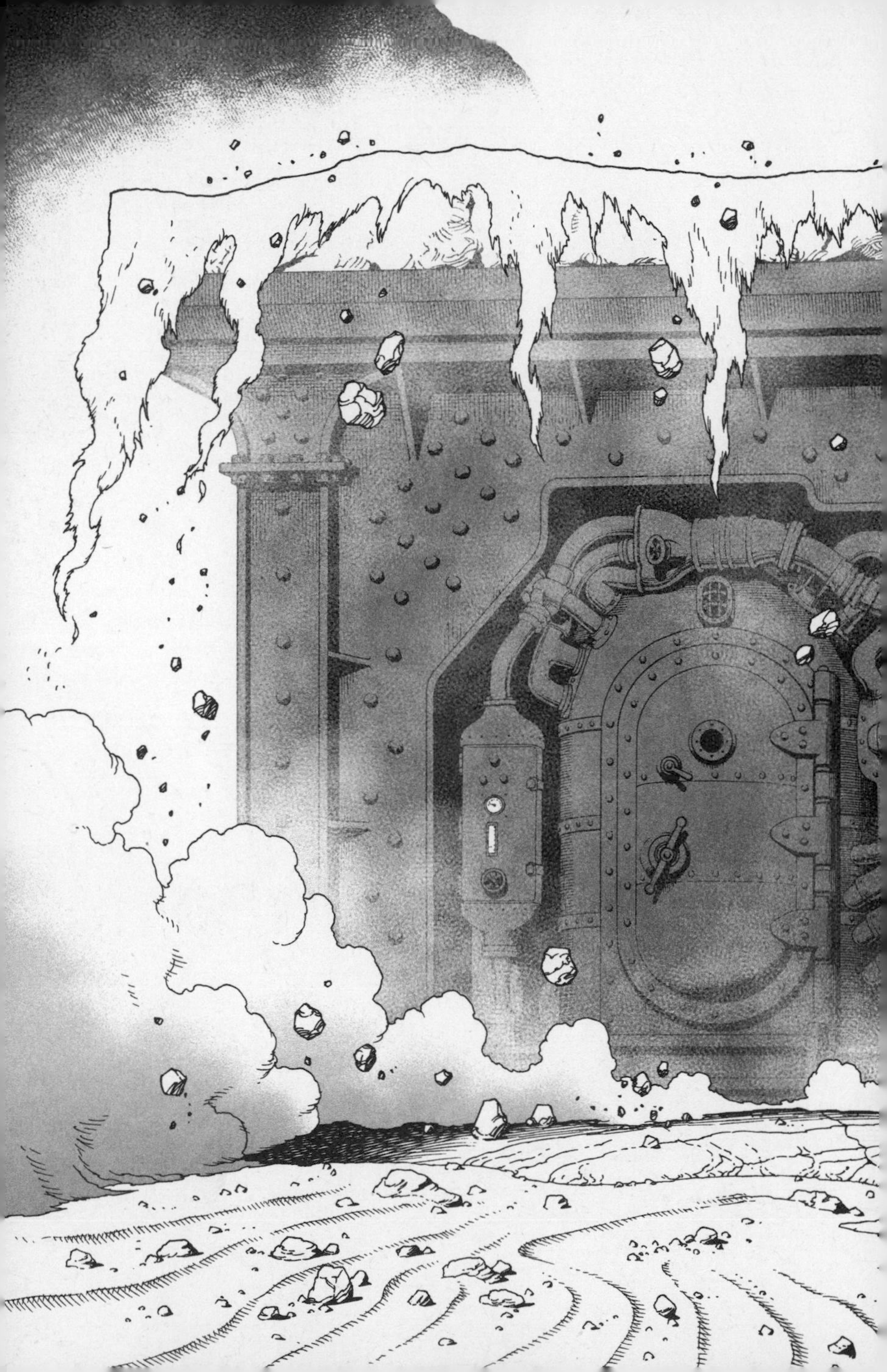

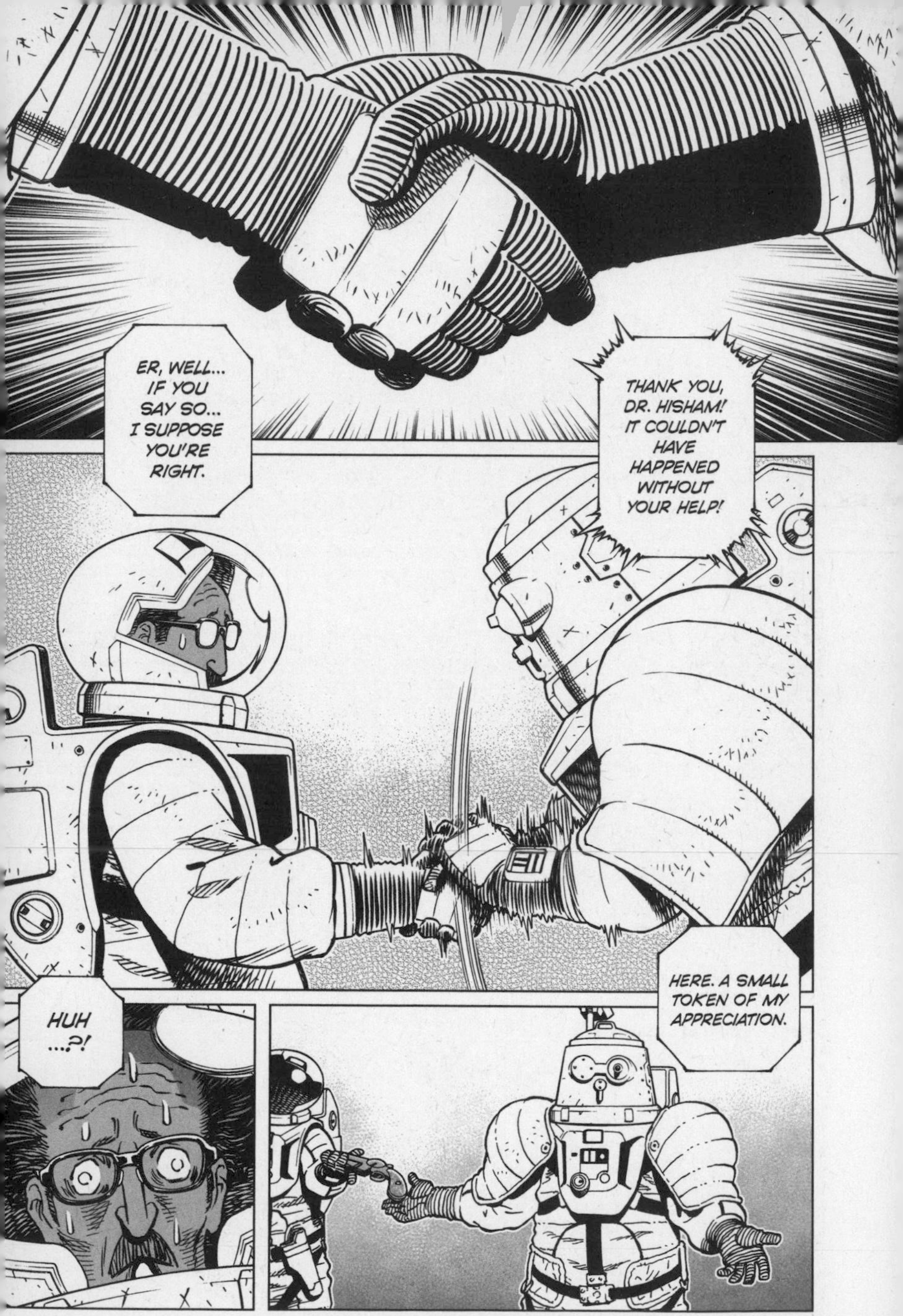
THANK YOU, DR. HISHAM! IT COULDN'T HAVE HAPPENED WITHOUT YOUR HELP!
ER, WELL... IF YOU SAY SO... I SUPPOSE YOU'RE RIGHT.
HERE. A SMALL TOKEN OF MY APPRECIATION.
HUH ...?!

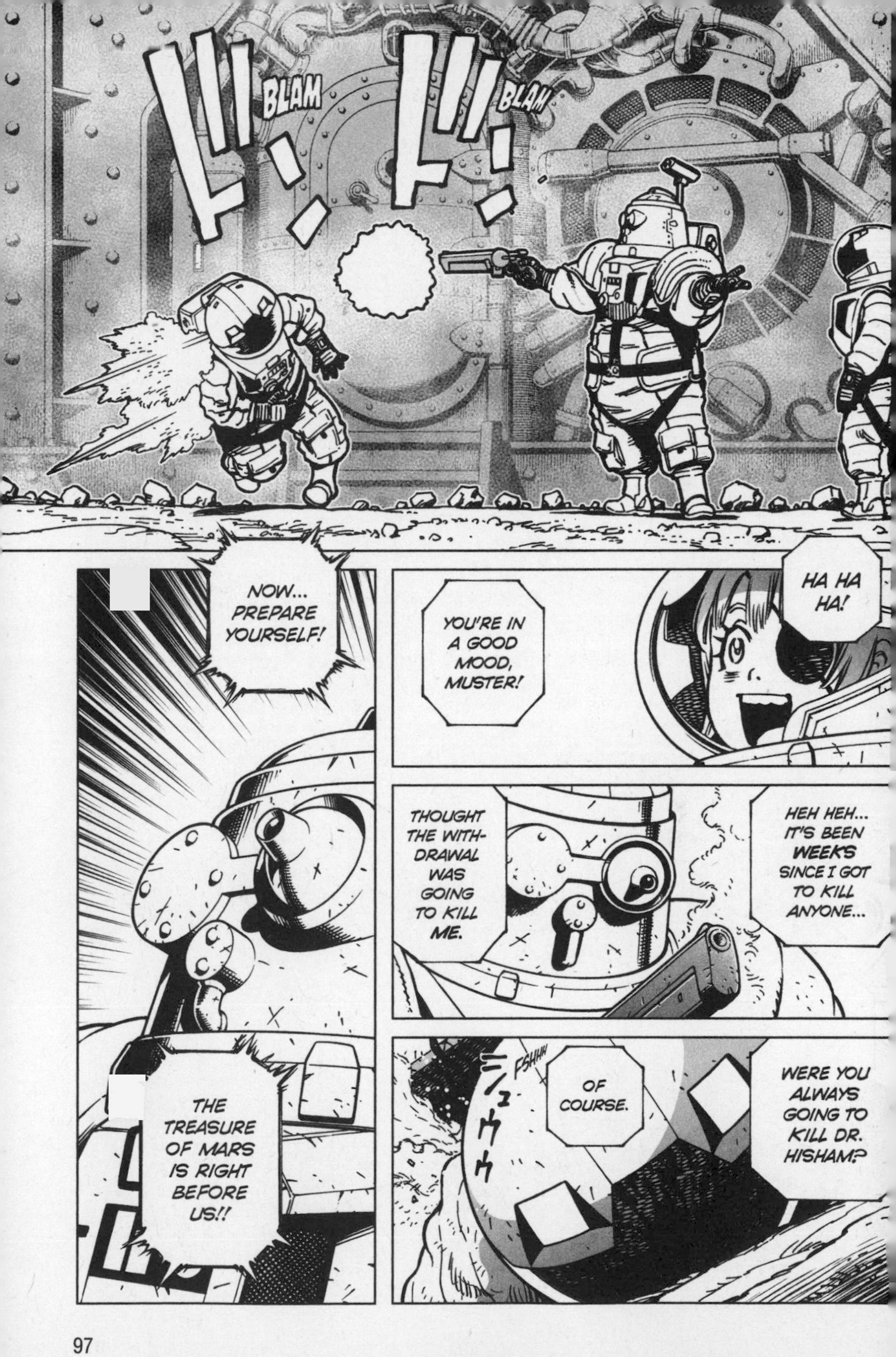
BLAM
BLAM
HA HA HA!
YOU'RE IN A GOOD MOOD, MUSTER!
HEH HEH... IT'S BEEN WEEKS SINCE I GOT TO KILL ANYONE...
THOUGHT THE WITH-DRAWAL WAS GOING TO KILL ME.
WERE YOU ALWAYS GOING TO KILL DR. HISHAM?
OF COURSE.
FSHHH
NOW... PREPARE YOURSELF!
THE TREASURE OF MARS IS RIGHT BEFORE US!!

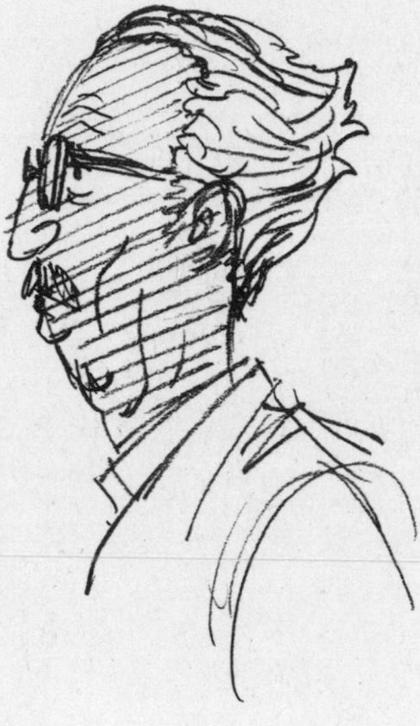

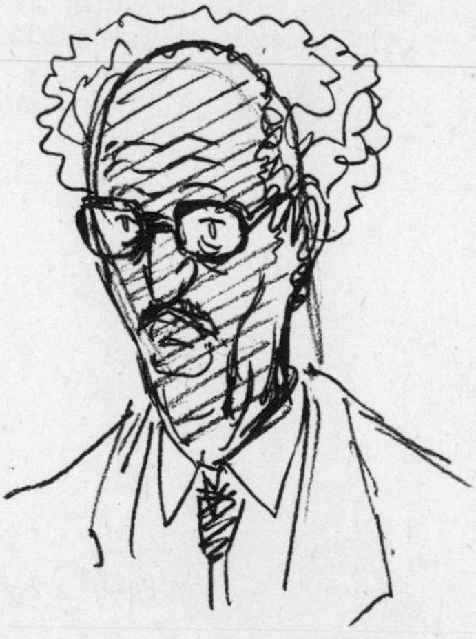

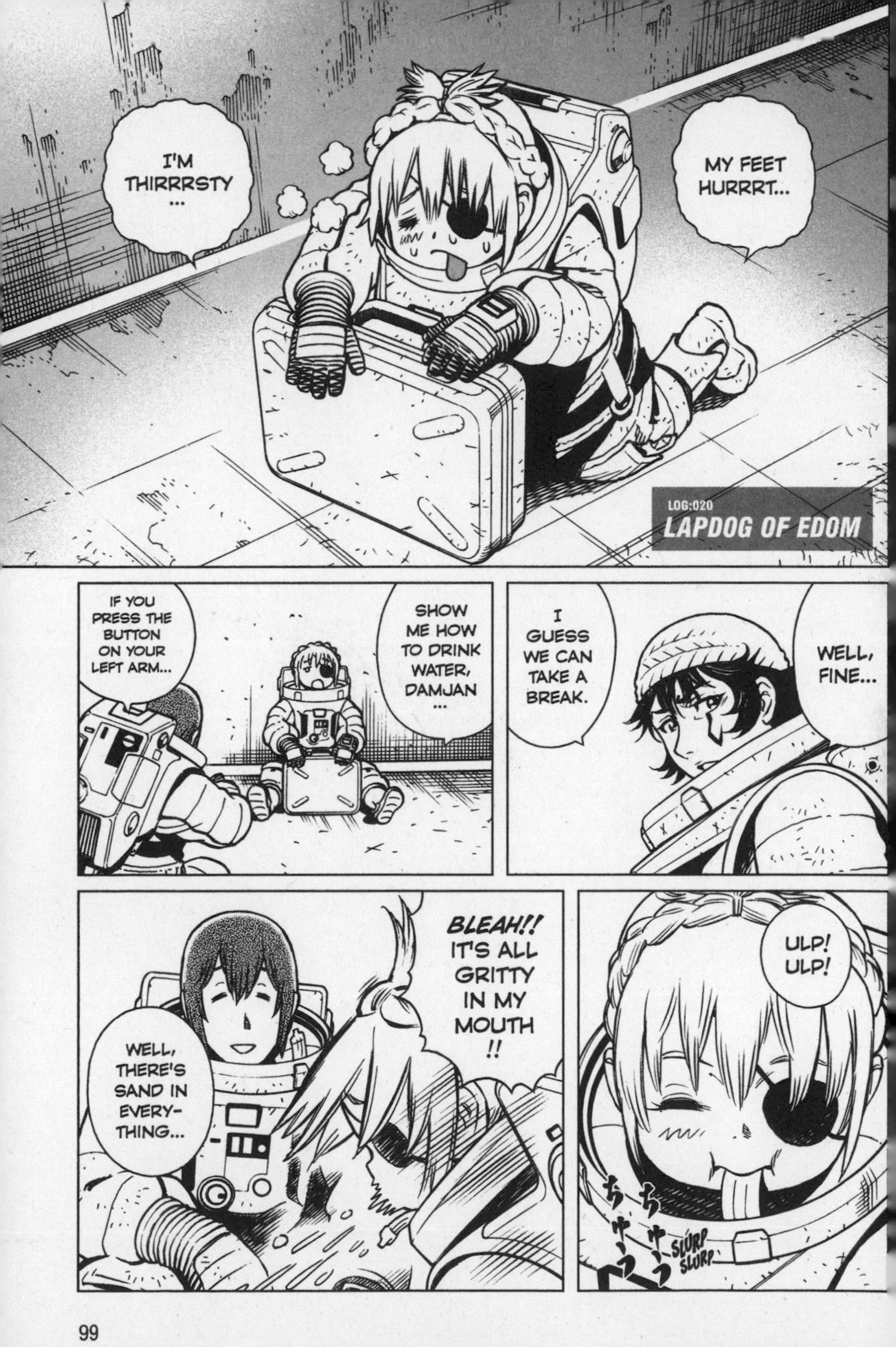
MY FEET HURRRT...
I'M THIRRRSTY ...
LOG:020
LAPDOG OF EDOM
WELL, FINE...
I GUESS WE CAN TAKE A BREAK.
SHOW ME HOW TO DRINK WATER, DAMJAN ...
IF YOU PRESS THE BUTTON ON YOUR LEFT ARM...
ULP! ULP!
SLURP SLURP
BLEAH!! IT'S ALL GRITTY IN MY MOUTH !!
WELL, THERE'S SAND IN EVERY-THING...

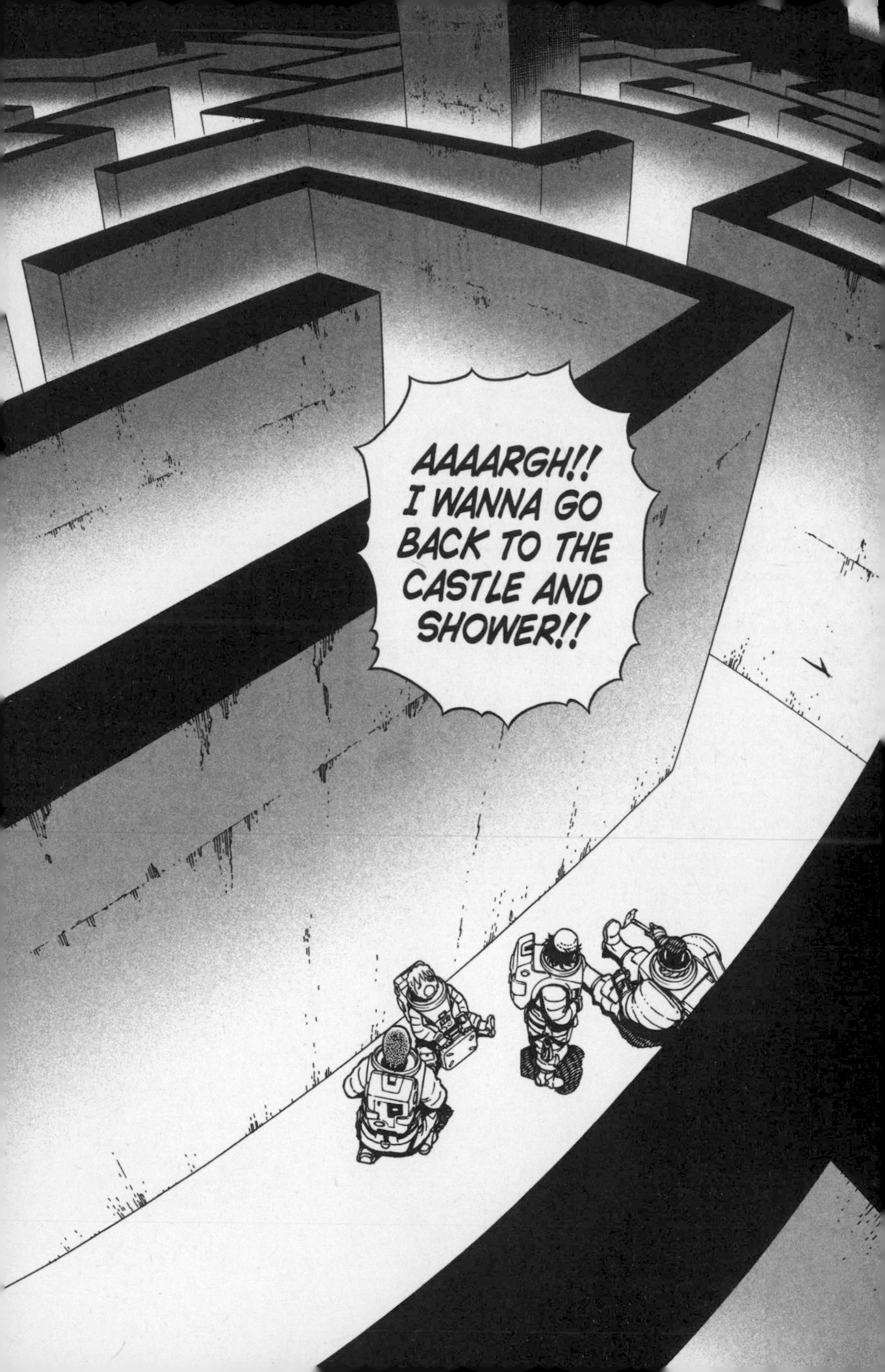
AAAARGH!! I WANNA GO BACK TO THE CASTLE AND SHOWER!!

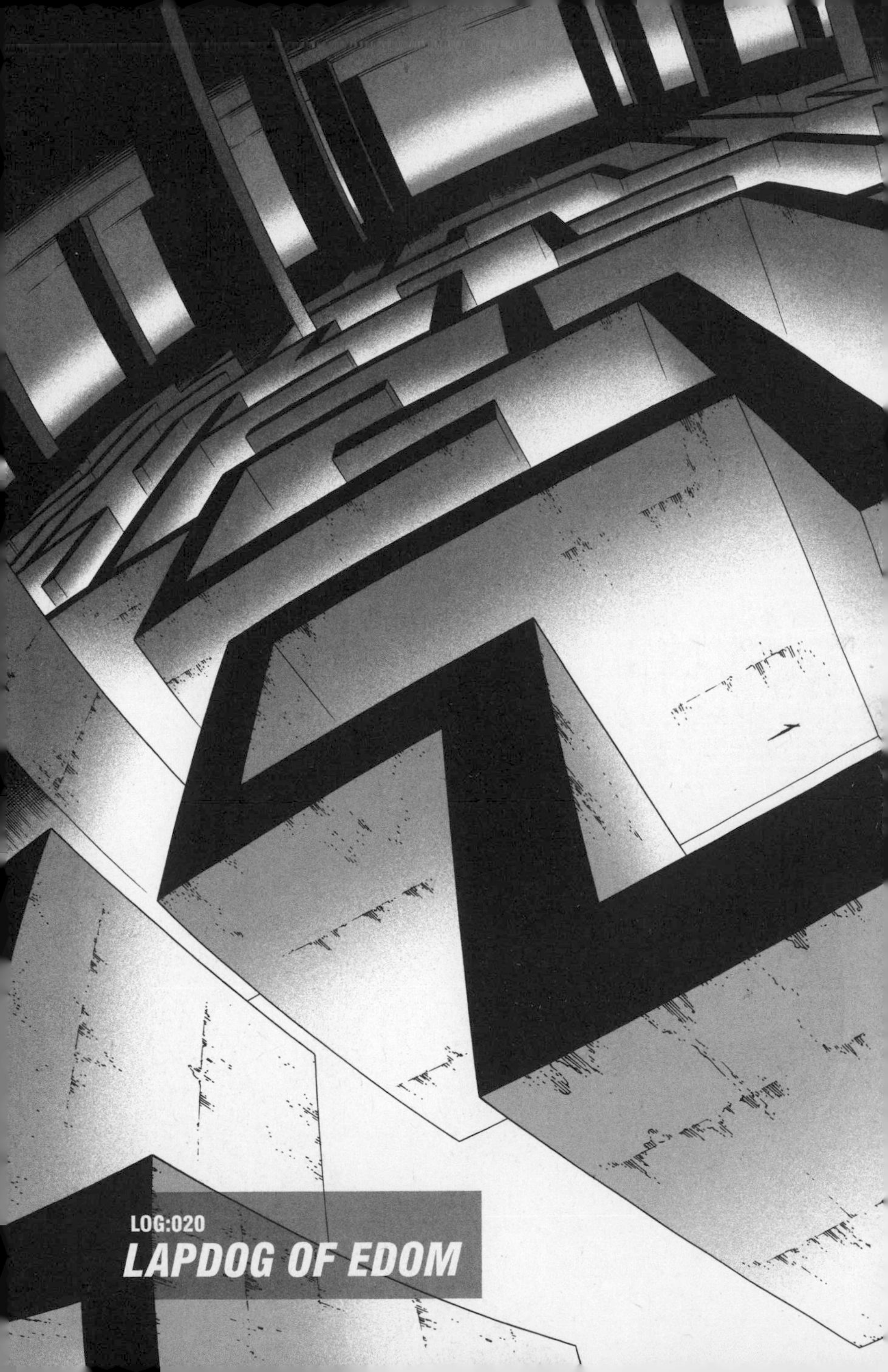
LOG:020
LAPDOG OF EDOM

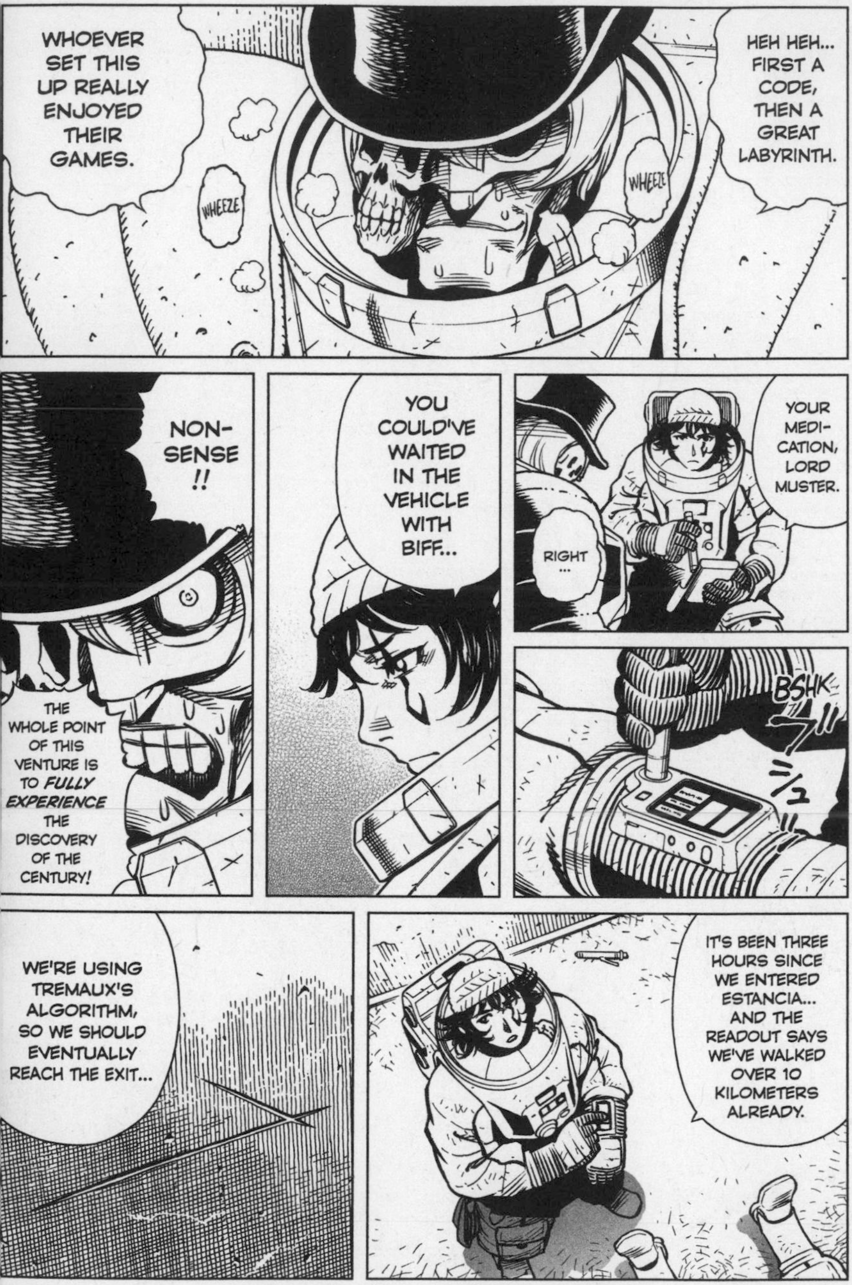
HEH HEH... FIRST A CODE, THEN A GREAT LABYRINTH.
WHEEZE
WHEEZE
WHOEVER SET THIS UP REALLY ENJOYED THEIR GAMES.
YOUR MEDICATION, LORD MUSTER.
RIGHT...
BSHK
YOU COULD'VE WAITED IN THE VEHICLE WITH BIFF...
NON-SENSE!!
THE WHOLE POINT OF THIS VENTURE IS TO *FULLY EXPERIENCE* THE DISCOVERY OF THE CENTURY!
IT'S BEEN THREE HOURS SINCE WE ENTERED ESTANCIA... AND THE READOUT SAYS WE'VE WALKED OVER 10 KILOMETERS ALREADY.
WE'RE USING TREMAUX'S ALGORITHM, SO WE SHOULD EVENTUALLY REACH THE EXIT...

*10 KM = 6.21 MI.

TREMAUX'S ALGORITHM

One of the more famous methods of solving a maze is the left-hand (or right-hand) method. By keeping your left (or right) hand on the wall as you go, it will eventually take you to the exit. The big flaw of this method is that in three-dimensional mazes, or cases when the goal or start is in the center of the maze, you may not be able to escape.

A French mathematician named Tremaux devised the Tremaux algorithm (expanded left-hand method) to solve for any maze. It works as follows.

1. Place an indicator on the wall and proceed left.
2. If you reach a branch you visited previously, treat it as a dead-end and turn around.
3. If you reach an actual dead-end, return to the last branch.

At the very worst, this will bring you to the exit of the maze having walked twice the length of all its paths.

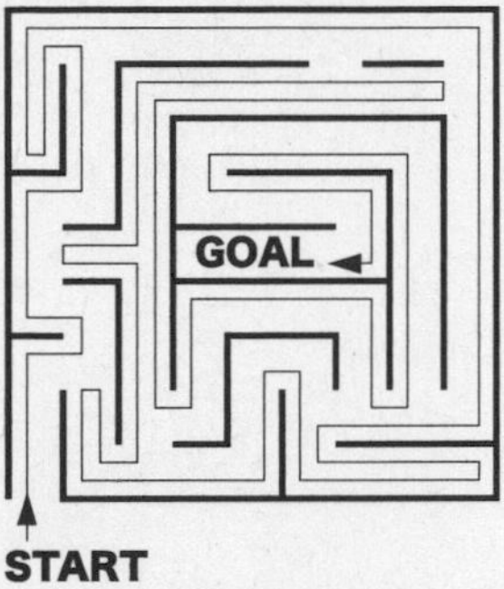
GOAL
START

EXAMPLE OF TREMAUX'S METHOD

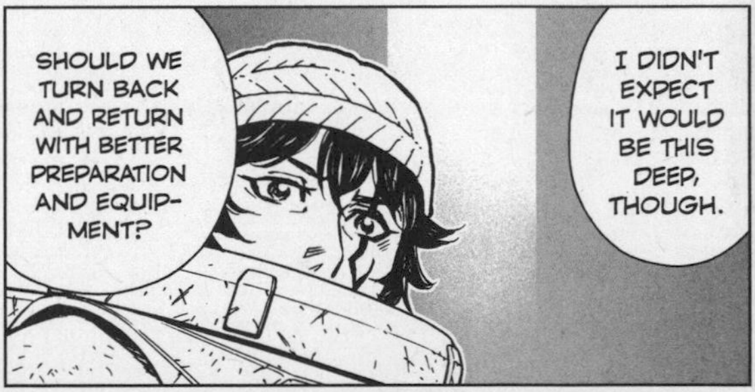
I DIDN'T EXPECT IT WOULD BE THIS DEEP, THOUGH.
SHOULD WE TURN BACK AND RETURN WITH BETTER PREPARATION AND EQUIPMENT?

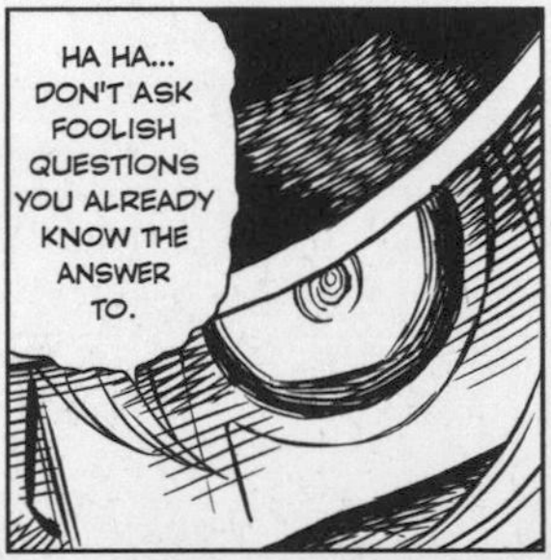
HA HA... DON'T ASK FOOLISH QUESTIONS YOU ALREADY KNOW THE ANSWER TO.

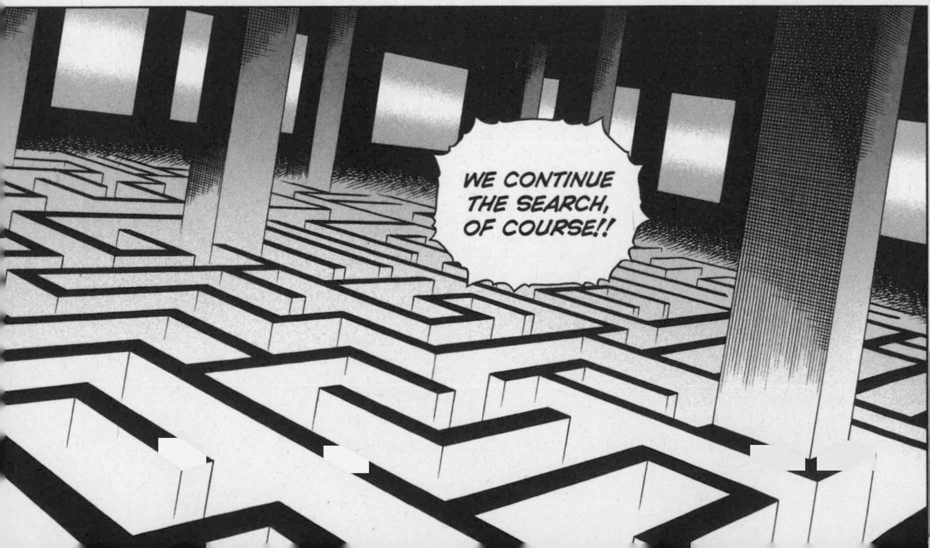
WE CONTINUE THE SEARCH, OF COURSE!!

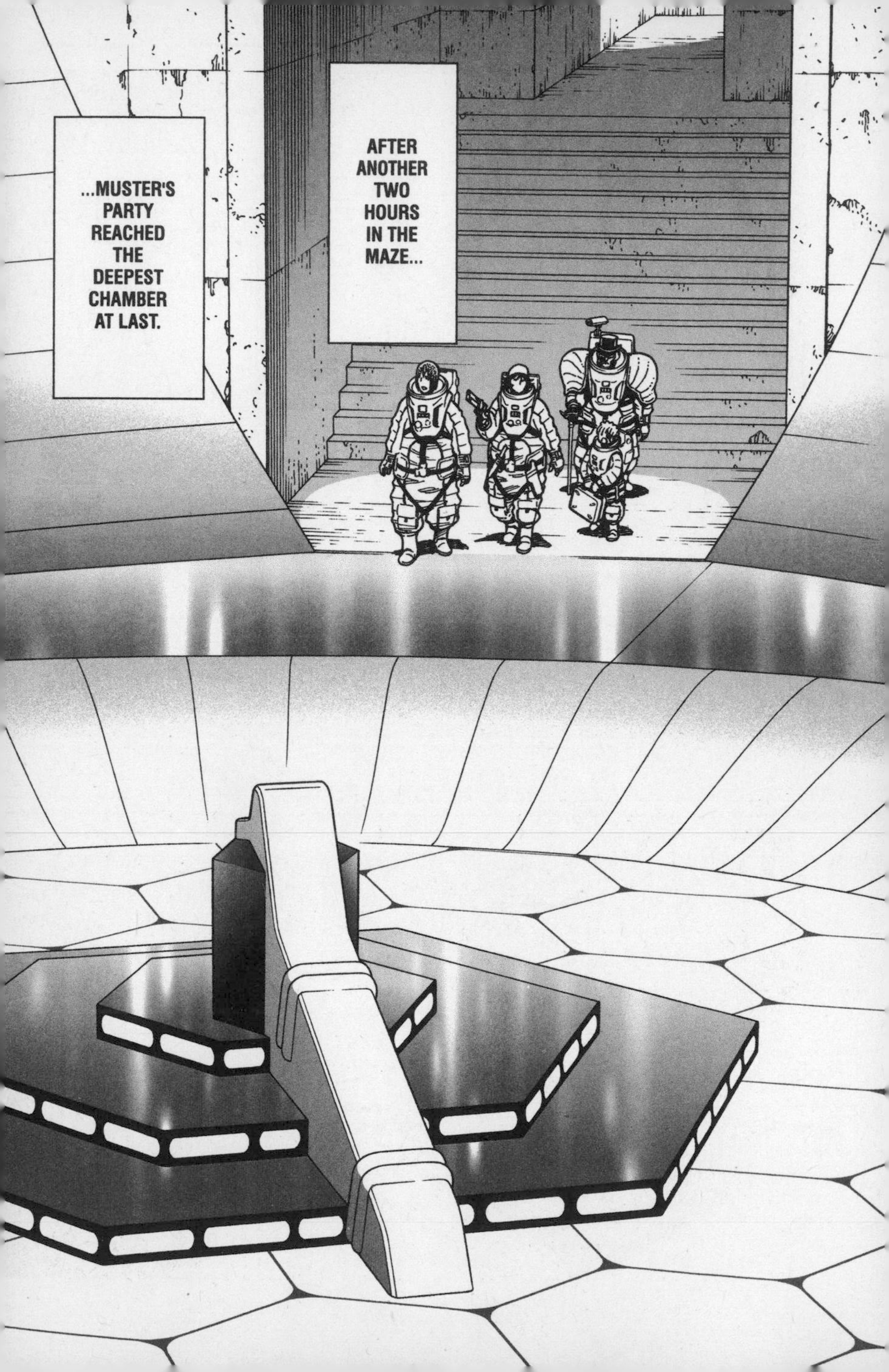
AFTER ANOTHER TWO HOURS IN THE MAZE...
...MUSTER'S PARTY REACHED THE DEEPEST CHAMBER AT LAST.

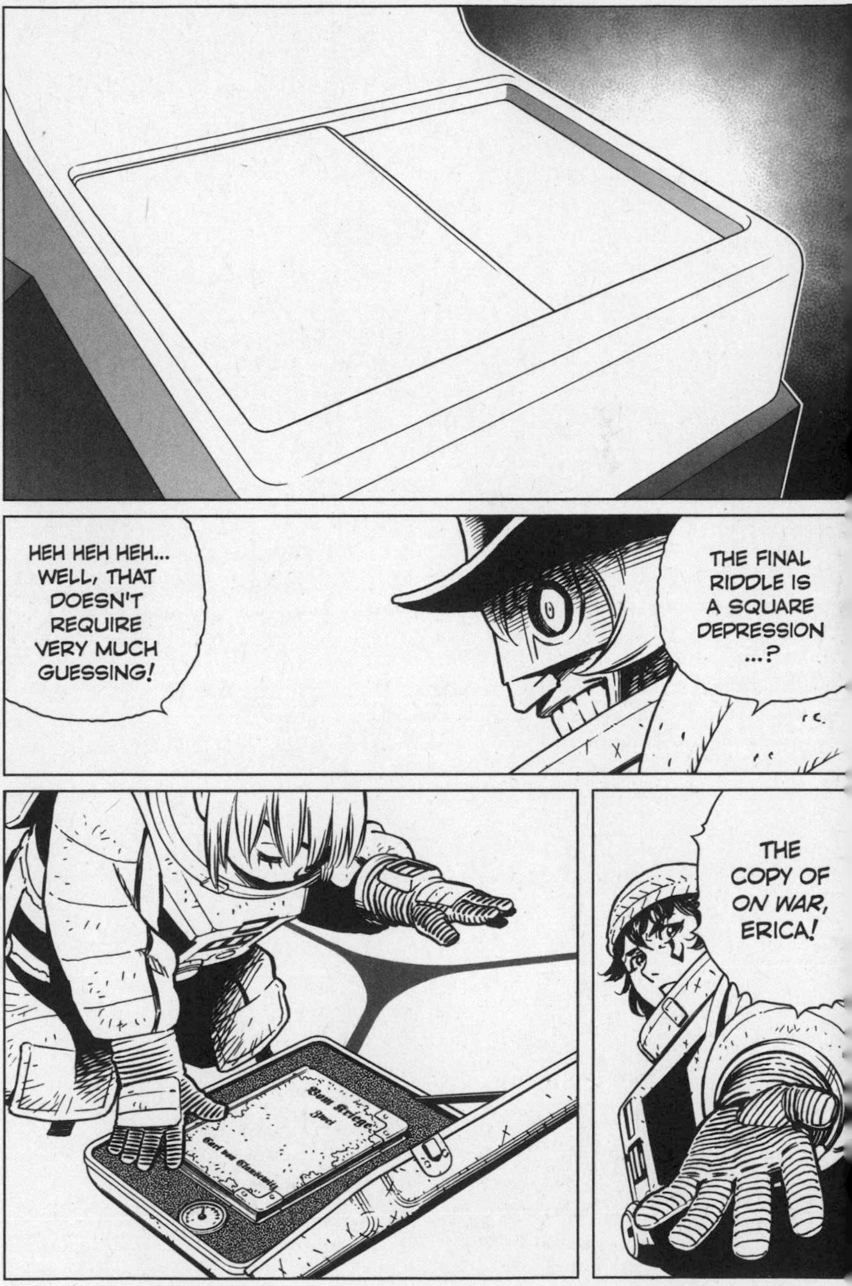
THE FINAL RIDDLE IS A SQUARE DEPRESSION ...?
HEH HEH HEH... WELL, THAT DOESN'T REQUIRE VERY MUCH GUESSING!
THE COPY OF ON WAR, ERICA!

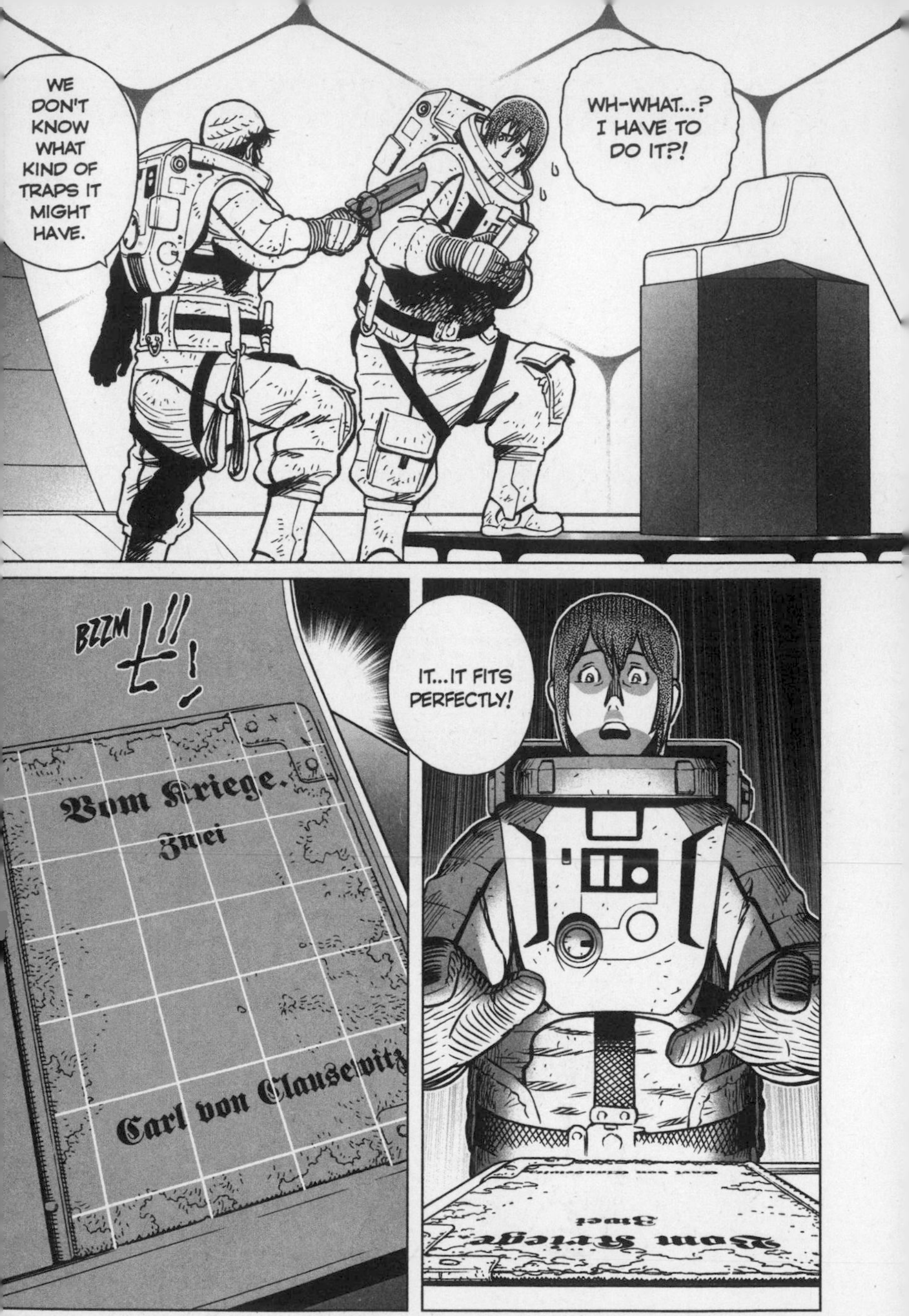

WH-WHAT...? I HAVE TO DO IT?!
WE DON'T KNOW WHAT KIND OF TRAPS IT MIGHT HAVE.
IT...IT FITS PERFECTLY!
BZZM
Vom Kriege.
Zwei
Carl von Clausewitz

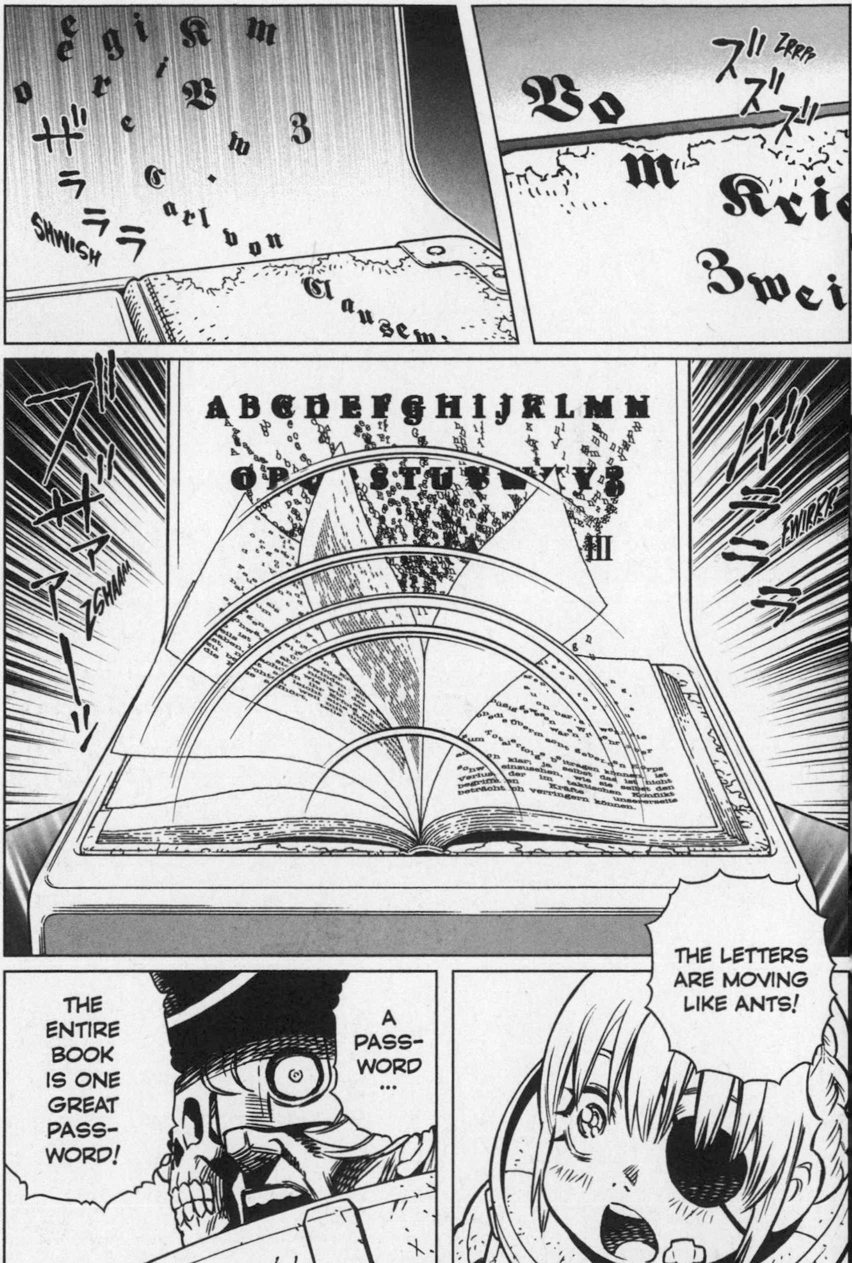
ZRRRP
SHWISH
FWIRRR
ZSHAAA
THE LETTERS ARE MOVING LIKE ANTS!
A PASSWORD...
THE ENTIRE BOOK IS ONE GREAT PASSWORD!

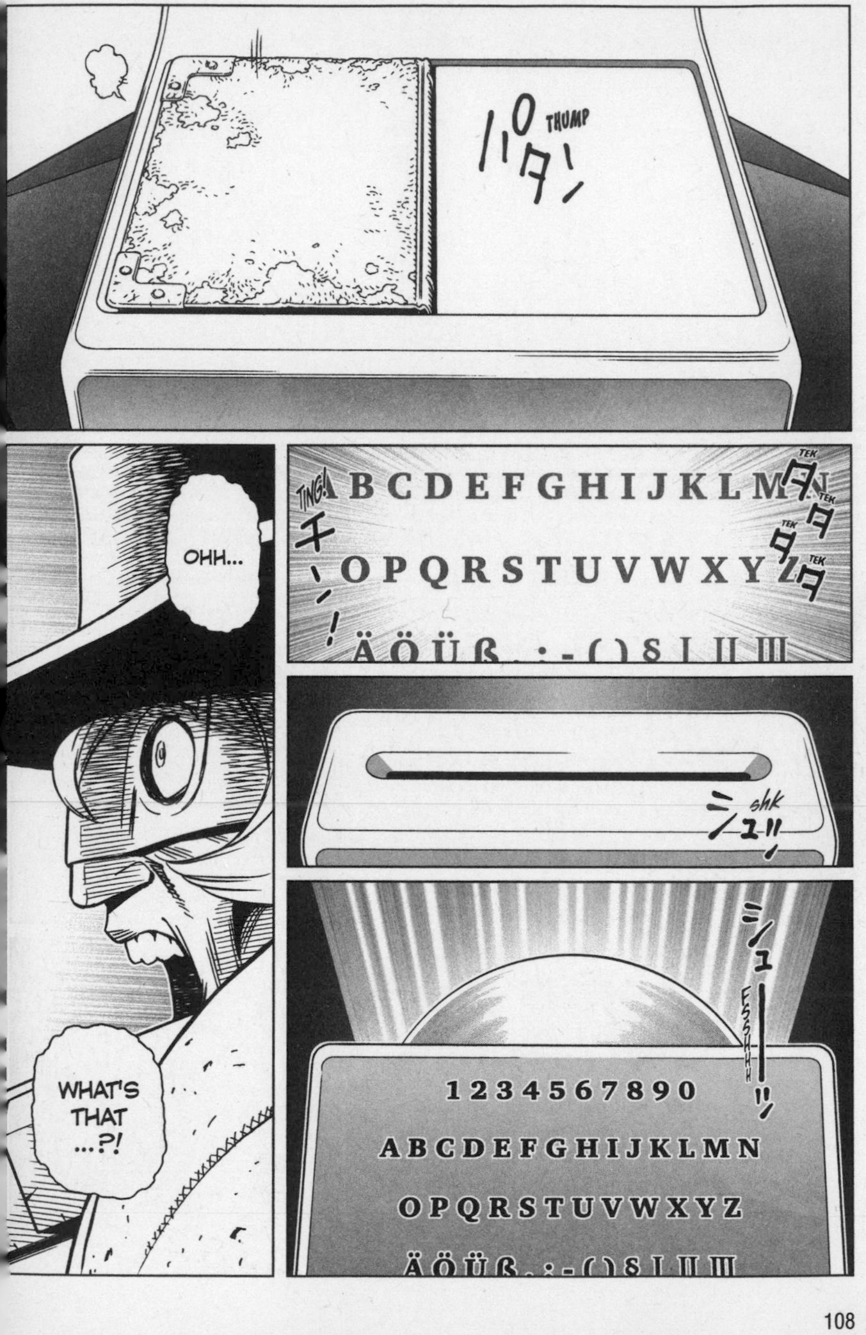
パタン
THUMP
チーン！
TING!
タタタタ
TEK TEK TEK TEK
A B C D E F G H I J K L M
O P Q R S T U V W X Y
シュッ
shk
シューーッ
FSSHHH
1 2 3 4 5 6 7 8 9 0
A B C D E F G H I J K L M N
O P Q R S T U V W X Y Z
OHH...
WHAT'S THAT ...?!

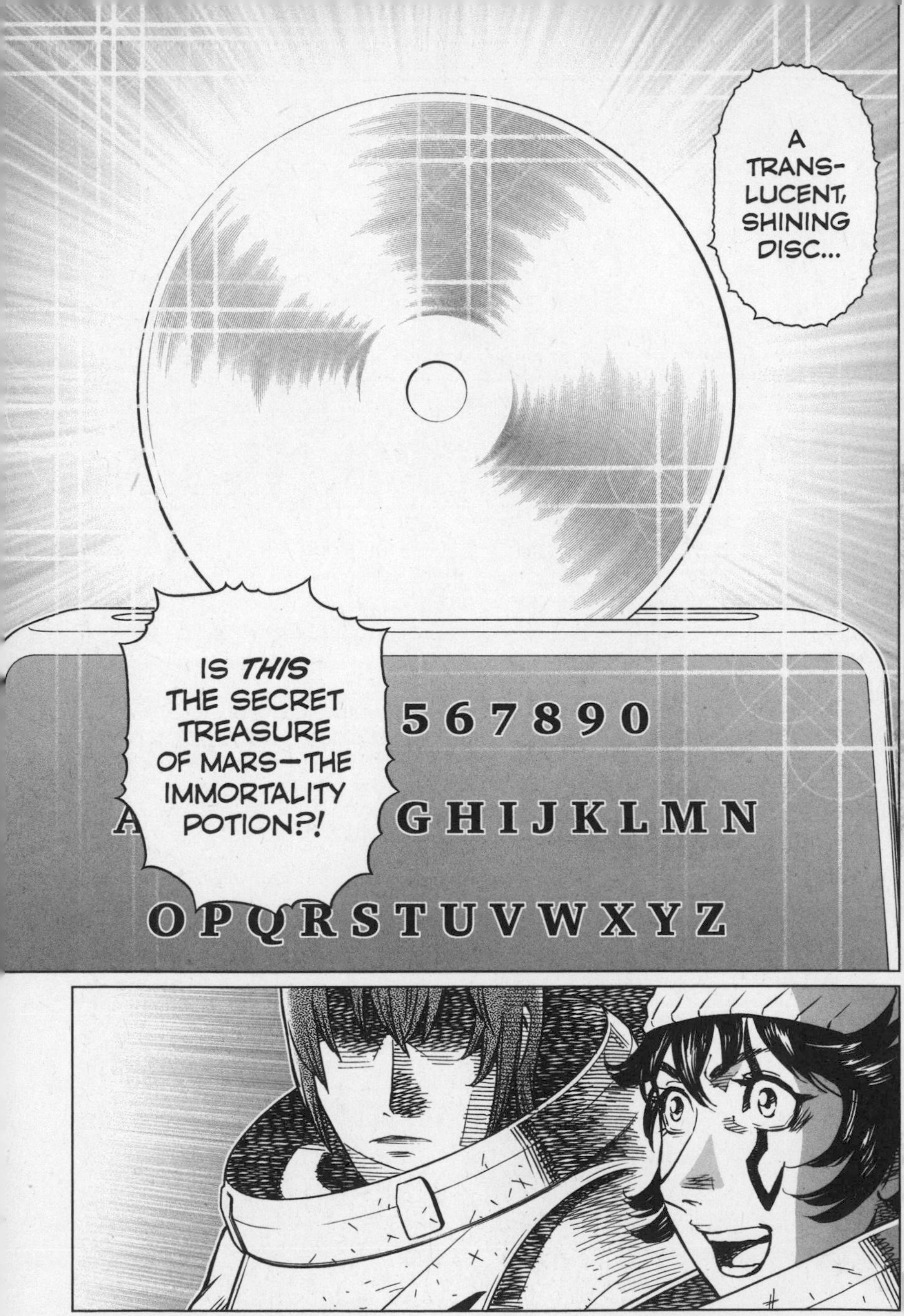
A TRANS-LUCENT, SHINING DISC...
IS *THIS* THE SECRET TREASURE OF MARS—THE IMMORTALITY POTION?!
5 6 7 8 9 0
A GHIJKLMN
OPQRSTUVWXYZ

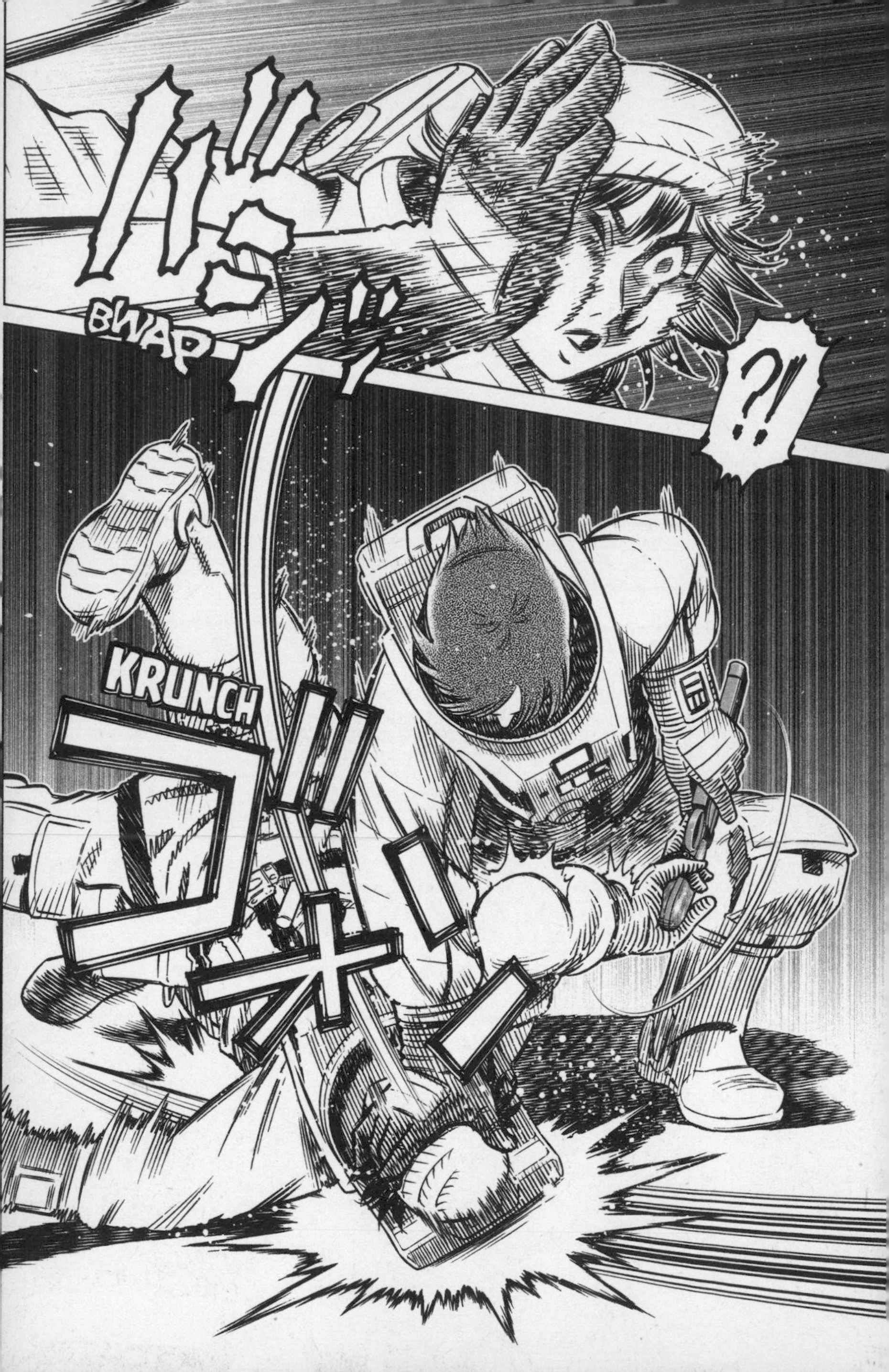
BWAP
?!
KRUNCH

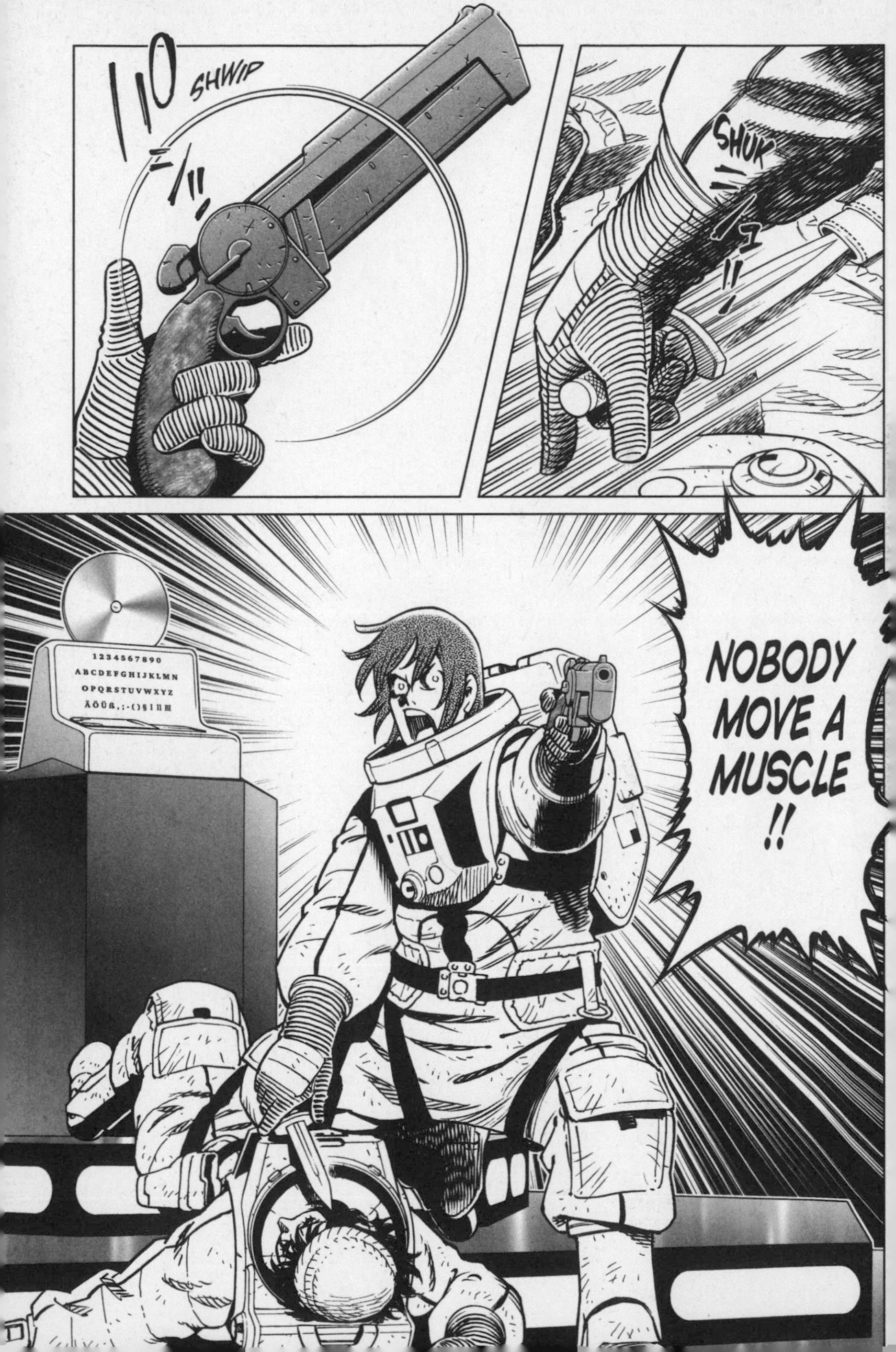
SHUK
SHWIP
1234567890
ABCDEFGHIJKLMN
OPQRSTUVWXYZ
NOBODY MOVE A MUSCLE !!

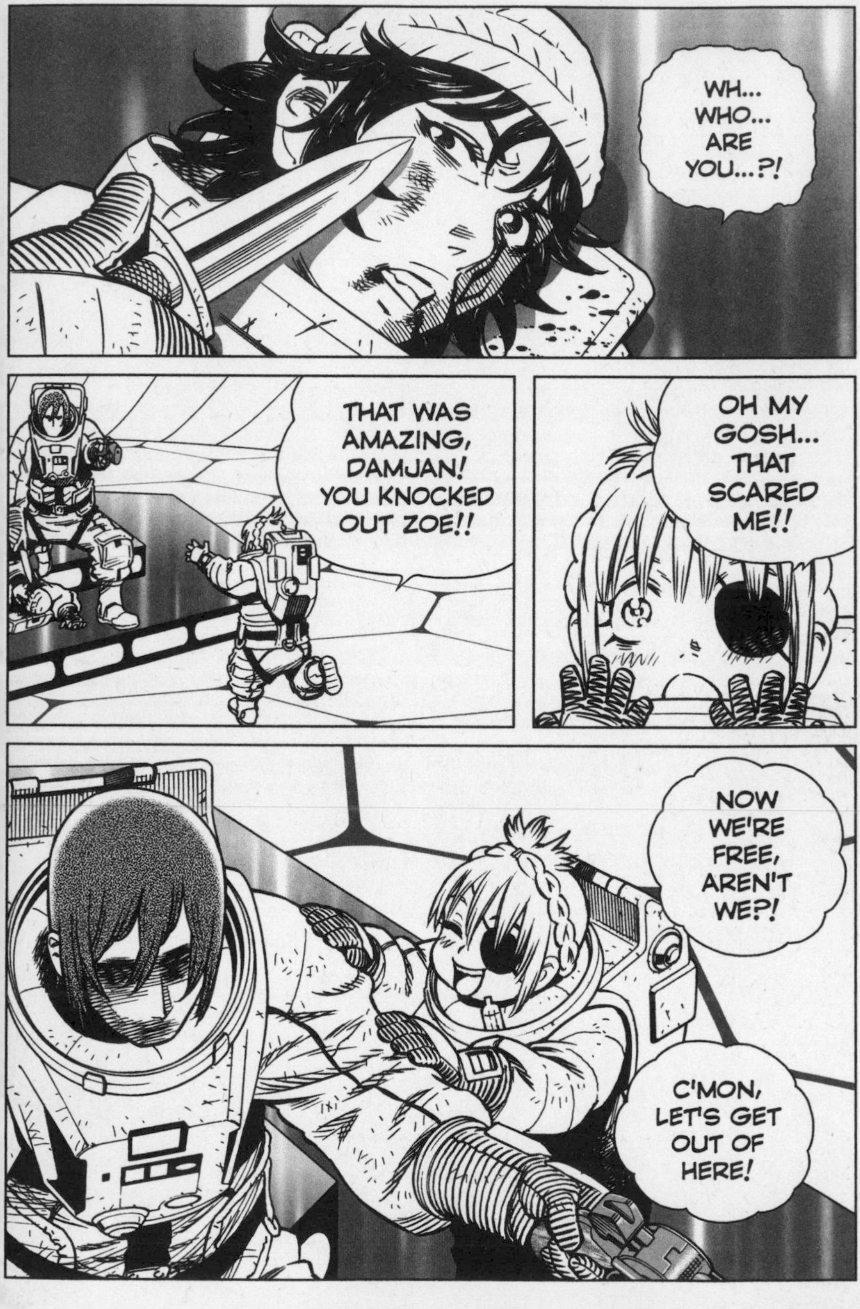
WH... WHO... ARE YOU...?!
OH MY GOSH... THAT SCARED ME!!
THAT WAS AMAZING, DAMJAN! YOU KNOCKED OUT ZOE!!
NOW WE'RE FREE, AREN'T WE?!
C'MON, LET'S GET OUT OF HERE!

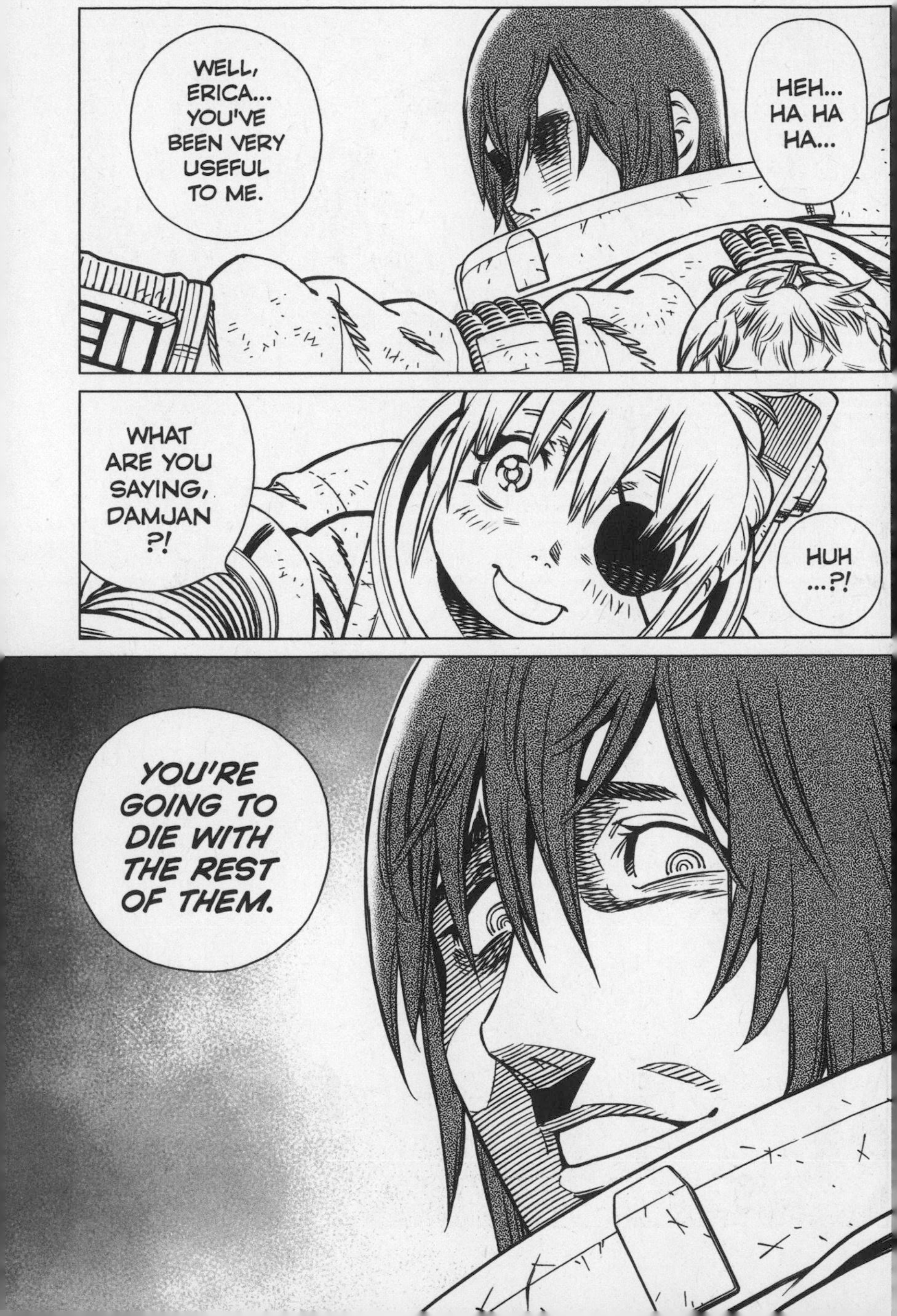
HEH... HA HA HA...
WELL, ERICA... YOU'VE BEEN VERY USEFUL TO ME.
HUH ...?!
WHAT ARE YOU SAYING, DAMJAN ?!
YOU'RE GOING TO DIE WITH THE REST OF THEM.

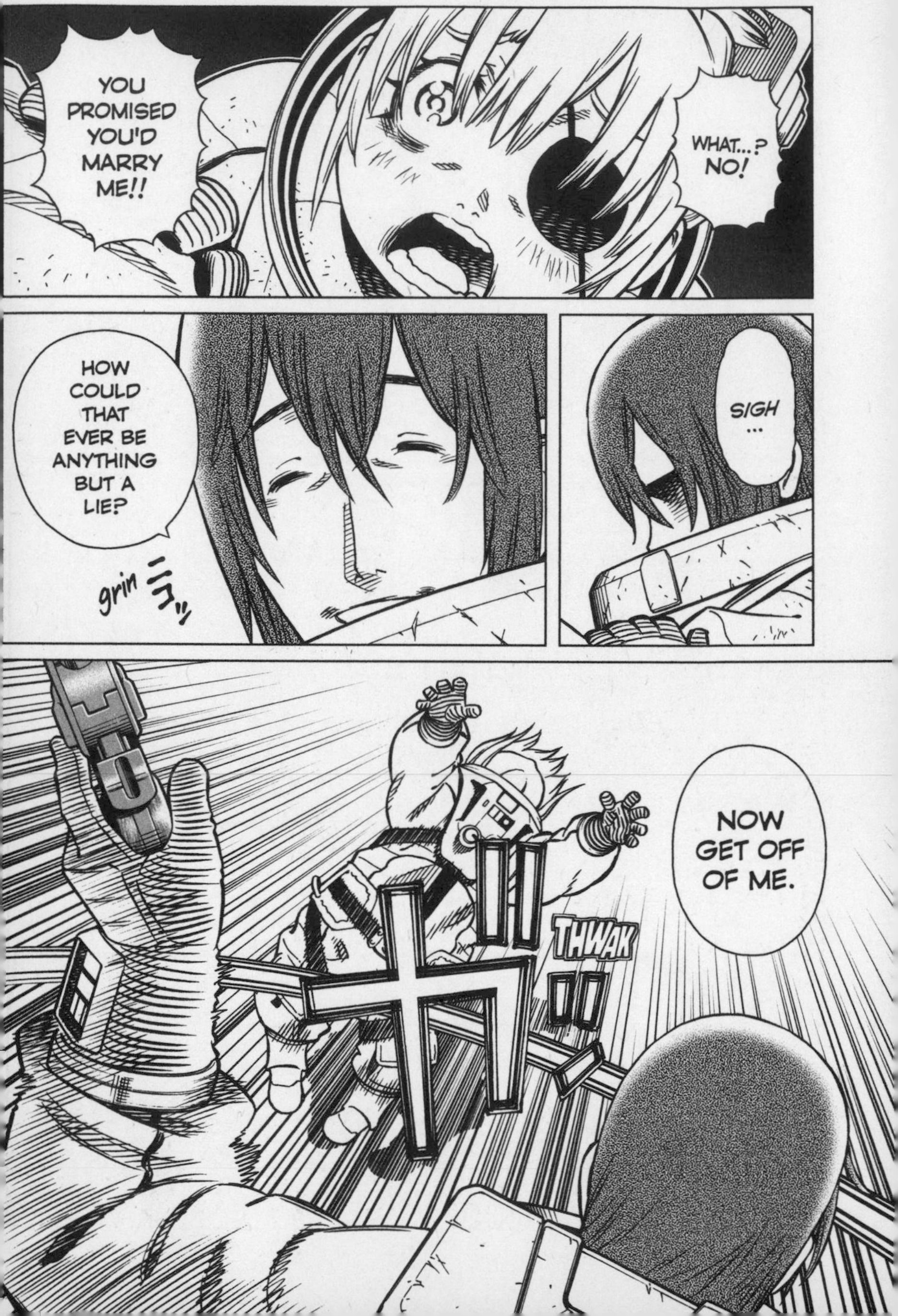
WHAT...? NO!
YOU PROMISED YOU'D MARRY ME!!
SIGH ...
HOW COULD THAT EVER BE ANYTHING BUT A LIE?
grin
NOW GET OFF OF ME.
THWAK

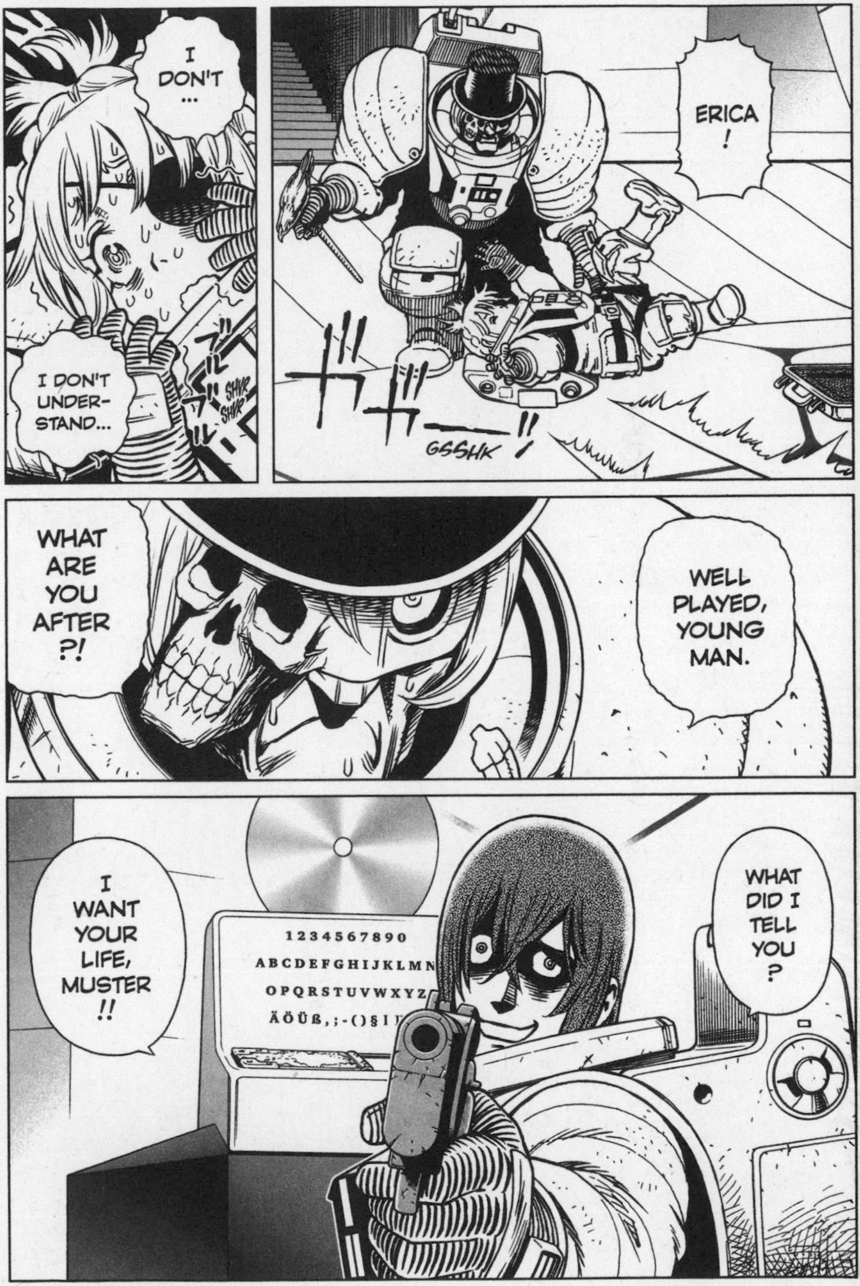
ERICA!
GSSHK!!
I DON'T ...
I DON'T UNDERSTAND...
SHVR SHVR
WELL PLAYED, YOUNG MAN.
WHAT ARE YOU AFTER?!
WHAT DID I TELL YOU?
1234567890
ABCDEFGHIJKLMN
OPQRSTUVWXYZ
I WANT YOUR LIFE, MUSTER!!

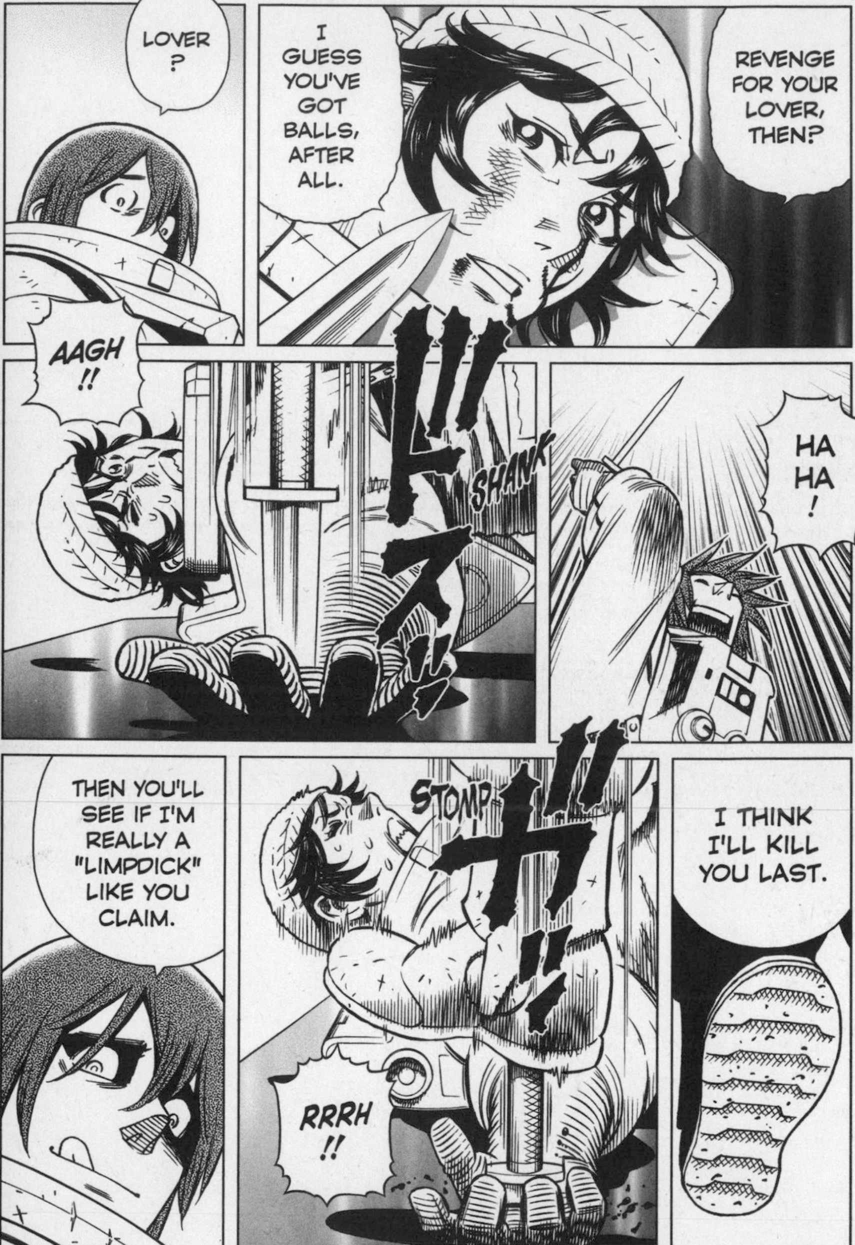

REVENGE FOR YOUR LOVER, THEN?
I GUESS YOU'VE GOT BALLS, AFTER ALL.
LOVER ?
HA HA !
SHANK
AAGH !!
I THINK I'LL KILL YOU LAST.
STOMP
RRRH !!
THEN YOU'LL SEE IF I'M REALLY A "LIMPDICK" LIKE YOU CLAIM.

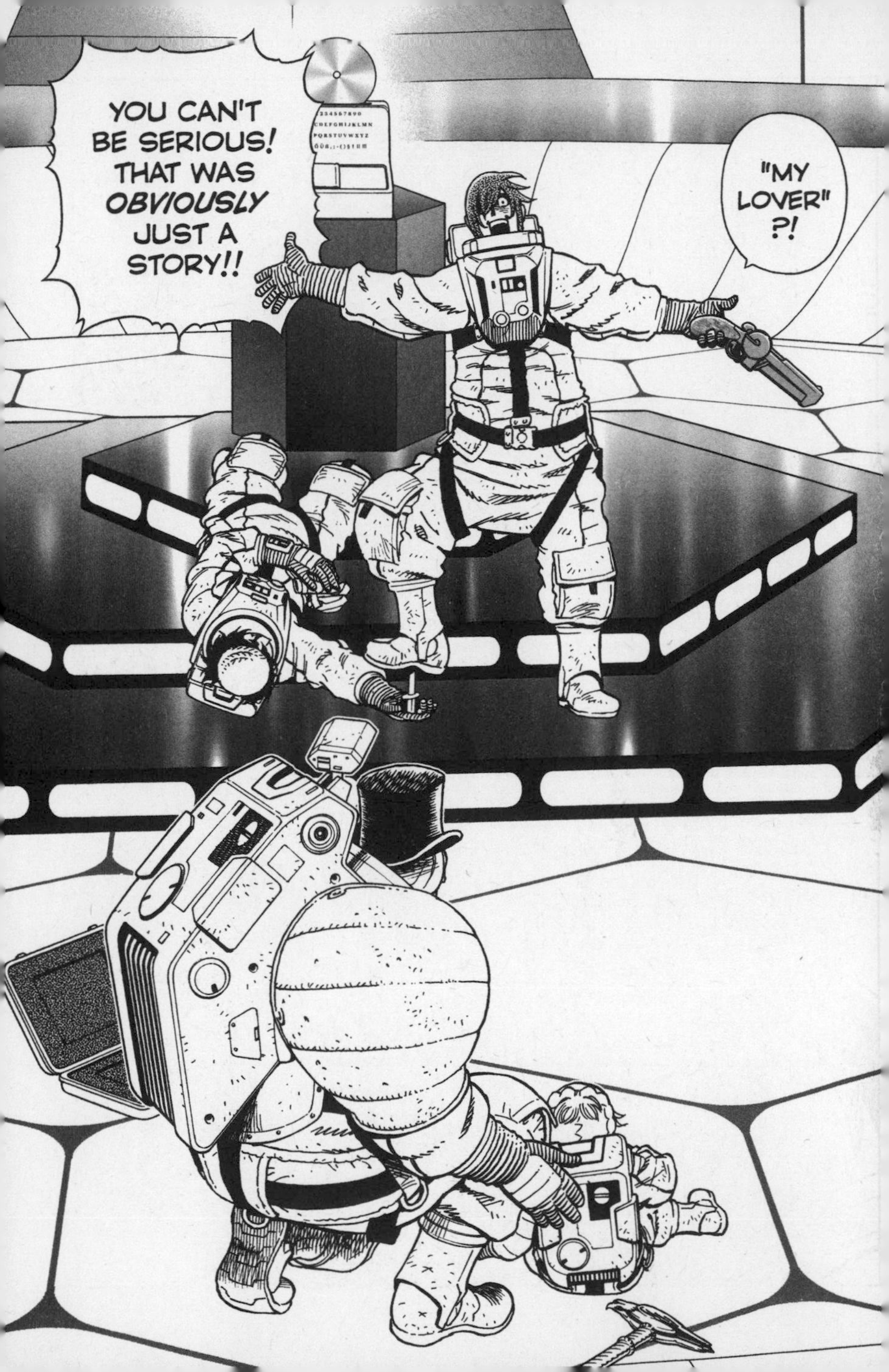
"MY LOVER" ?!
YOU CAN'T BE SERIOUS! THAT WAS *OBVIOUSLY* JUST A STORY!!

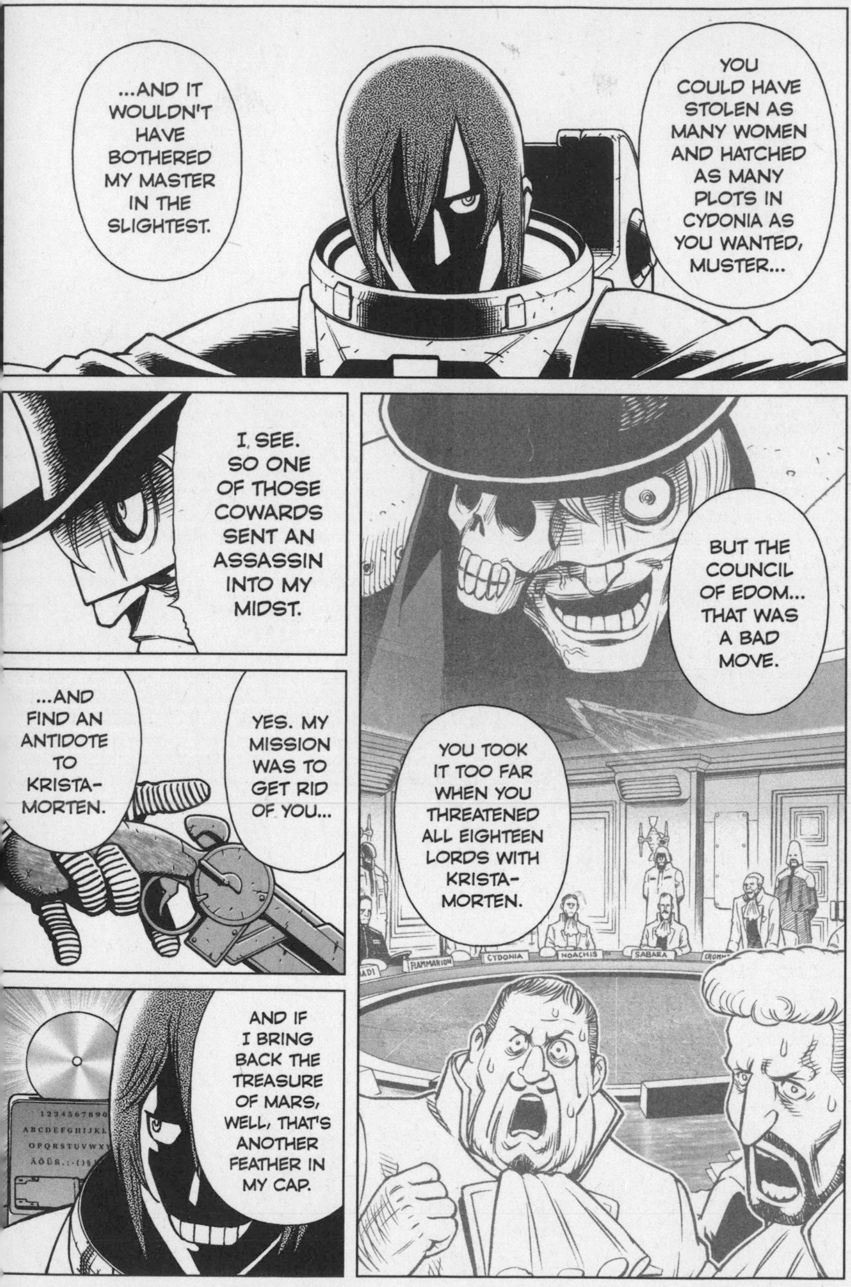
YOU COULD HAVE STOLEN AS MANY WOMEN AND HATCHED AS MANY PLOTS IN CYDONIA AS YOU WANTED, MUSTER...
...AND IT WOULDN'T HAVE BOTHERED MY MASTER IN THE SLIGHTEST.
BUT THE COUNCIL OF EDOM... THAT WAS A BAD MOVE.
YOU TOOK IT TOO FAR WHEN YOU THREATENED ALL EIGHTEEN LORDS WITH KRISTA-MORTEN.
I SEE. SO ONE OF THOSE COWARDS SENT AN ASSASSIN INTO MY MIDST.
YES. MY MISSION WAS TO GET RID OF YOU...
...AND FIND AN ANTIDOTE TO KRISTA-MORTEN.
AND IF I BRING BACK THE TREASURE OF MARS, WELL, THAT'S ANOTHER FEATHER IN MY CAP.

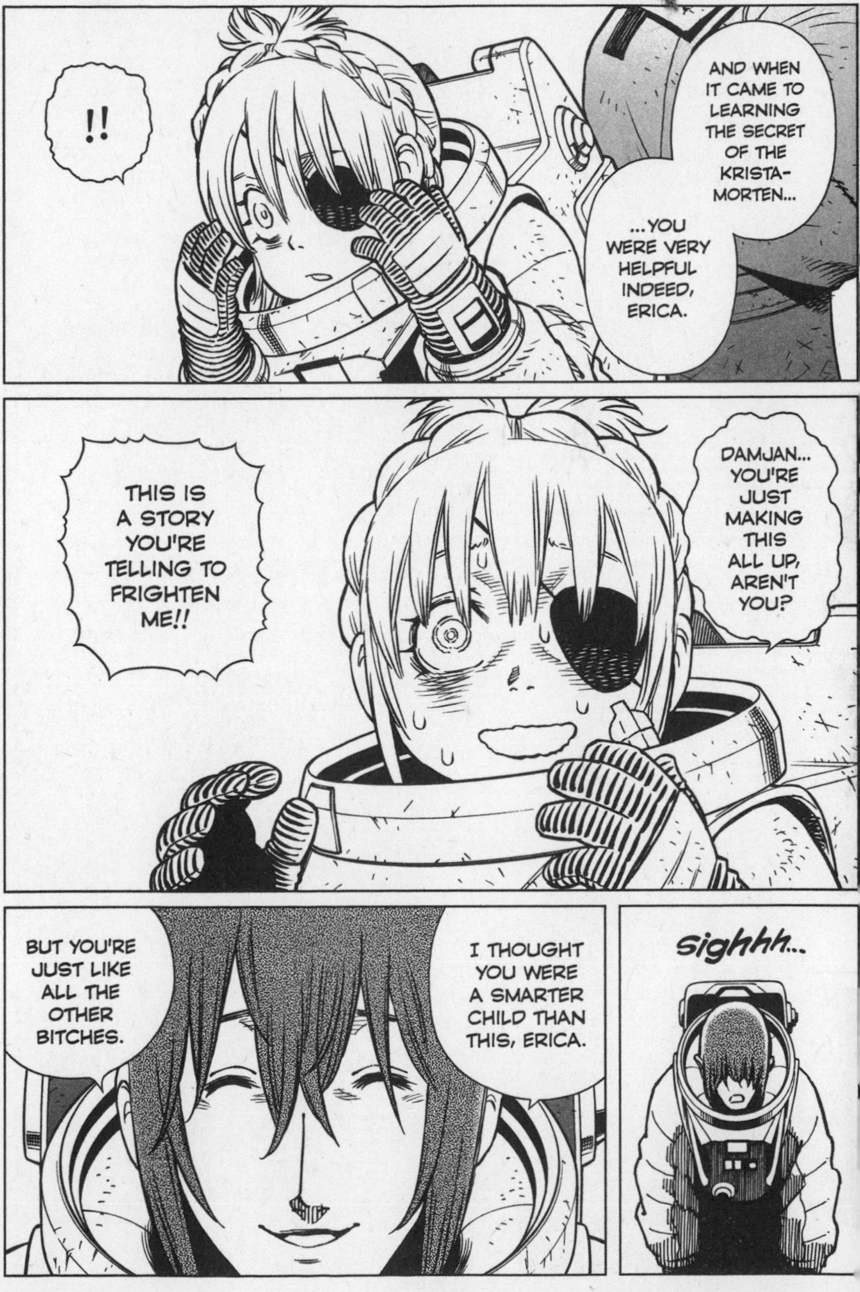
AND WHEN IT CAME TO LEARNING THE SECRET OF THE KRISTA-MORTEN...
...YOU WERE VERY HELPFUL INDEED, ERICA.
!!
DAMJAN... YOU'RE JUST MAKING THIS ALL UP, AREN'T YOU?
THIS IS A STORY YOU'RE TELLING TO FRIGHTEN ME!!
Sighhh...
I THOUGHT YOU WERE A SMARTER CHILD THAN THIS, ERICA.
BUT YOU'RE JUST LIKE ALL THE OTHER BITCHES.

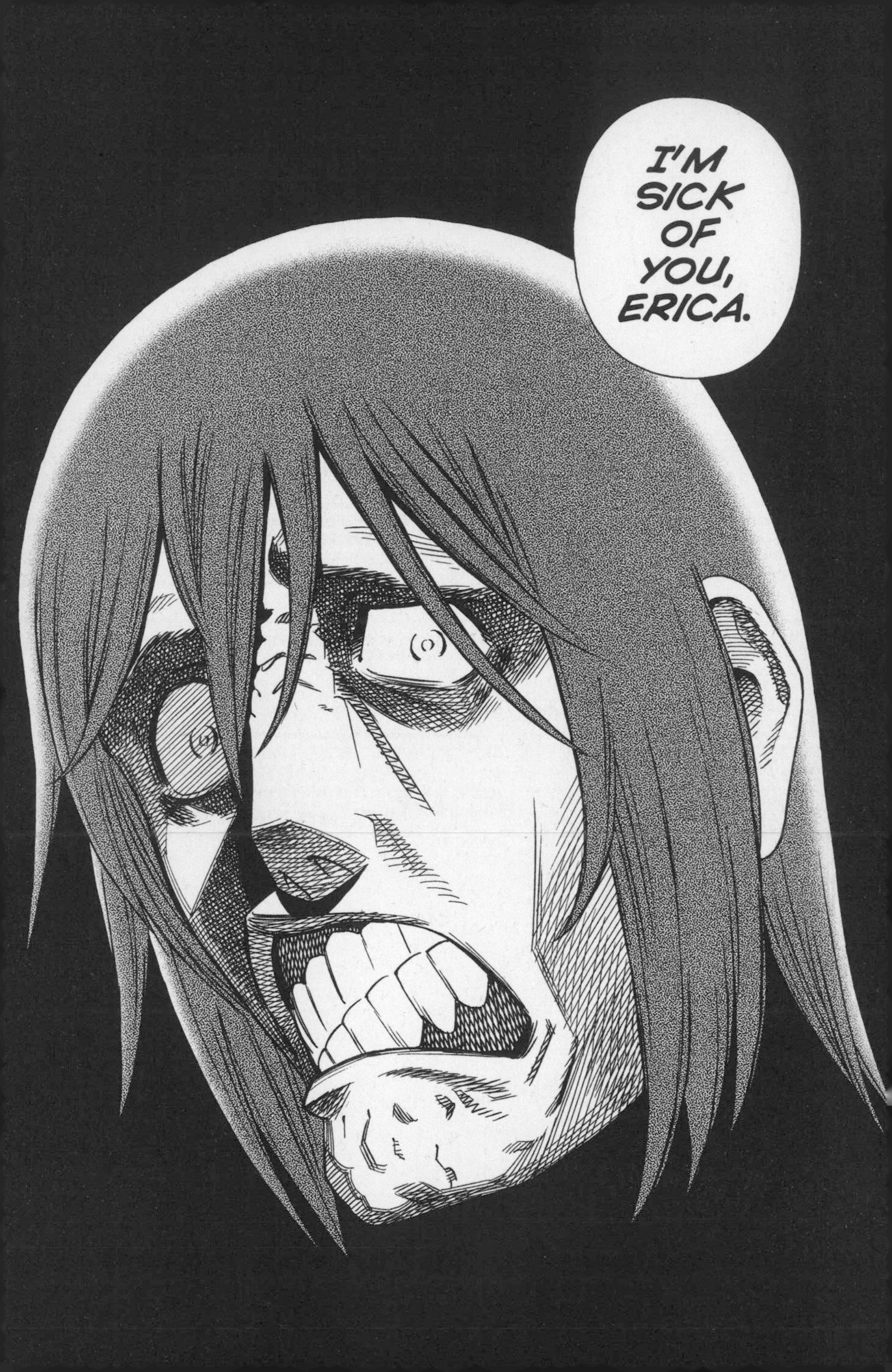
I'M SICK OF YOU, ERICA.

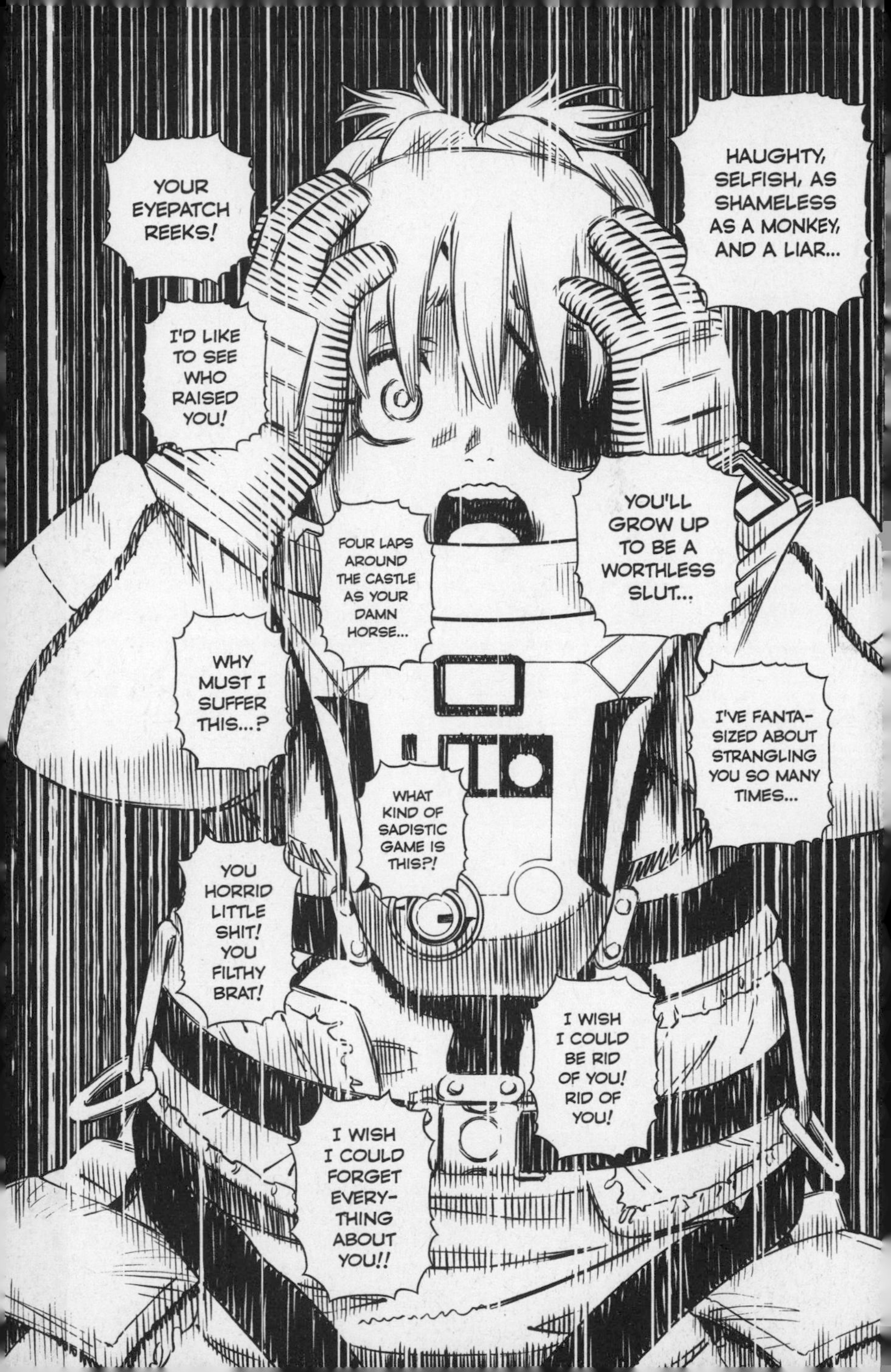
HAUGHTY, SELFISH, AS SHAMELESS AS A MONKEY, AND A LIAR...
YOUR EYEPATCH REEKS!
I'D LIKE TO SEE WHO RAISED YOU!
YOU'LL GROW UP TO BE A WORTHLESS SLUT...
FOUR LAPS AROUND THE CASTLE AS YOUR DAMN HORSE...
WHY MUST I SUFFER THIS...?
I'VE FANTA-SIZED ABOUT STRANGLING YOU SO MANY TIMES...
WHAT KIND OF SADISTIC GAME IS THIS?!
YOU HORRID LITTLE SHIT! YOU FILTHY BRAT!
I WISH I COULD BE RID OF YOU! RID OF YOU!
I WISH I COULD FORGET EVERY-THING ABOUT YOU!!

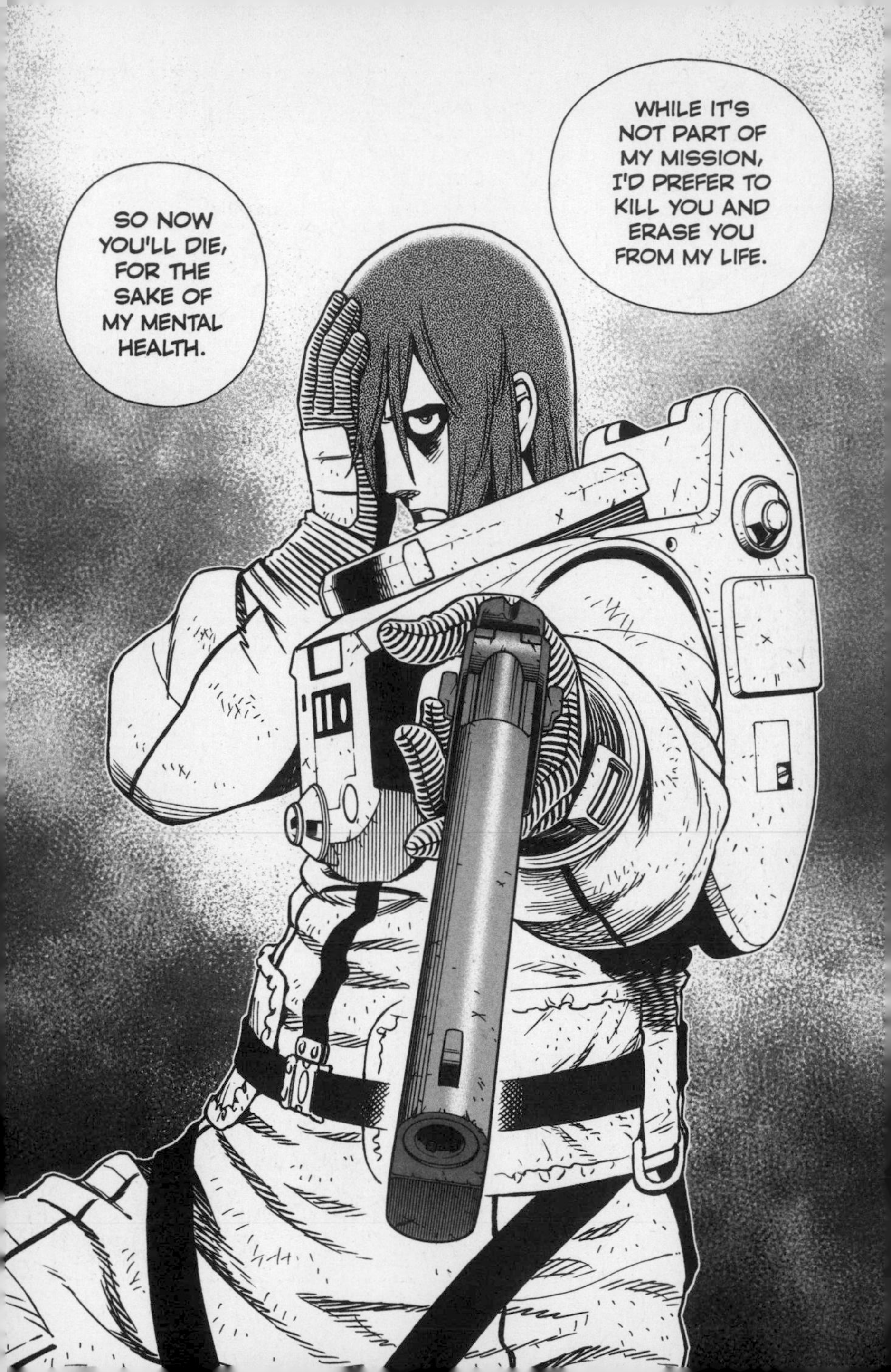
WHILE IT'S NOT PART OF MY MISSION, I'D PREFER TO KILL YOU AND ERASE YOU FROM MY LIFE.
SO NOW YOU'LL DIE, FOR THE SAKE OF MY MENTAL HEALTH.

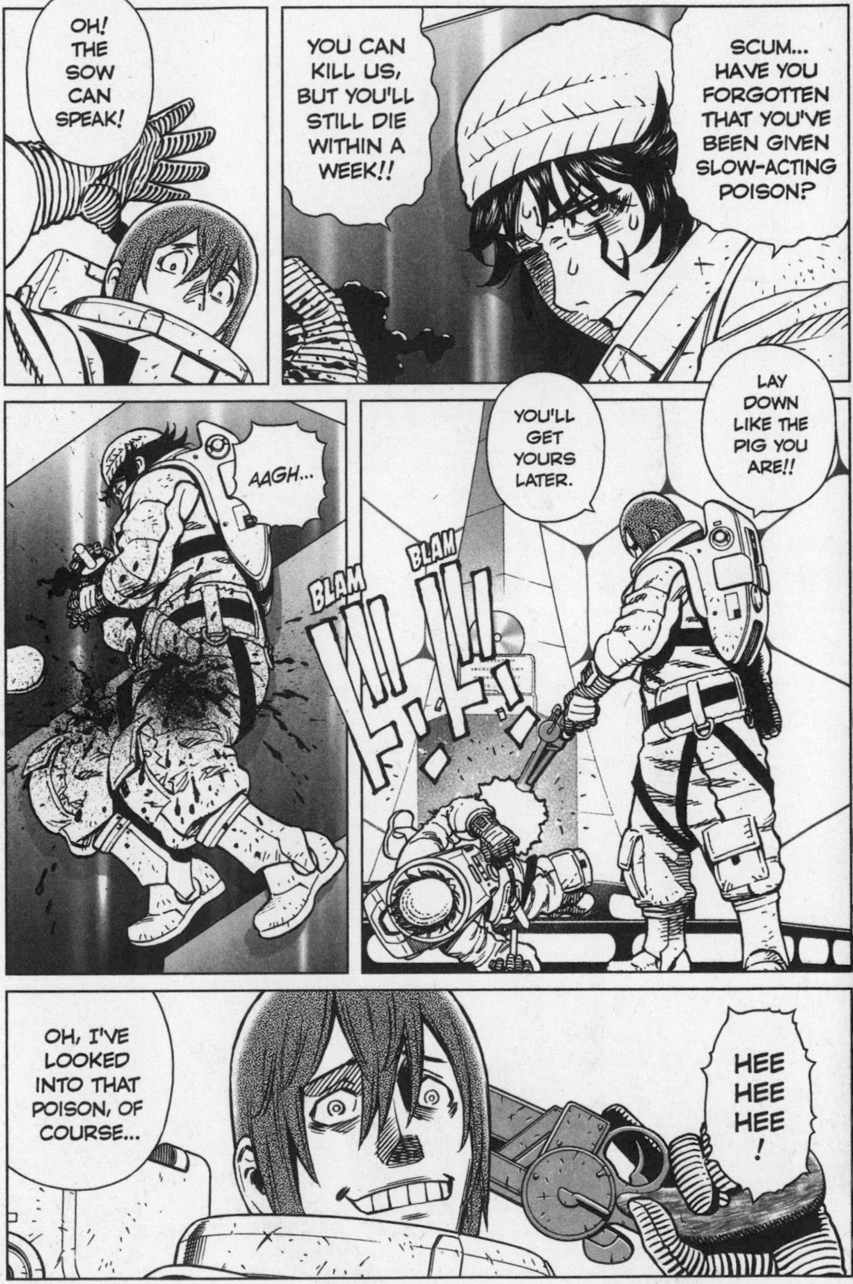
SCUM... HAVE YOU FORGOTTEN THAT YOU'VE BEEN GIVEN SLOW-ACTING POISON?
YOU CAN KILL US, BUT YOU'LL STILL DIE WITHIN A WEEK!!
OH! THE SOW CAN SPEAK!
LAY DOWN LIKE THE PIG YOU ARE!!
YOU'LL GET YOURS LATER.
BLAM
BLAM
AAGH...
HEE HEE HEE!
OH, I'VE LOOKED INTO THAT POISON, OF COURSE...

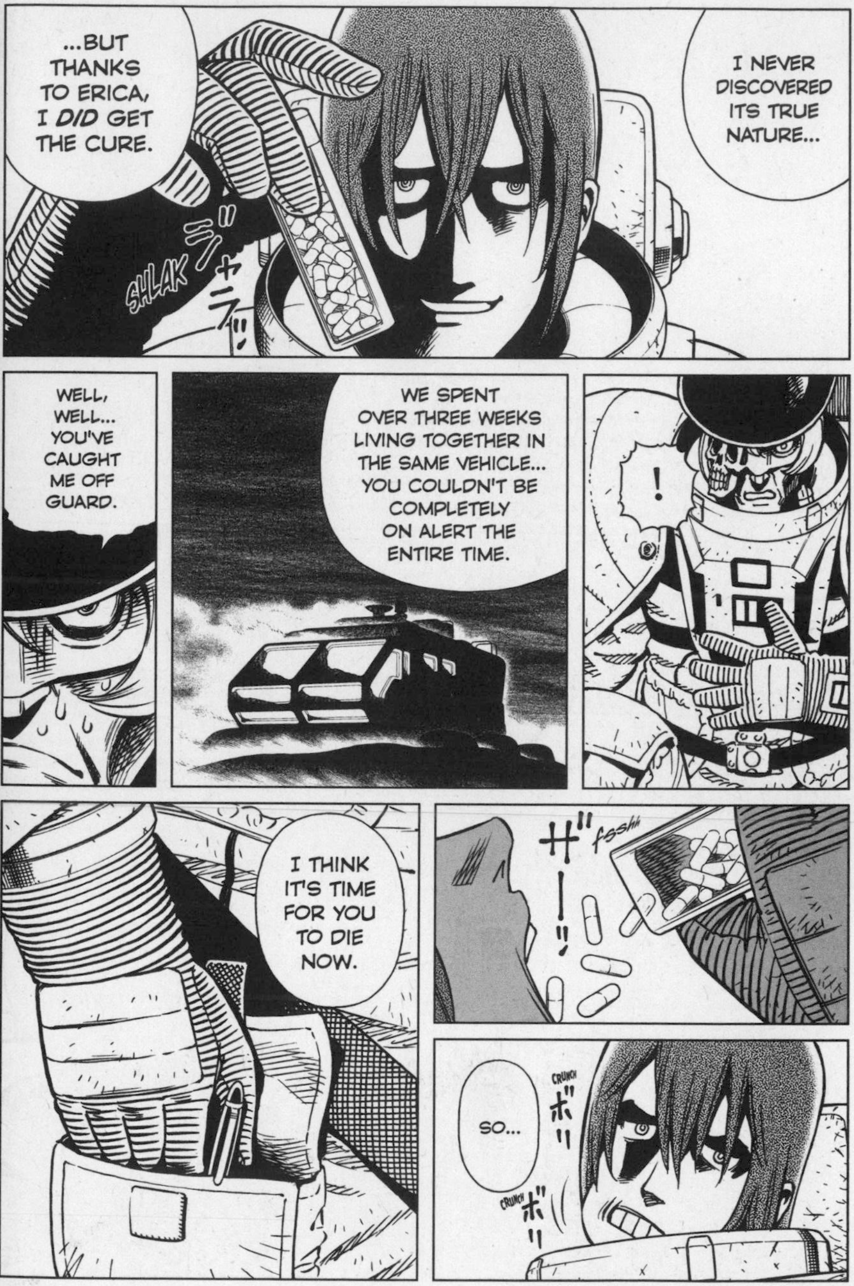
I NEVER DISCOVERED ITS TRUE NATURE...
...BUT THANKS TO ERICA, I *DID* GET THE CURE.
SHLAK
!
WE SPENT OVER THREE WEEKS LIVING TOGETHER IN THE SAME VEHICLE... YOU COULDN'T BE COMPLETELY ON ALERT THE ENTIRE TIME.
WELL, WELL... YOU'VE CAUGHT ME OFF GUARD.
fsshh
CRUNCH
SO...
CRUNCH
I THINK IT'S TIME FOR YOU TO DIE NOW.

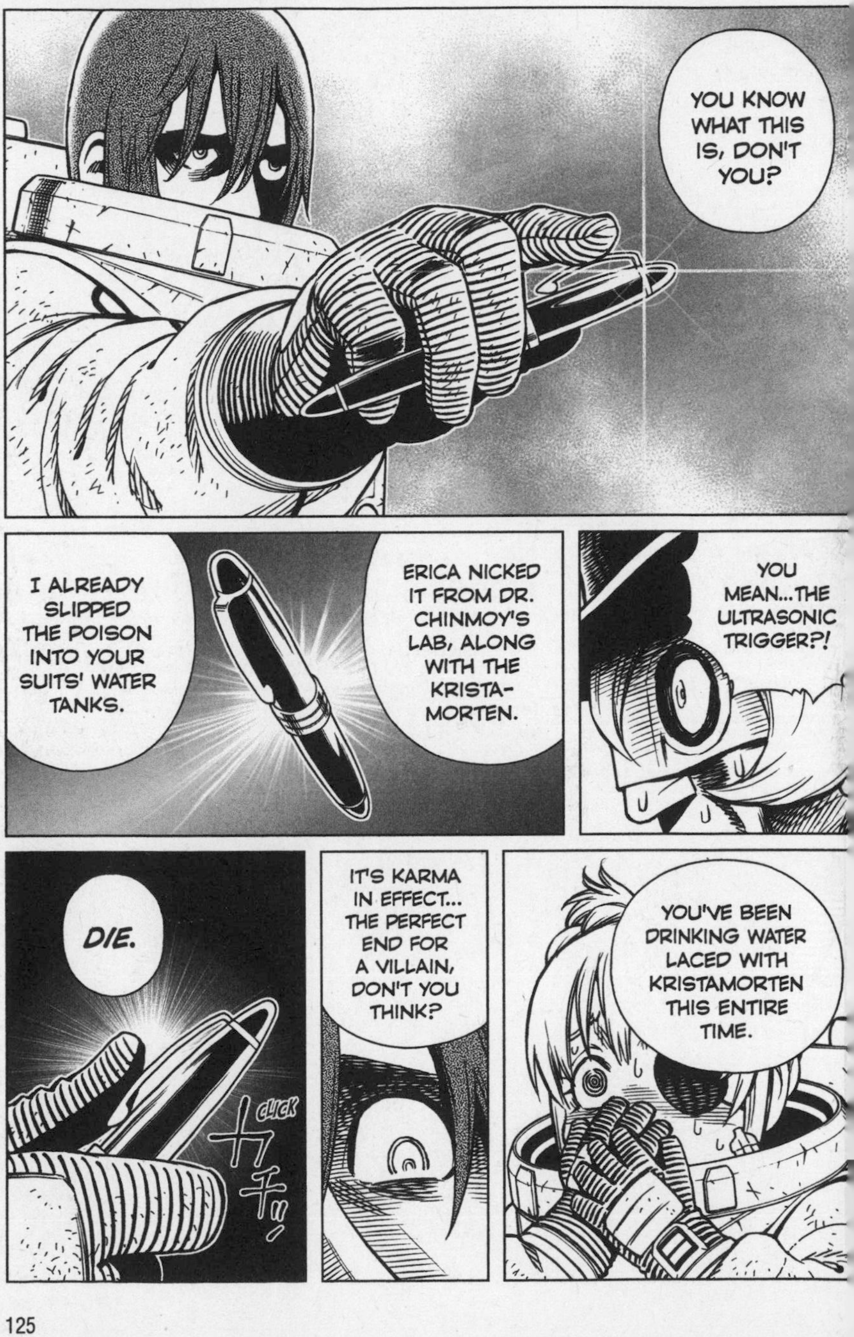
YOU KNOW WHAT THIS IS, DON'T YOU?
YOU MEAN...THE ULTRASONIC TRIGGER?!
ERICA NICKED IT FROM DR. CHINMOY'S LAB, ALONG WITH THE KRISTA-MORTEN.
I ALREADY SLIPPED THE POISON INTO YOUR SUITS' WATER TANKS.
YOU'VE BEEN DRINKING WATER LACED WITH KRISTAMORTEN THIS ENTIRE TIME.
IT'S KARMA IN EFFECT... THE PERFECT END FOR A VILLAIN, DON'T YOU THINK?
DIE.
CLICK
カチ!!

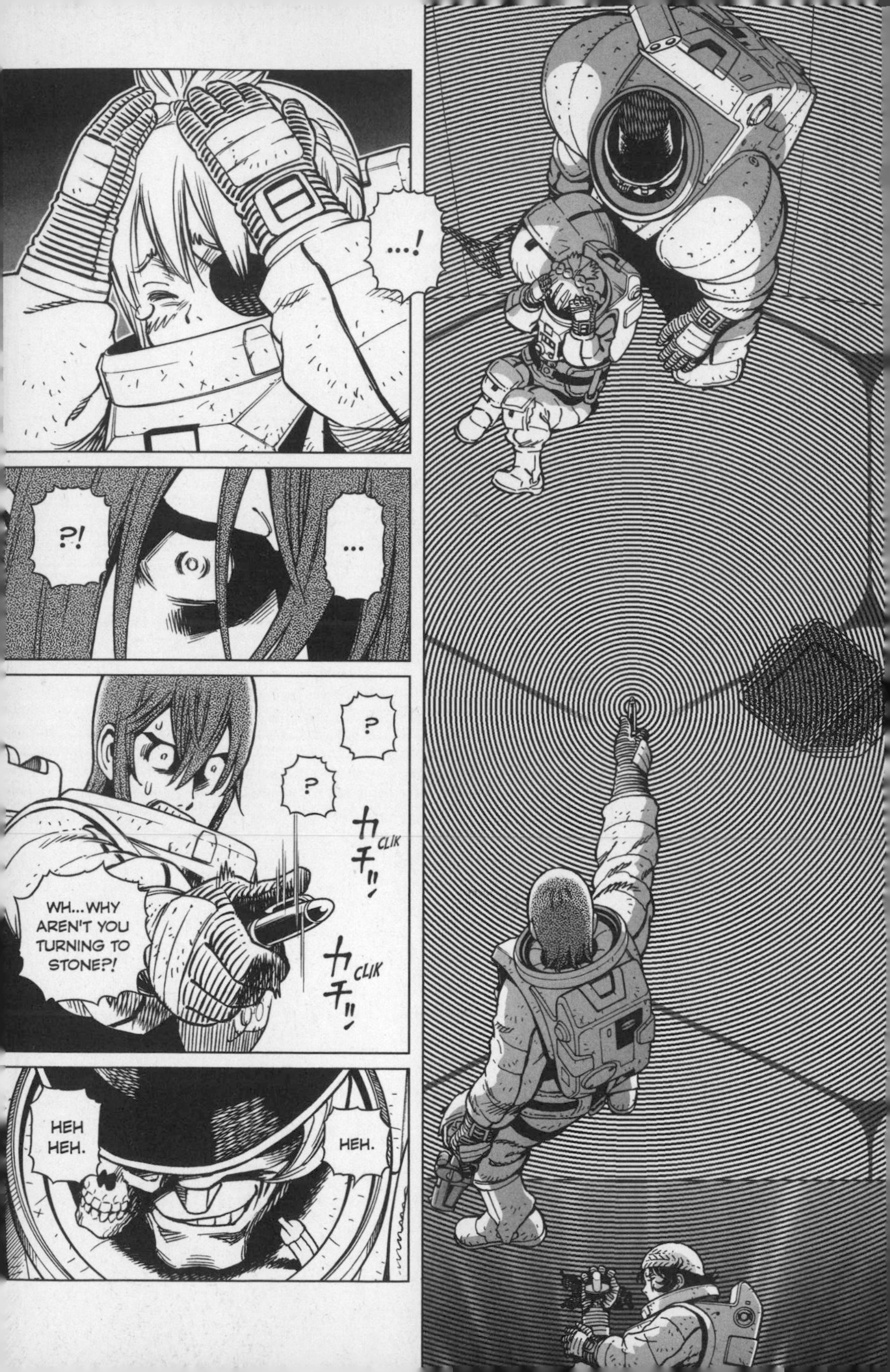
...!
...
?!
?
?
カチ!!
CLIK
カチ!!
CLIK
WH...WHY AREN'T YOU TURNING TO STONE?!
HEH.
HEH HEH.

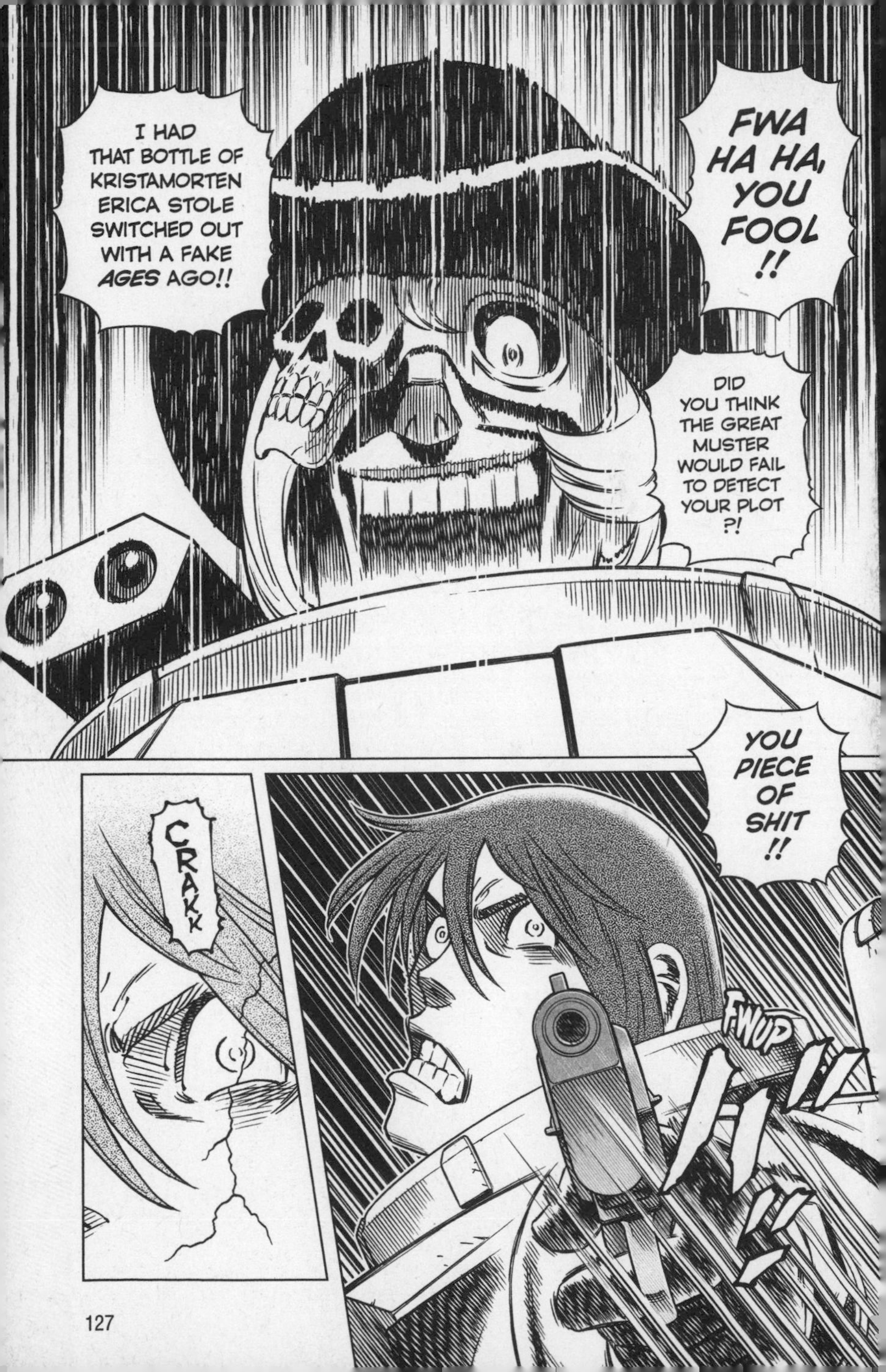
FWA HA HA, YOU FOOL!!
DID YOU THINK THE GREAT MUSTER WOULD FAIL TO DETECT YOUR PLOT?!
I HAD THAT BOTTLE OF KRISTAMORTEN ERICA STOLE SWITCHED OUT WITH A FAKE AGES AGO!!
YOU PIECE OF SHIT!!
FWUP
CRAKK

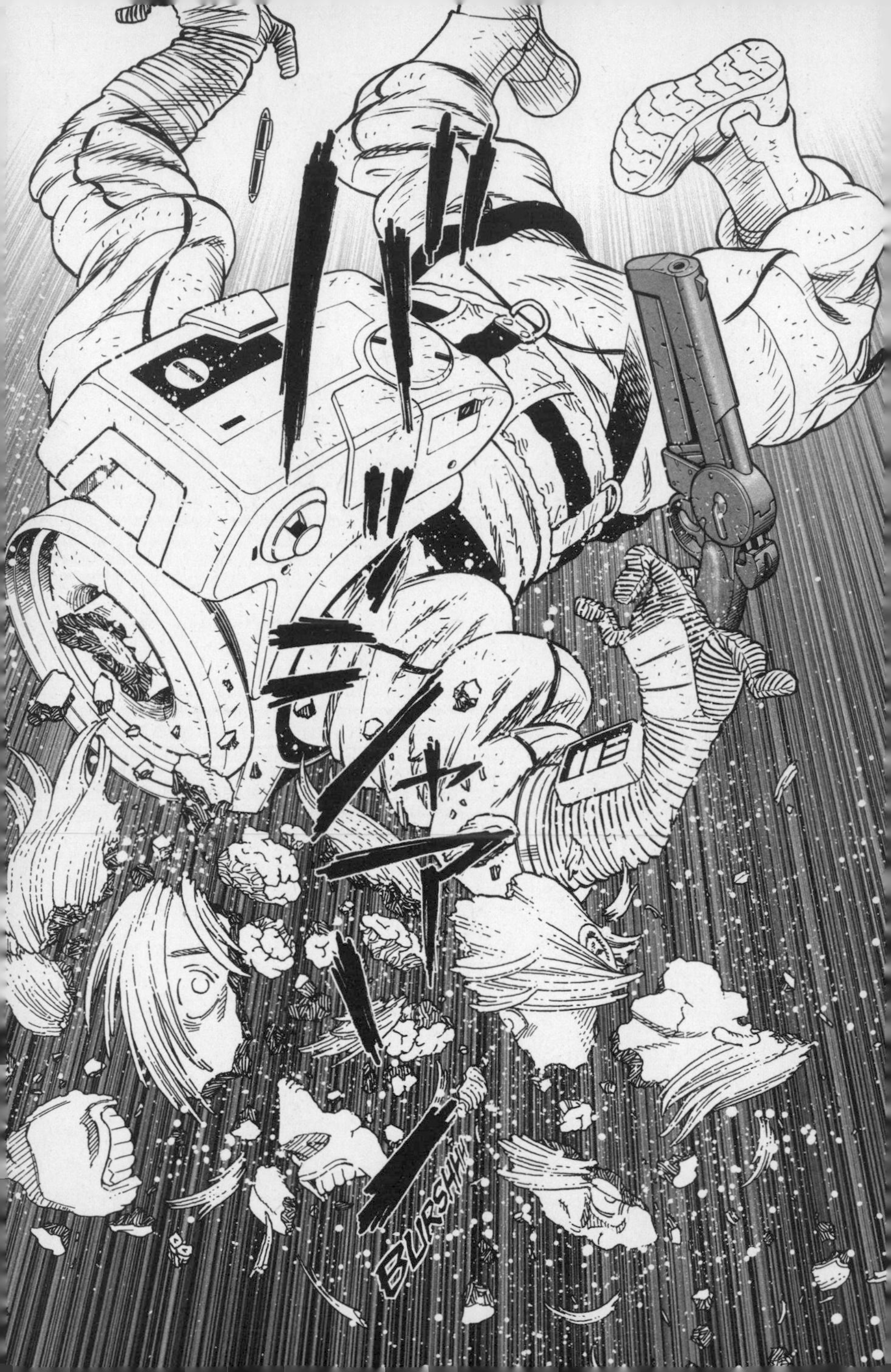
BURSHH

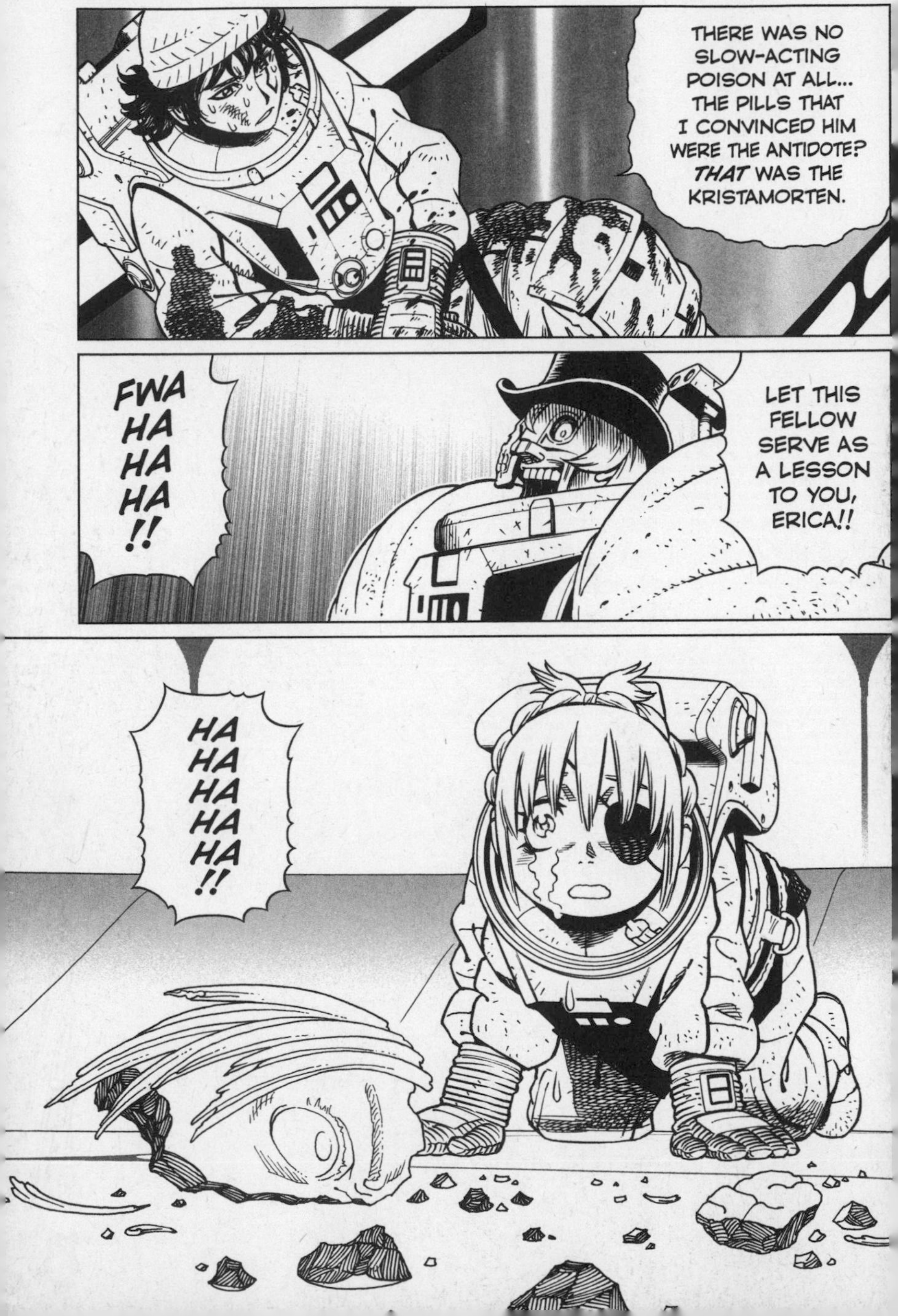
THERE WAS NO SLOW-ACTING POISON AT ALL... THE PILLS THAT I CONVINCED HIM WERE THE ANTIDOTE? *THAT* WAS THE KRISTAMORTEN.
LET THIS FELLOW SERVE AS A LESSON TO YOU, ERICA!!
FWA HA HA HA!!
HA HA HA HA HA!!

LOG:021

THE SORROWS OF YOUNG ITALL

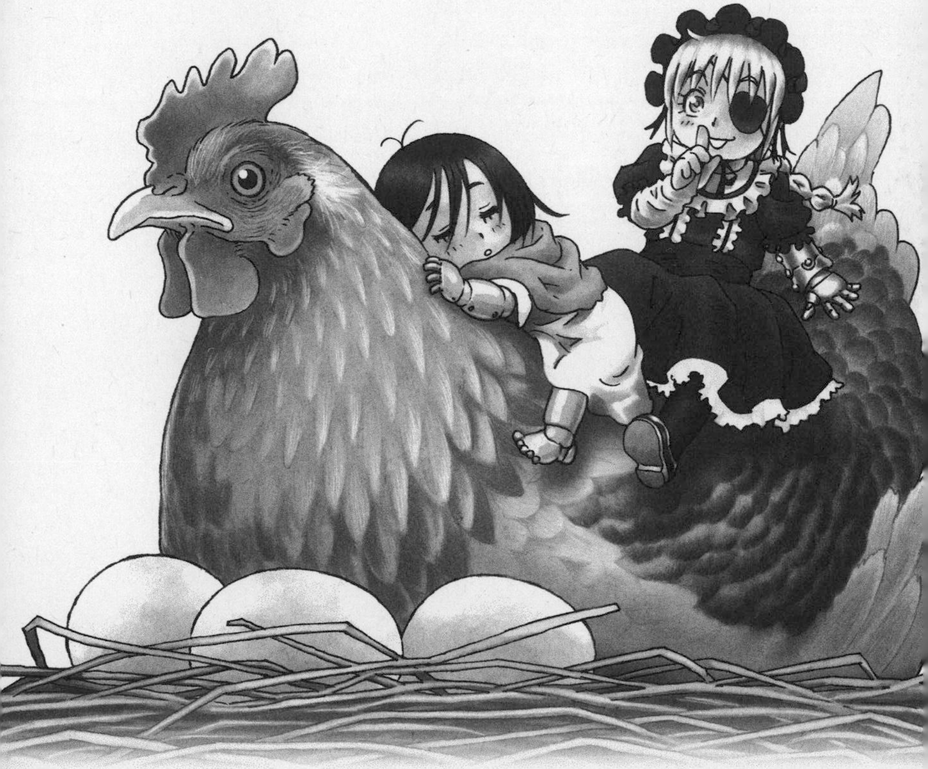

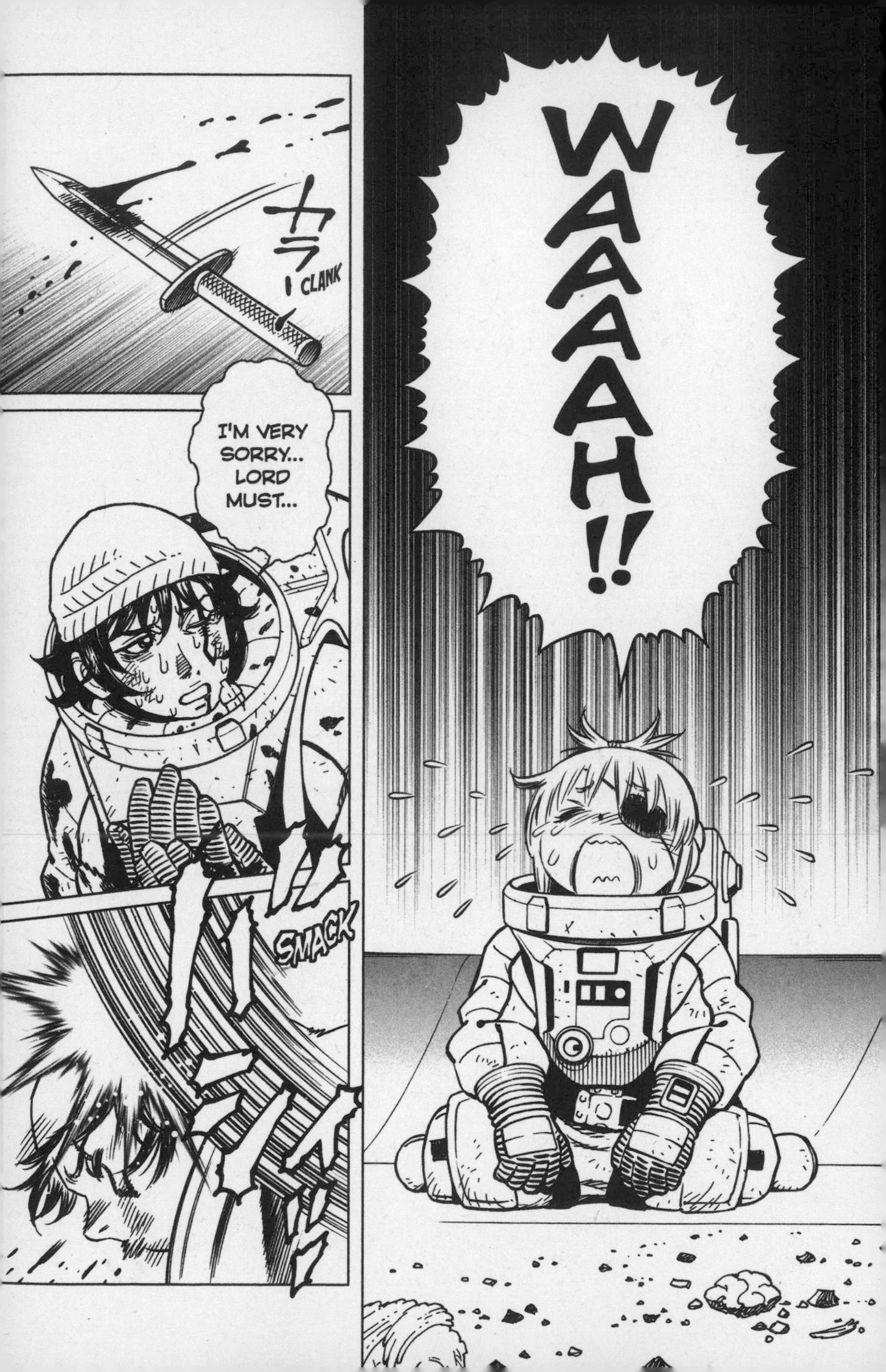

WAAAAH!!
カラ
CLANK
I'M VERY SORRY... LORD MUST...
SMACK

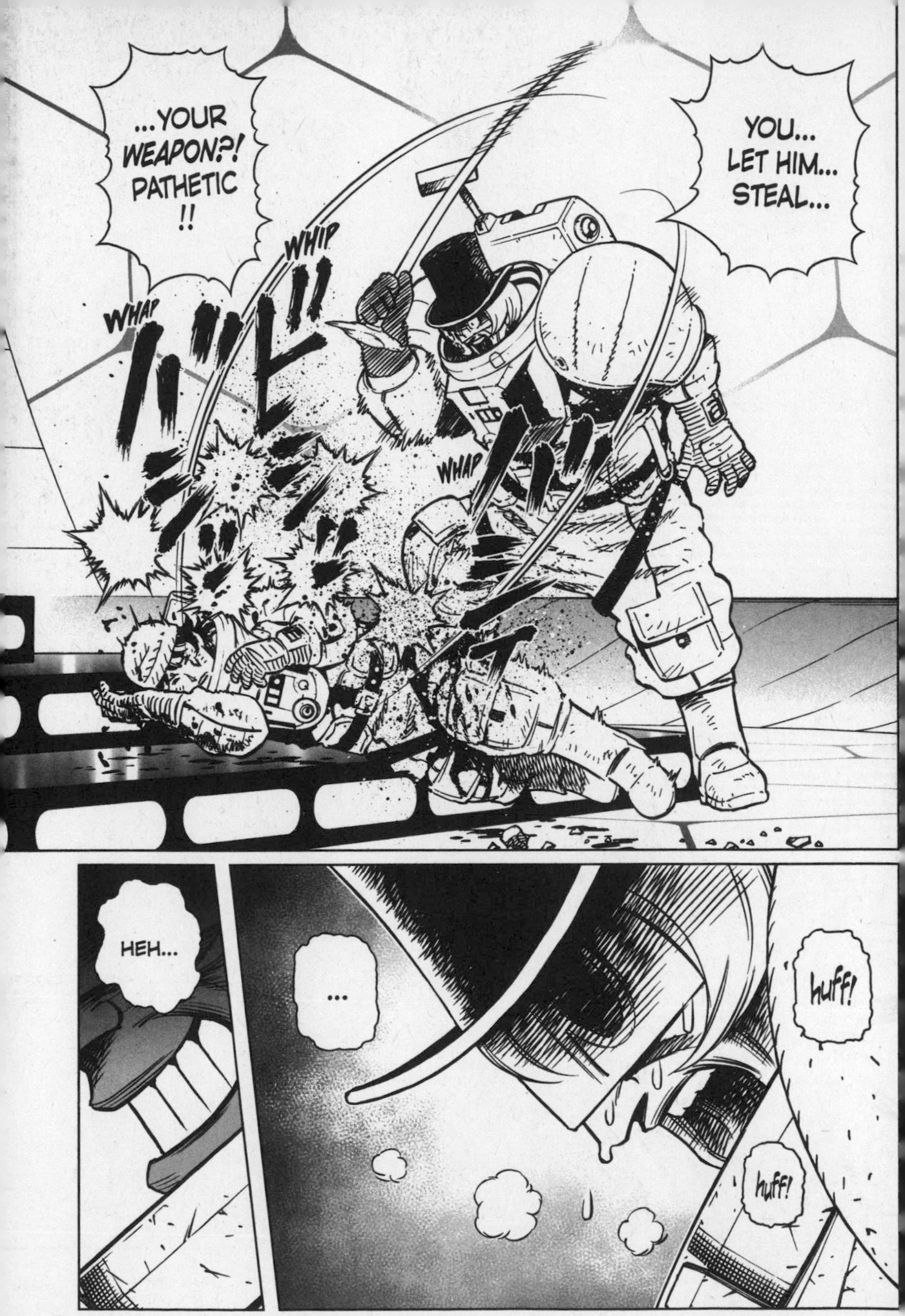
YOU... LET HIM... STEAL...
...YOUR WEAPON?! PATHETIC !!
WHIP
WHAP
WHAP
huff!
...
huff!
HEH...

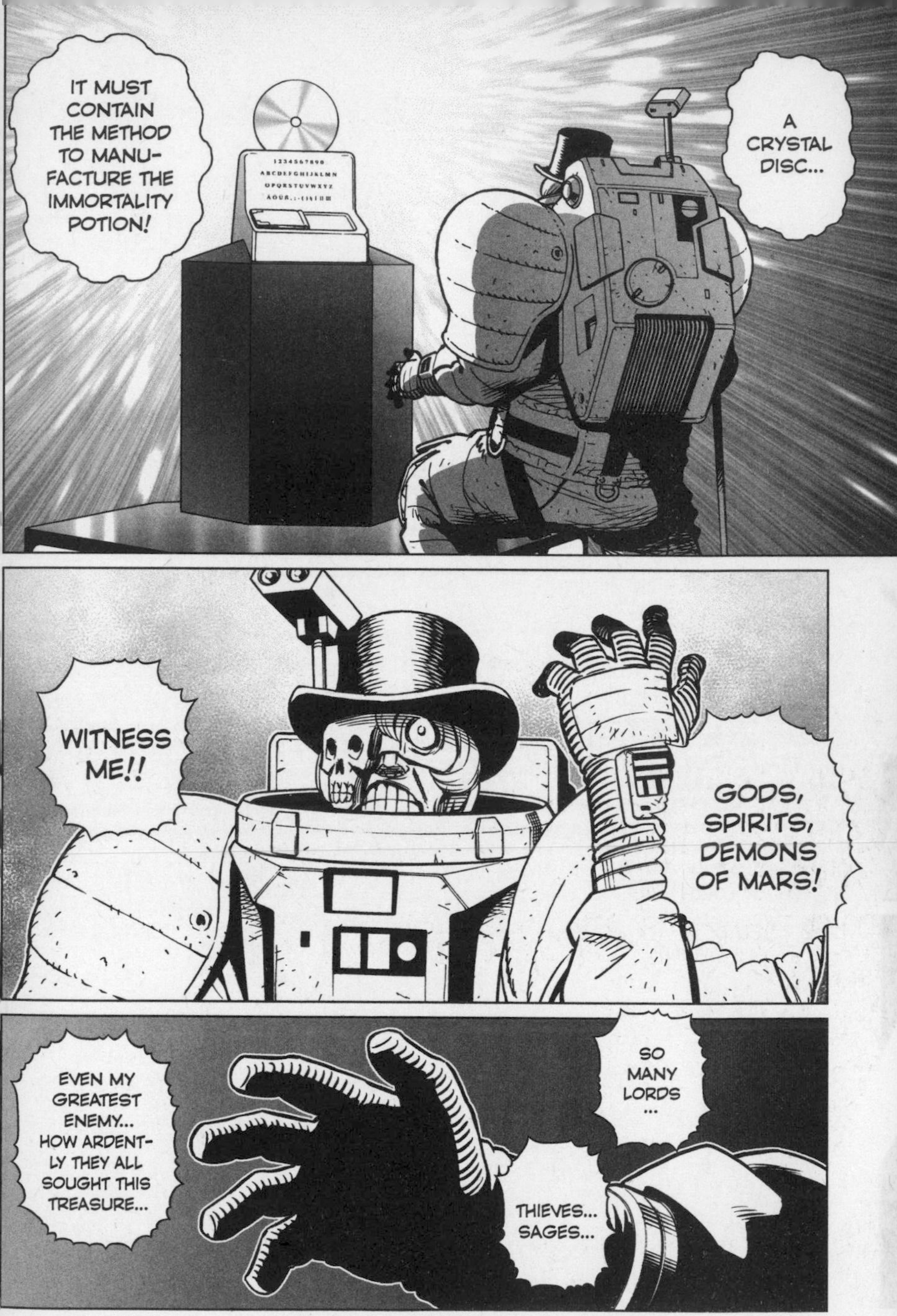
A CRYSTAL DISC...
IT MUST CONTAIN THE METHOD TO MANU-FACTURE THE IMMORTALITY POTION!
GODS, SPIRITS, DEMONS OF MARS!
WITNESS ME!!
SO MANY LORDS ...
THIEVES... SAGES...
EVEN MY GREATEST ENEMY... HOW ARDENT-LY THEY ALL SOUGHT THIS TREASURE...

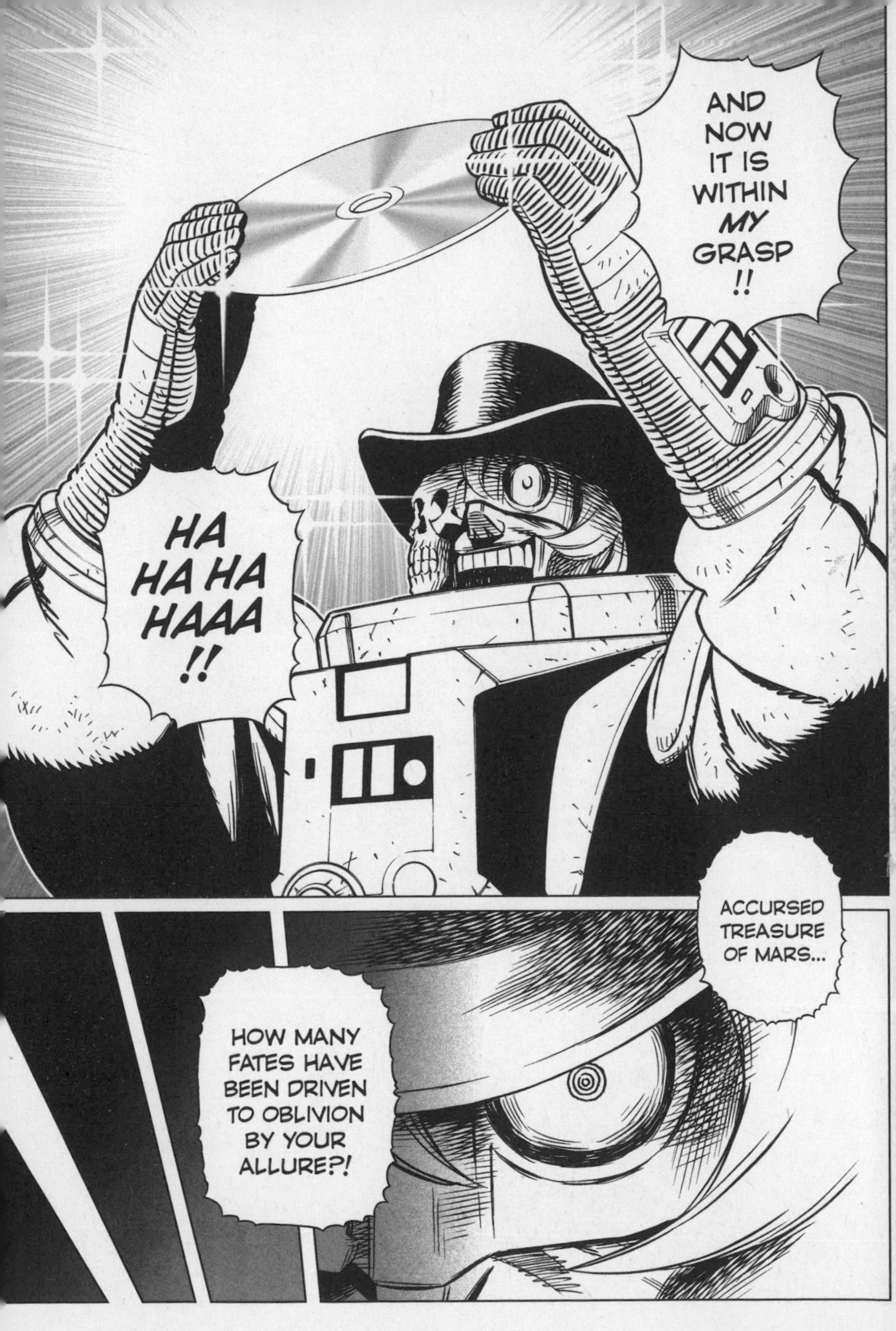
AND NOW IT IS WITHIN *MY* GRASP!!
HA HA HA HAAA!!
ACCURSED TREASURE OF MARS...
HOW MANY FATES HAVE BEEN DRIVEN TO OBLIVION BY YOUR ALLURE?!

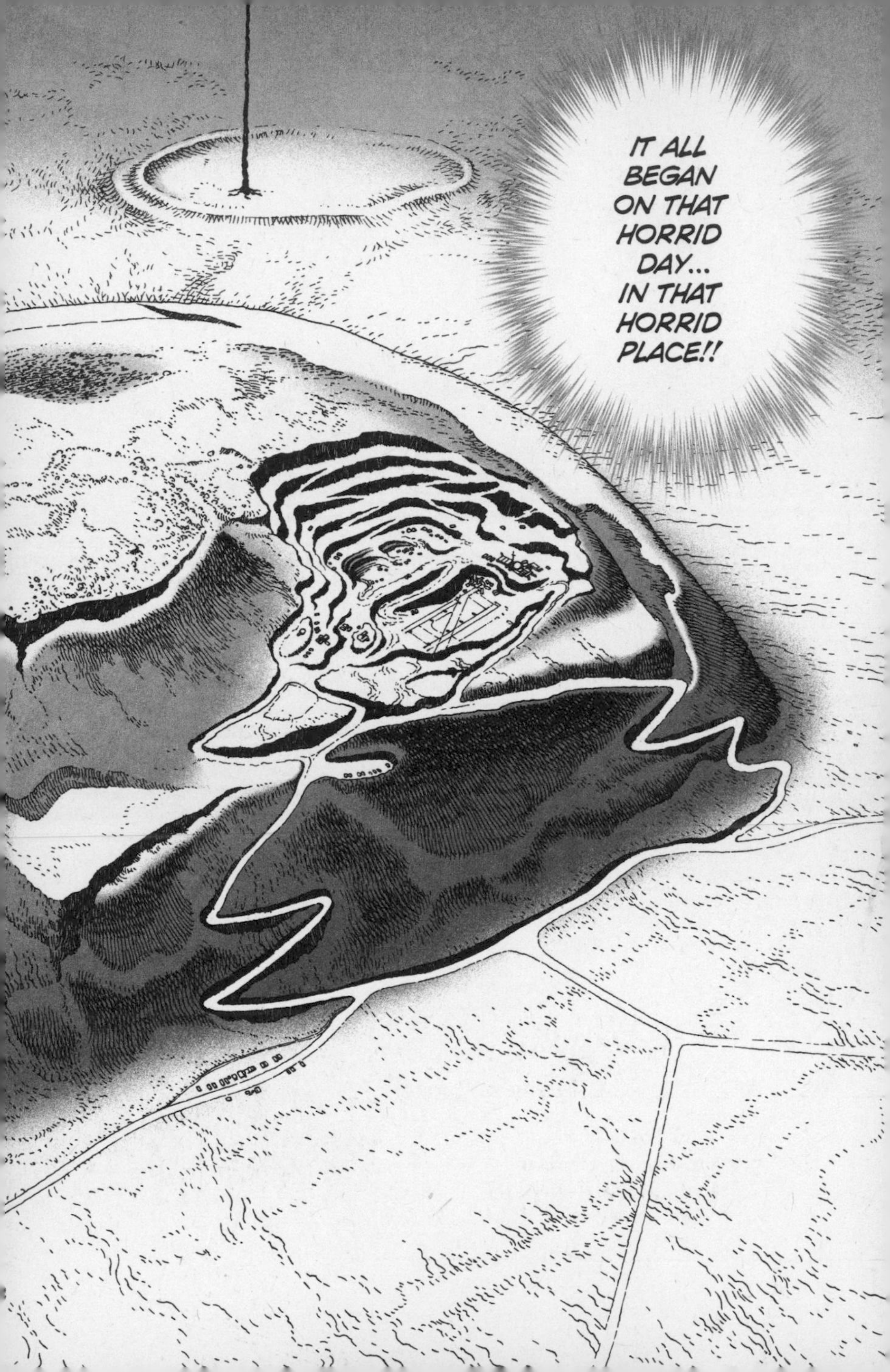
IT ALL BEGAN ON THAT HORRID DAY... IN THAT HORRID PLACE!!

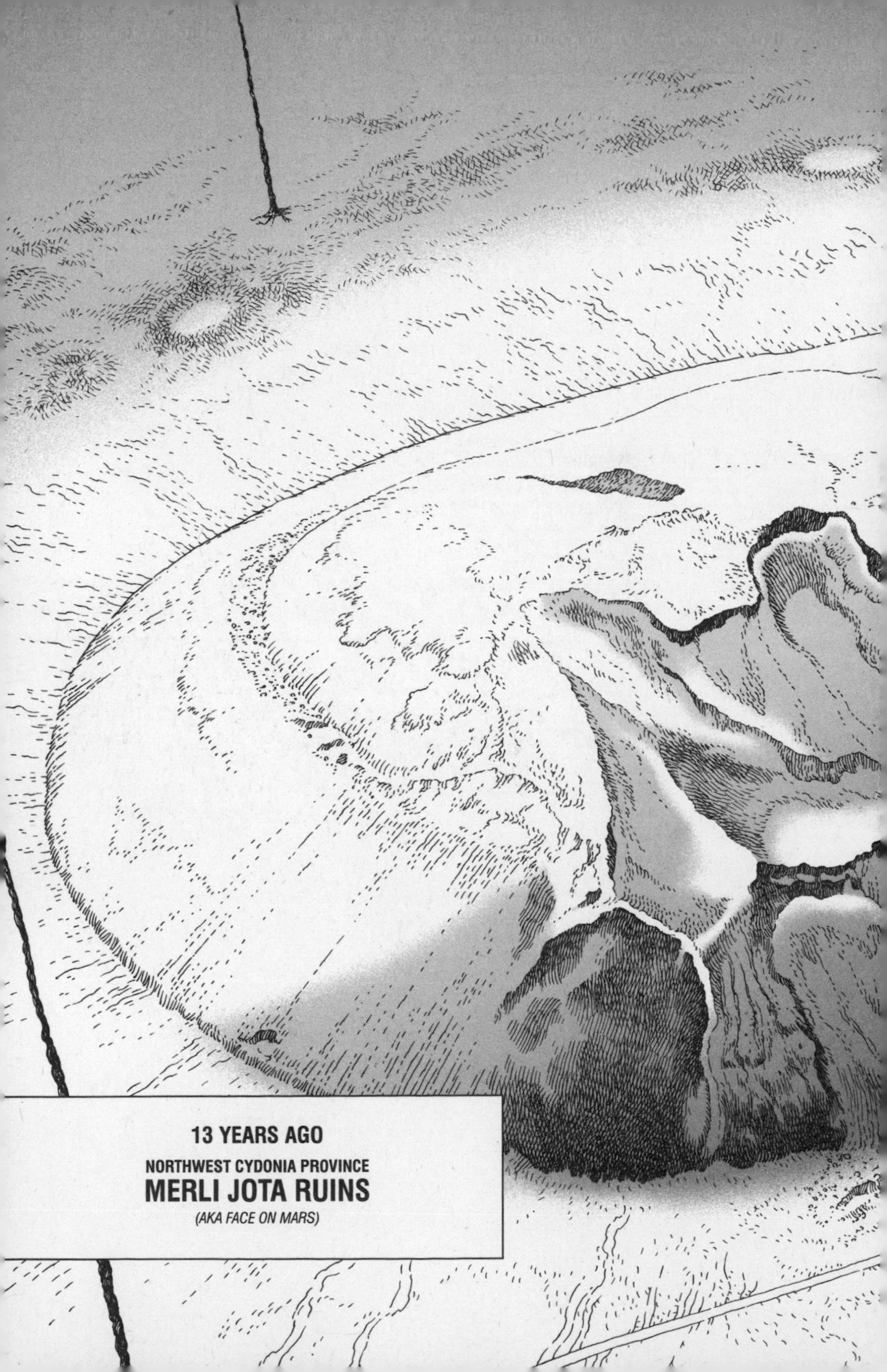
13 YEARS AGO
NORTHWEST CYDONIA PROVINCE
MERLI JOTA RUINS
(AKA FACE ON MARS)

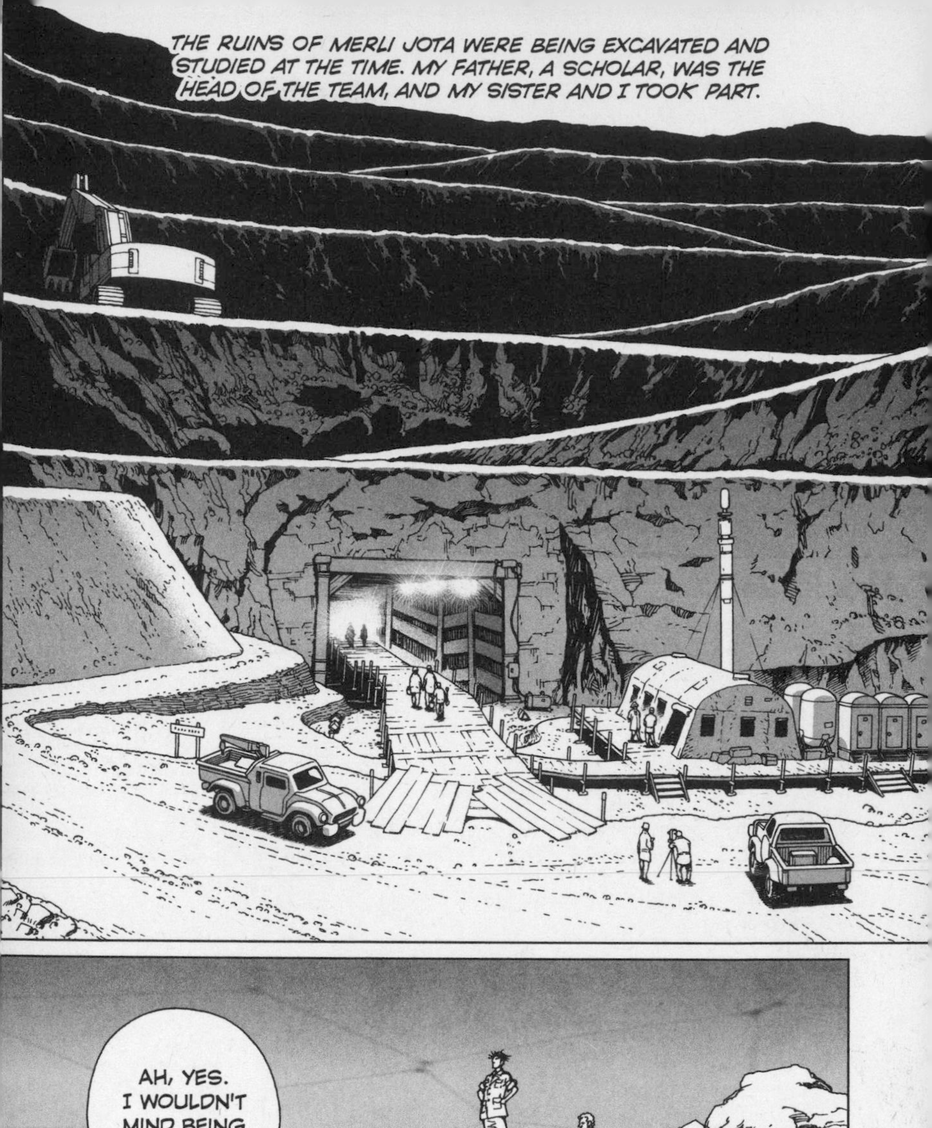
THE RUINS OF MERLI JOTA WERE BEING EXCAVATED AND STUDIED AT THE TIME. MY FATHER, A SCHOLAR, WAS THE HEAD OF THE TEAM, AND MY SISTER AND I TOOK PART.

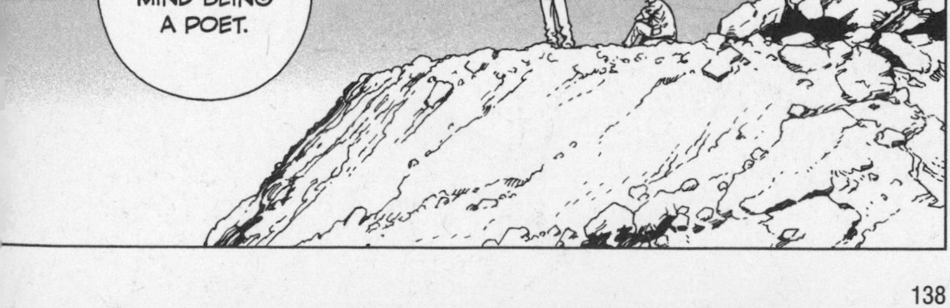
AH, YES. I WOULDN'T MIND BEING A POET.

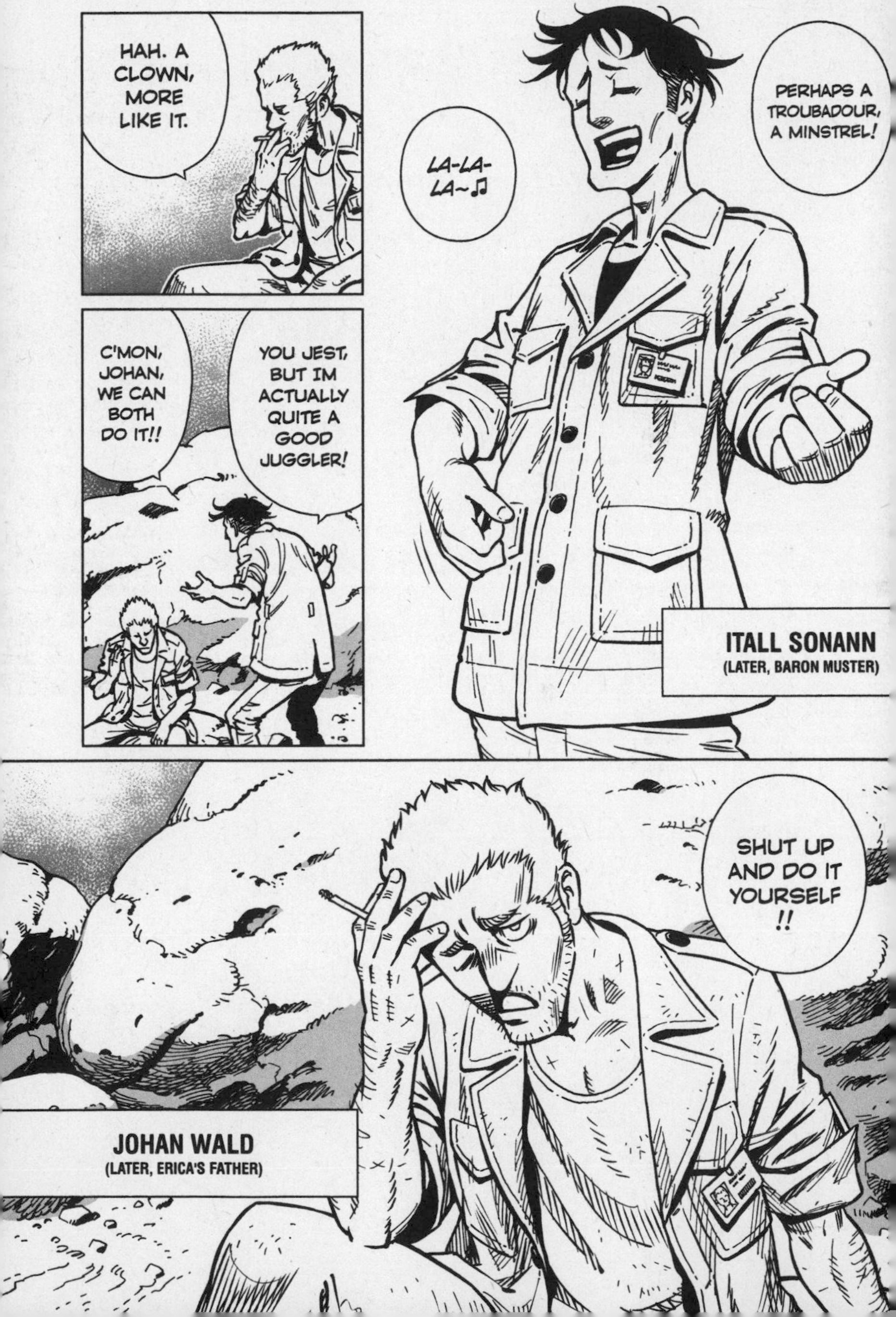
PERHAPS A TROUBADOUR, A MINSTREL!
LA-LA-LA~♫
ITALL SONANN
(LATER, BARON MUSTER)
HAH. A CLOWN, MORE LIKE IT.
YOU JEST, BUT IM ACTUALLY QUITE A GOOD JUGGLER!
C'MON, JOHAN, WE CAN BOTH DO IT!!
SHUT UP AND DO IT YOURSELF !!
JOHAN WALD
(LATER, ERICA'S FATHER)

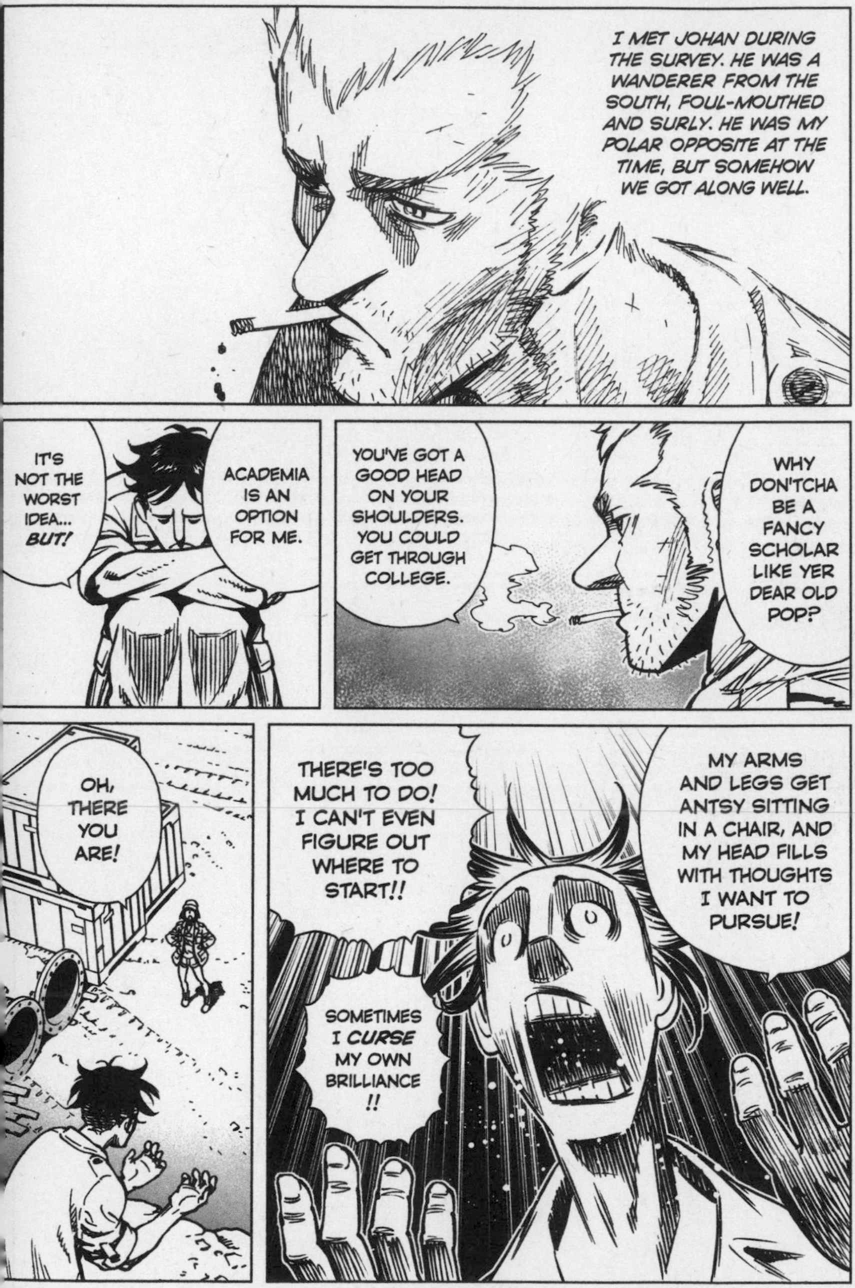
I MET JOHAN DURING THE SURVEY. HE WAS A WANDERER FROM THE SOUTH, FOUL-MOUTHED AND SURLY. HE WAS MY POLAR OPPOSITE AT THE TIME, BUT SOMEHOW WE GOT ALONG WELL.
WHY DON'TCHA BE A FANCY SCHOLAR LIKE YER DEAR OLD POP?
YOU'VE GOT A GOOD HEAD ON YOUR SHOULDERS. YOU COULD GET THROUGH COLLEGE.
ACADEMIA IS AN OPTION FOR ME.
IT'S NOT THE WORST IDEA... *BUT!*
MY ARMS AND LEGS GET ANTSY SITTING IN A CHAIR, AND MY HEAD FILLS WITH THOUGHTS I WANT TO PURSUE!
THERE'S TOO MUCH TO DO! I CAN'T EVEN FIGURE OUT WHERE TO START!!
SOMETIMES I *CURSE* MY OWN BRILLIANCE!!
OH, THERE YOU ARE!

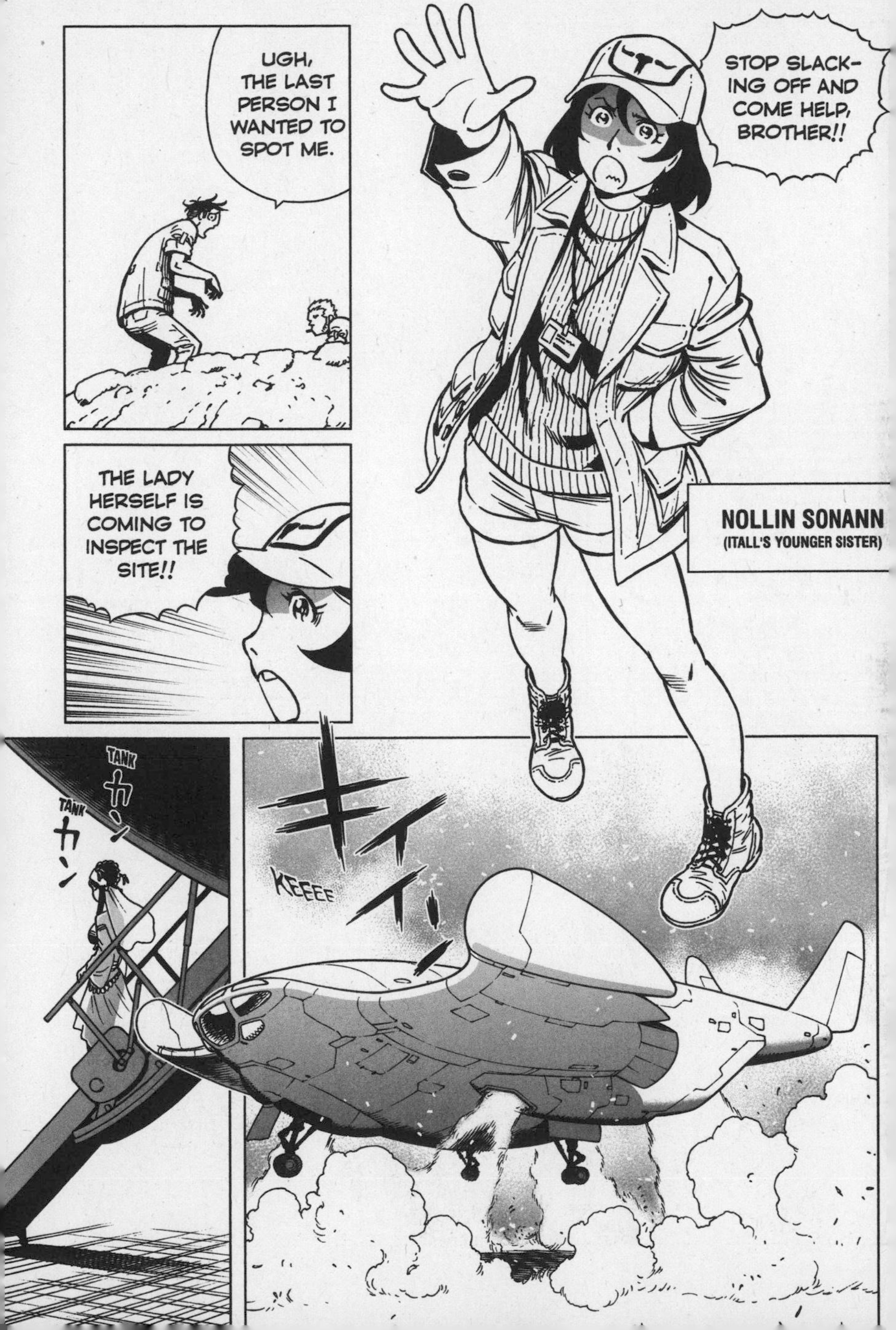
STOP SLACKING OFF AND COME HELP, BROTHER!!
NOLLIN SONANN
(ITALL'S YOUNGER SISTER)
UGH, THE LAST PERSON I WANTED TO SPOT ME.
THE LADY HERSELF IS COMING TO INSPECT THE SITE!!
KEEEE
TANK
カン
TANK
カン

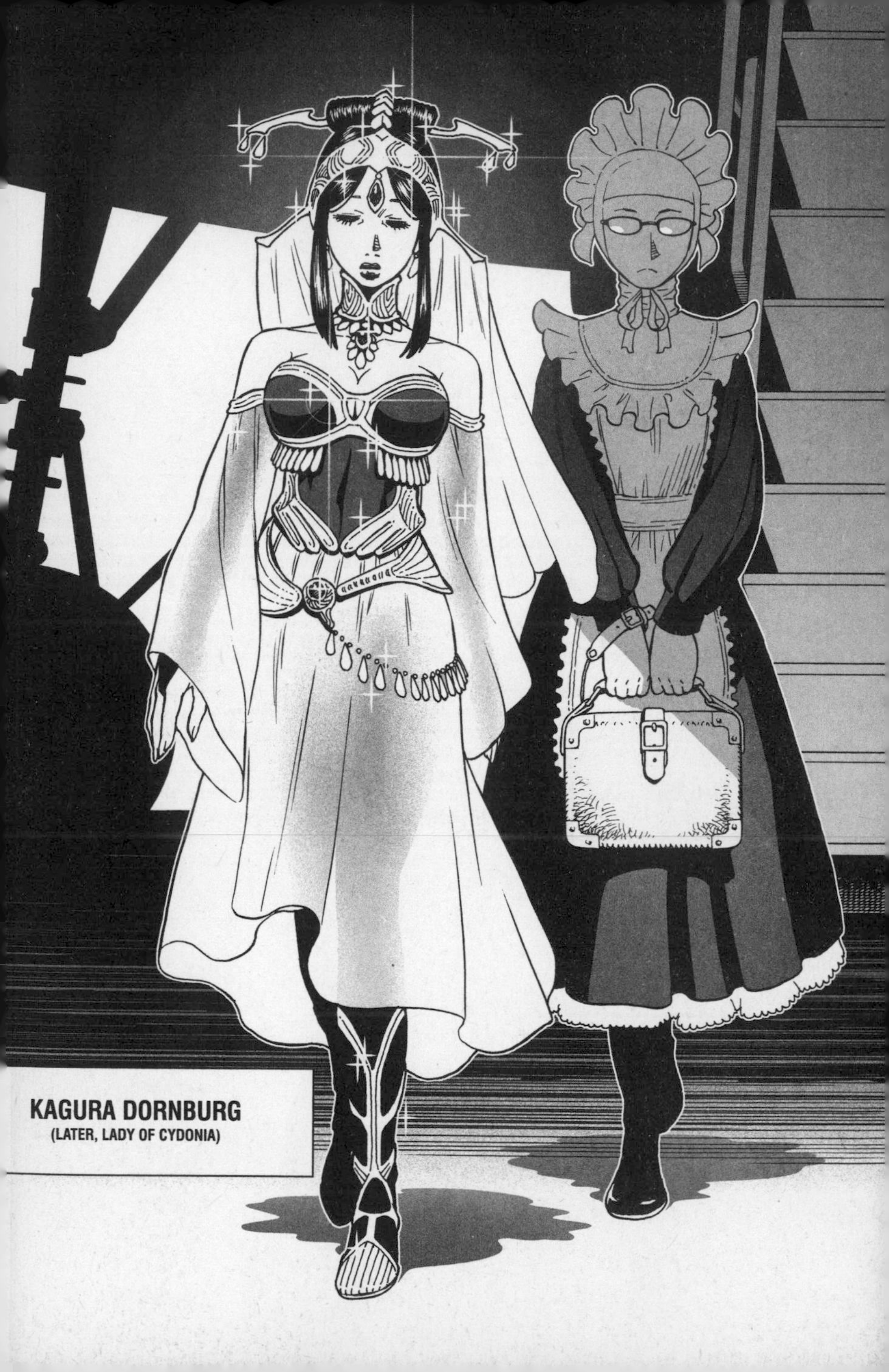
KAGURA DORNBURG
(LATER, LADY OF CYDONIA)

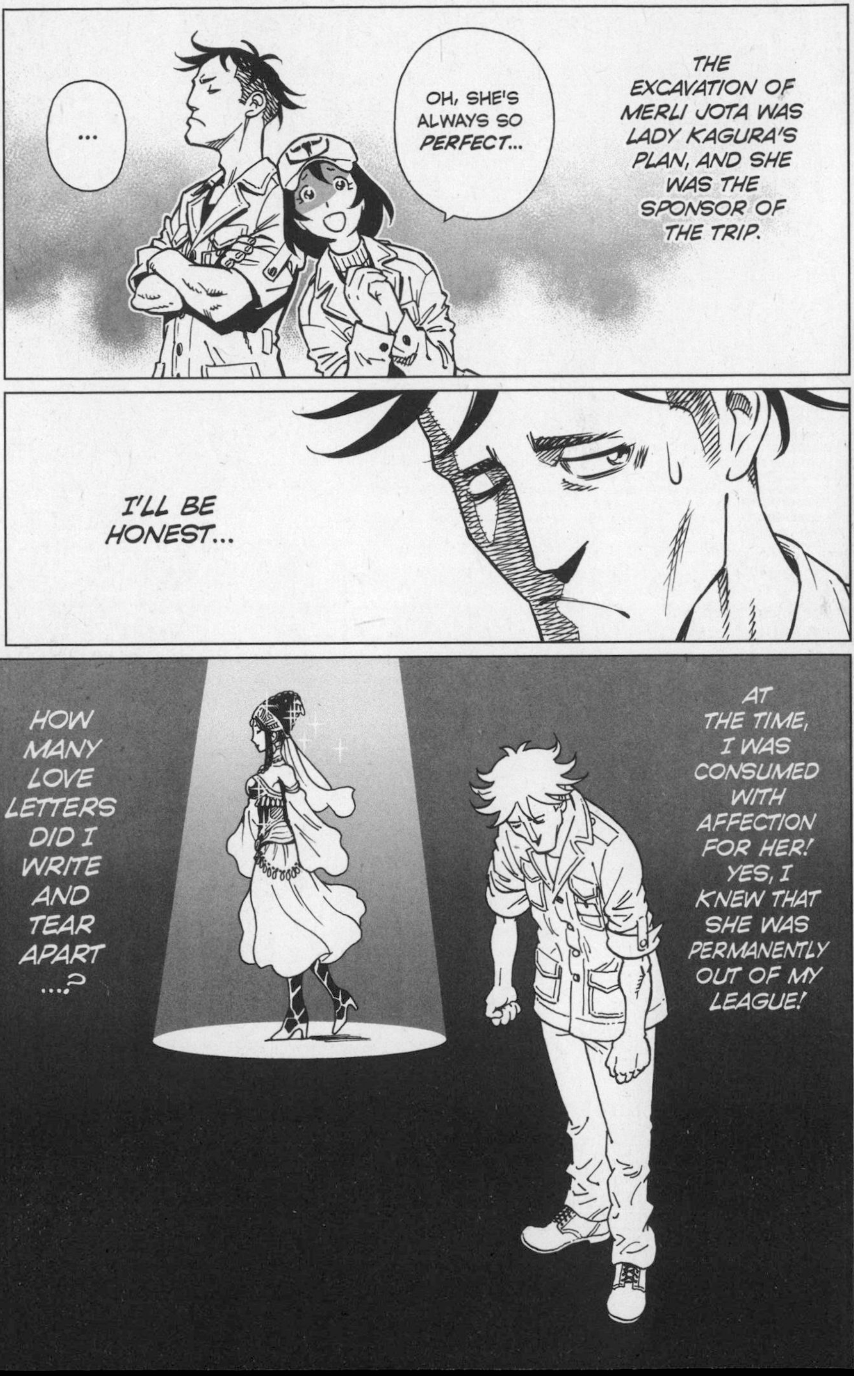
THE EXCAVATION OF MERLI JOTA WAS LADY KAGURA'S PLAN, AND SHE WAS THE SPONSOR OF THE TRIP.
OH, SHE'S ALWAYS SO PERFECT...
...
I'LL BE HONEST...
AT THE TIME, I WAS CONSUMED WITH AFFECTION FOR HER! YES, I KNEW THAT SHE WAS PERMANENTLY OUT OF MY LEAGUE!
HOW MANY LOVE LETTERS DID I WRITE AND TEAR APART ...?

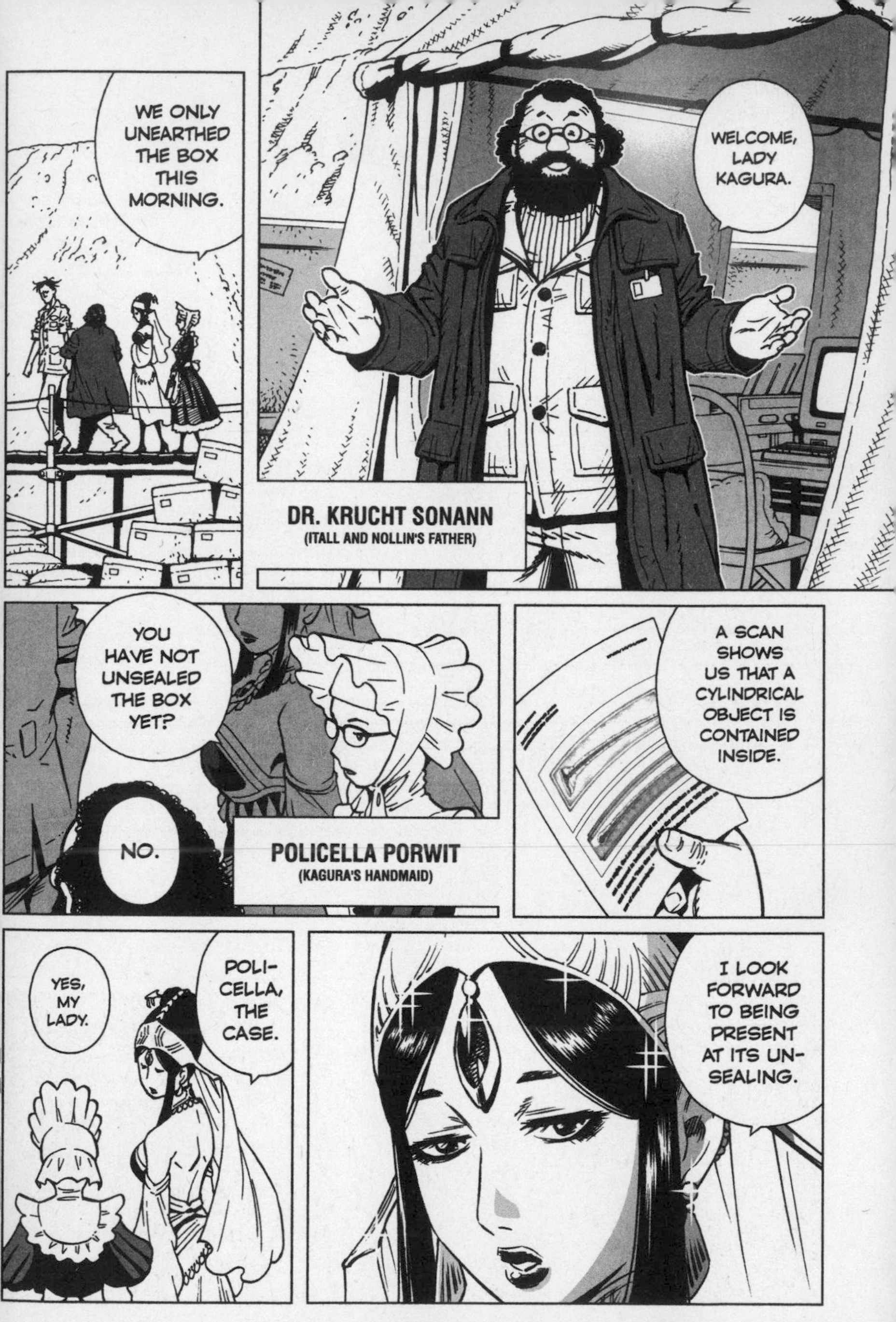
WELCOME, LADY KAGURA.
DR. KRUCHT SONANN
(ITALL AND NOLLIN'S FATHER)
WE ONLY UNEARTHED THE BOX THIS MORNING.
A SCAN SHOWS US THAT A CYLINDRICAL OBJECT IS CONTAINED INSIDE.
YOU HAVE NOT UNSEALED THE BOX YET?
NO.
POLICELLA PORWIT
(KAGURA'S HANDMAID)
I LOOK FORWARD TO BEING PRESENT AT ITS UN-SEALING.
POLI-CELLA, THE CASE.
YES, MY LADY.

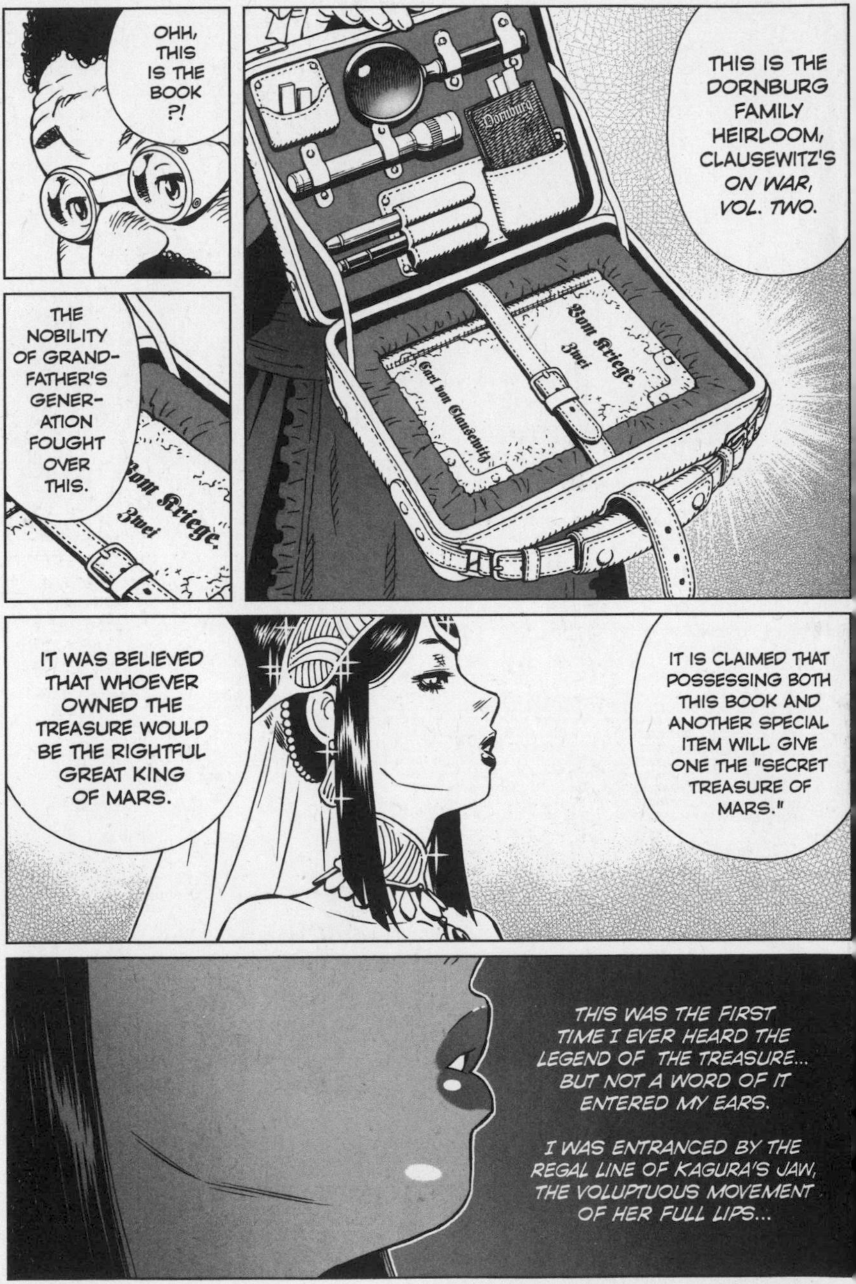
THIS IS THE DORNBURG FAMILY HEIRLOOM, CLAUSEWITZ'S *ON WAR*, VOL. TWO.
Dornburg
Vom Kriege.
Zwei
Carl von Clausewitz
OHH, THIS IS THE BOOK ?!
THE NOBILITY OF GRAND-FATHER'S GENER-ATION FOUGHT OVER THIS.
Vom Kriege.
Zwei
IT IS CLAIMED THAT POSSESSING BOTH THIS BOOK AND ANOTHER SPECIAL ITEM WILL GIVE ONE THE "SECRET TREASURE OF MARS."
IT WAS BELIEVED THAT WHOEVER OWNED THE TREASURE WOULD BE THE RIGHTFUL GREAT KING OF MARS.
THIS WAS THE FIRST TIME I EVER HEARD THE LEGEND OF THE TREASURE... BUT NOT A WORD OF IT ENTERED MY EARS.
I WAS ENTRANCED BY THE REGAL LINE OF KAGURA'S JAW, THE VOLUPTUOUS MOVEMENT OF HER FULL LIPS...

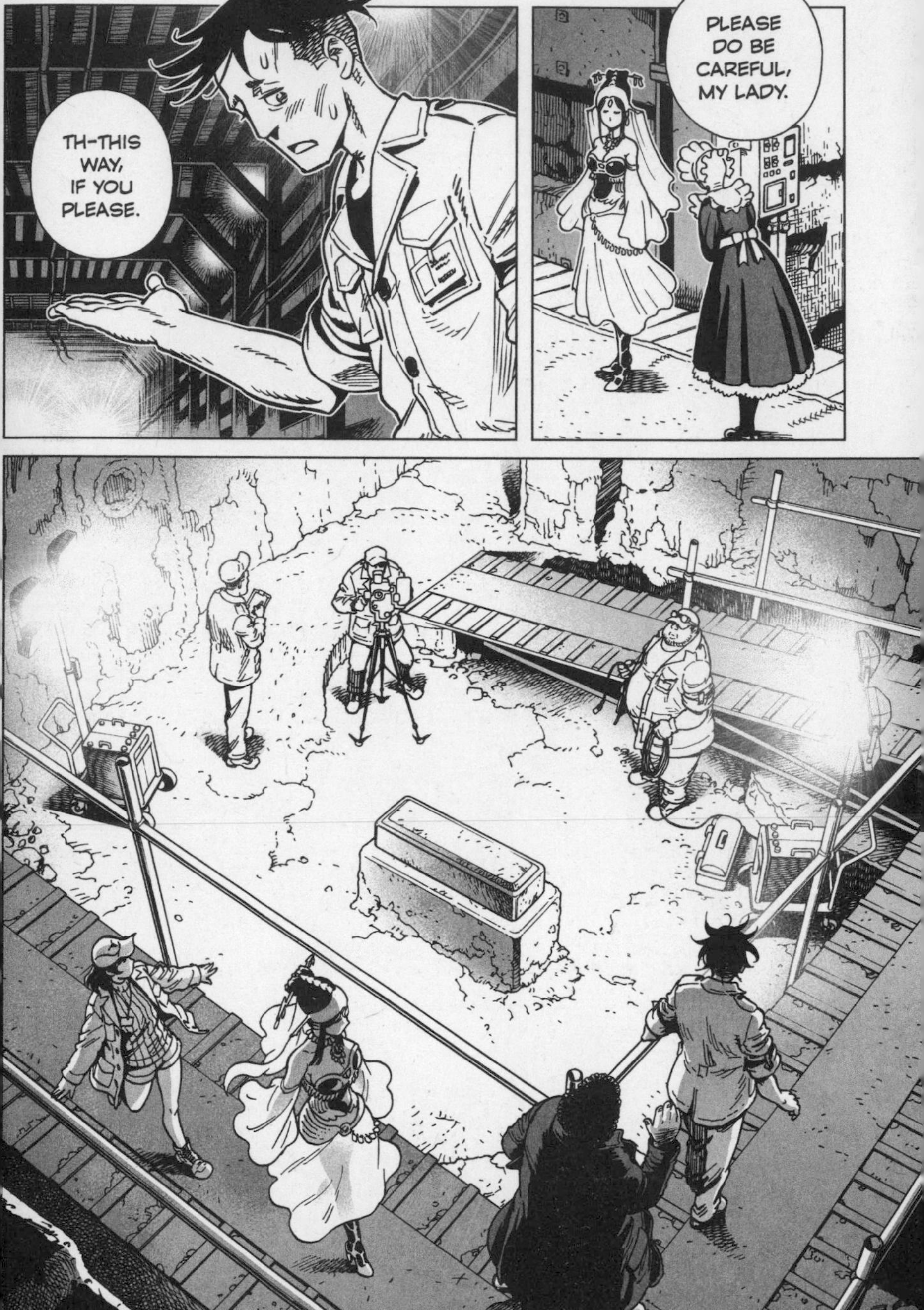
PLEASE DO BE CAREFUL, MY LADY.
TH-THIS WAY, IF YOU PLEASE.

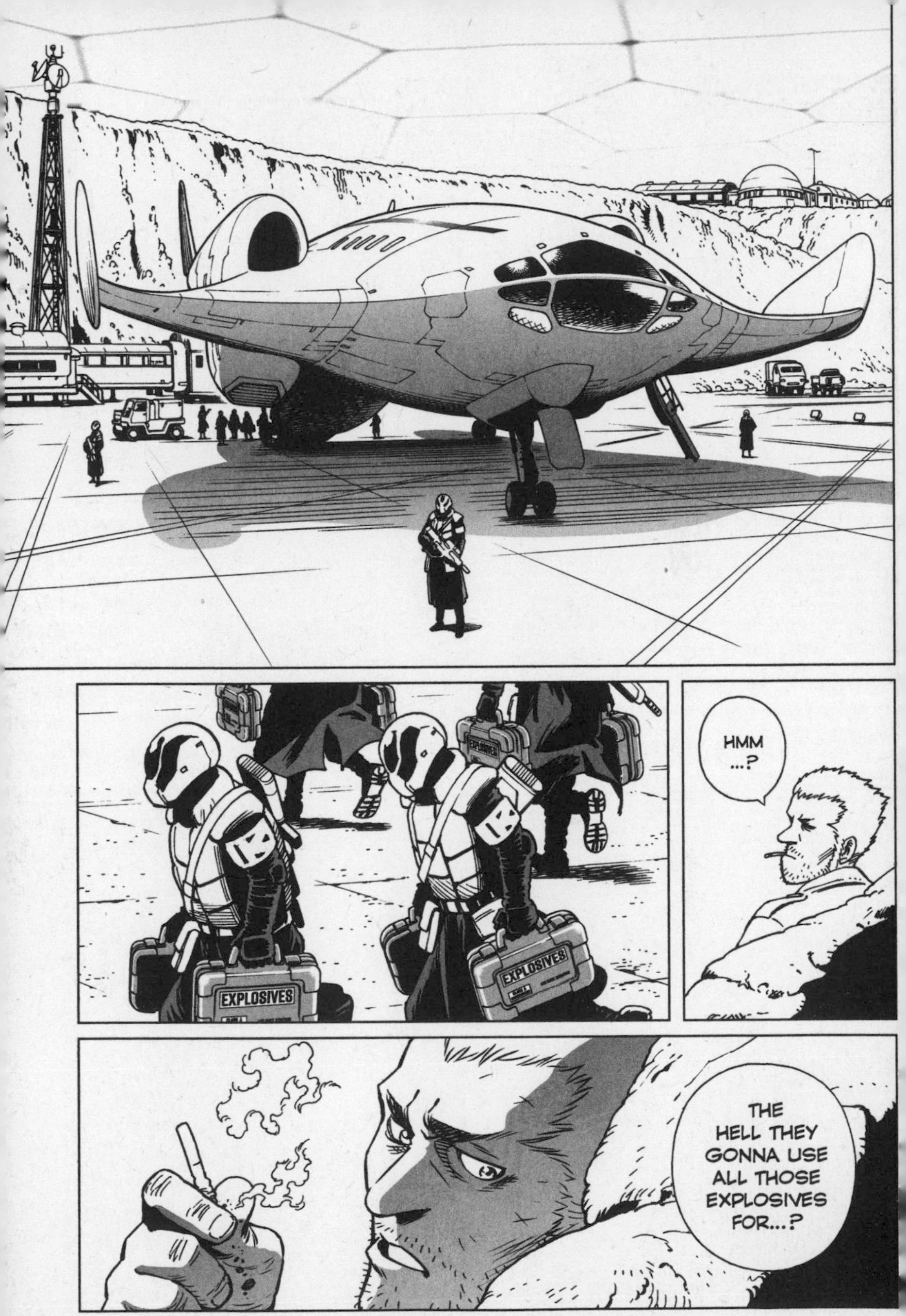
HMM ...?
EXPLOSIVES
EXPLOSIVES
EXPLOSIVES
THE HELL THEY GONNA USE ALL THOSE EXPLOSIVES FOR...?

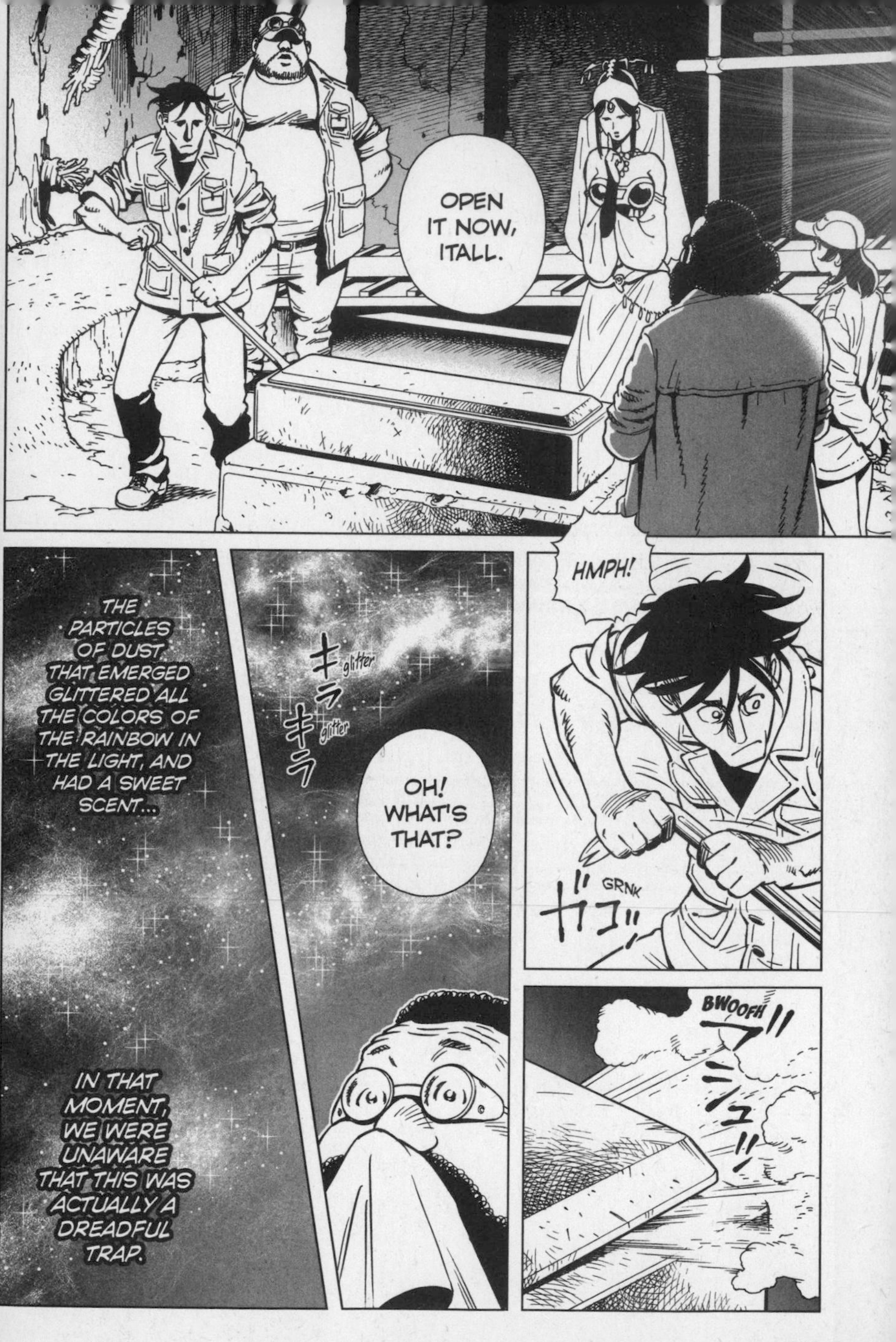
OPEN IT NOW, ITALL.
HMPH!
ガコッ
GRNK
BWOOFH
ブシュ!!
キラ glitter
キラ glitter
OH! WHAT'S THAT?
THE PARTICLES OF DUST THAT EMERGED GLITTERED ALL THE COLORS OF THE RAINBOW IN THE LIGHT, AND HAD A SWEET SCENT...
IN THAT MOMENT, WE WERE UNAWARE THAT THIS WAS ACTUALLY A DREADFUL TRAP.

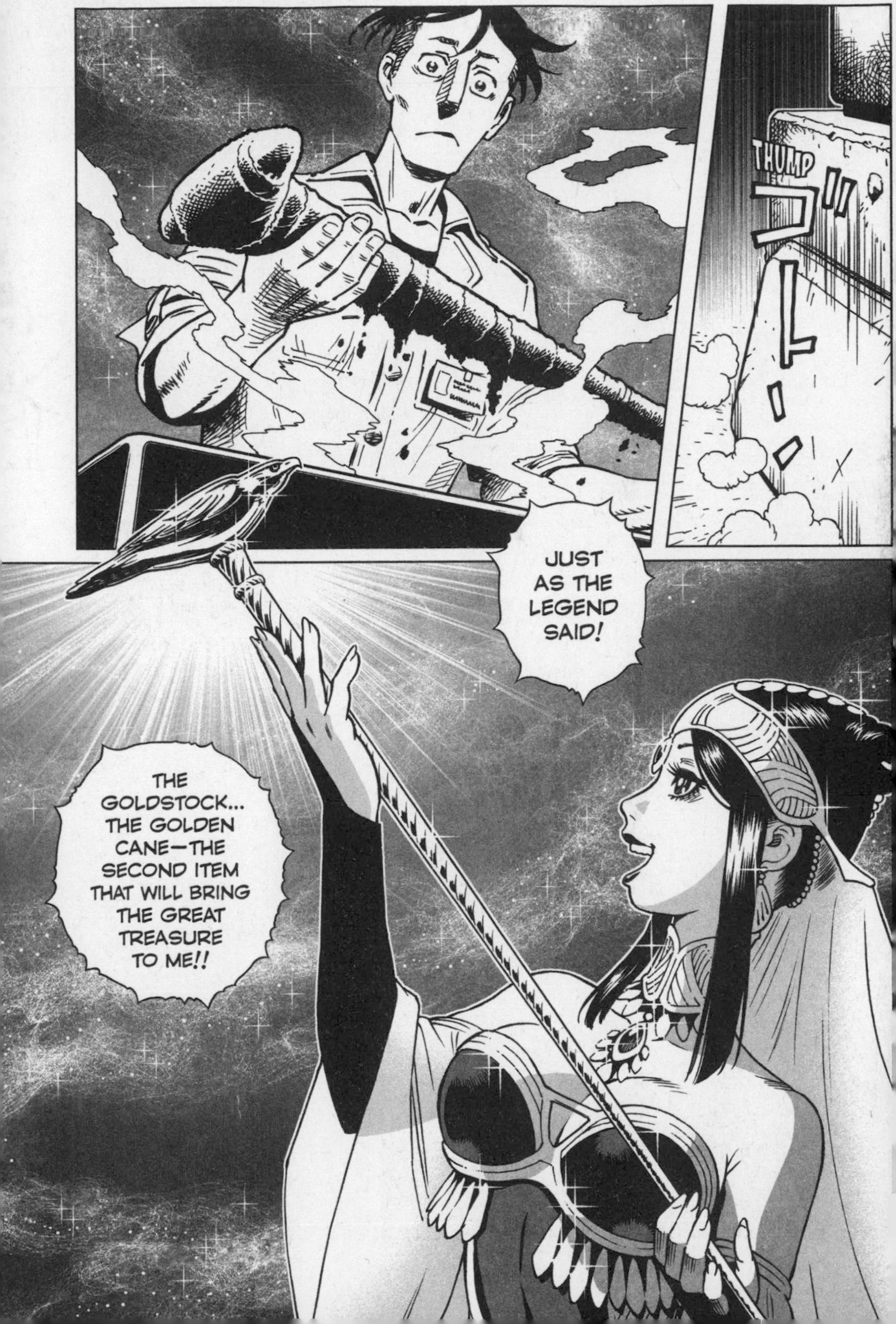
THUMP
JUST AS THE LEGEND SAID!
THE GOLDSTOCK... THE GOLDEN CANE—THE SECOND ITEM THAT WILL BRING THE GREAT TREASURE TO ME!!

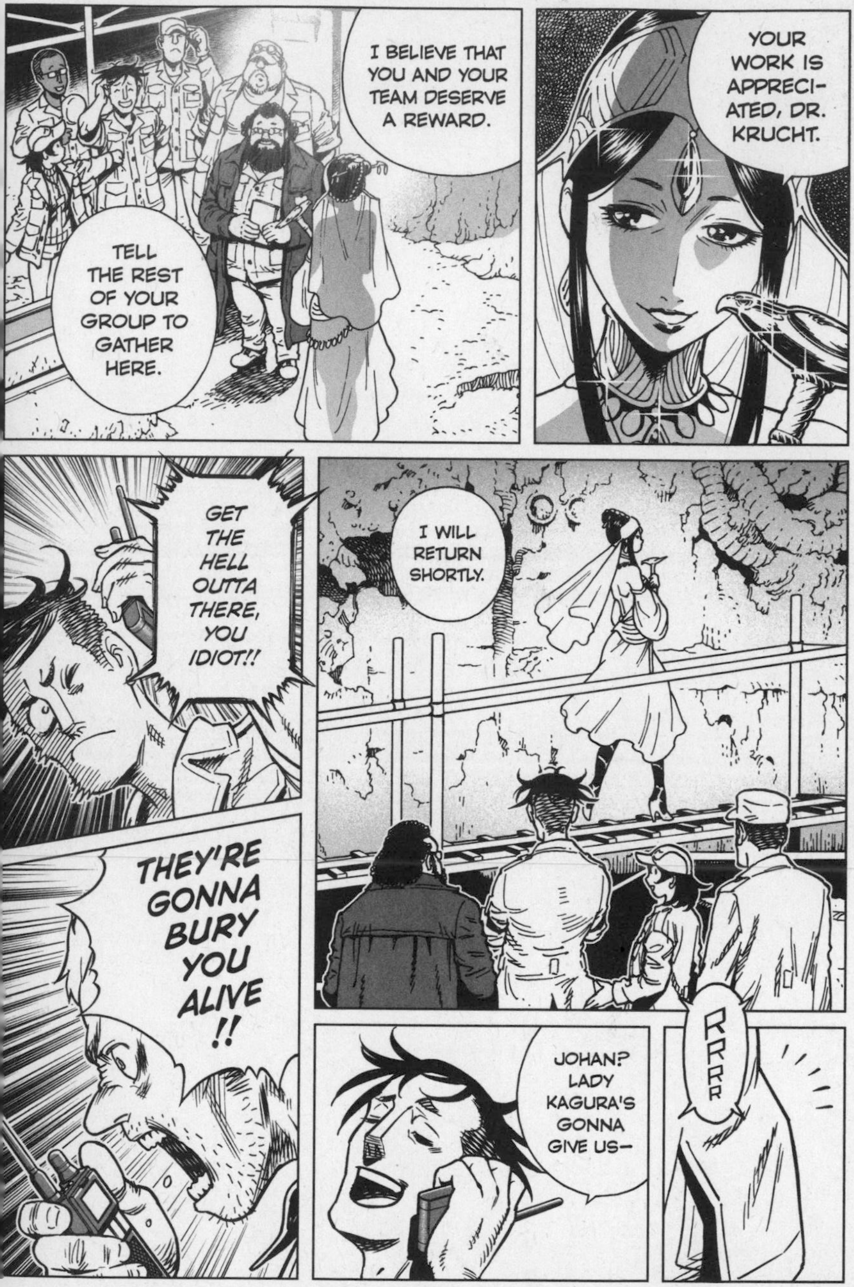
YOUR WORK IS APPRECI-ATED, DR. KRUCHT.
I BELIEVE THAT YOU AND YOUR TEAM DESERVE A REWARD.
TELL THE REST OF YOUR GROUP TO GATHER HERE.
I WILL RETURN SHORTLY.
RRRR
JOHAN? LADY KAGURA'S GONNA GIVE US—
GET THE HELL OUTTA THERE, YOU IDIOT!!
THEY'RE GONNA BURY YOU ALIVE!!

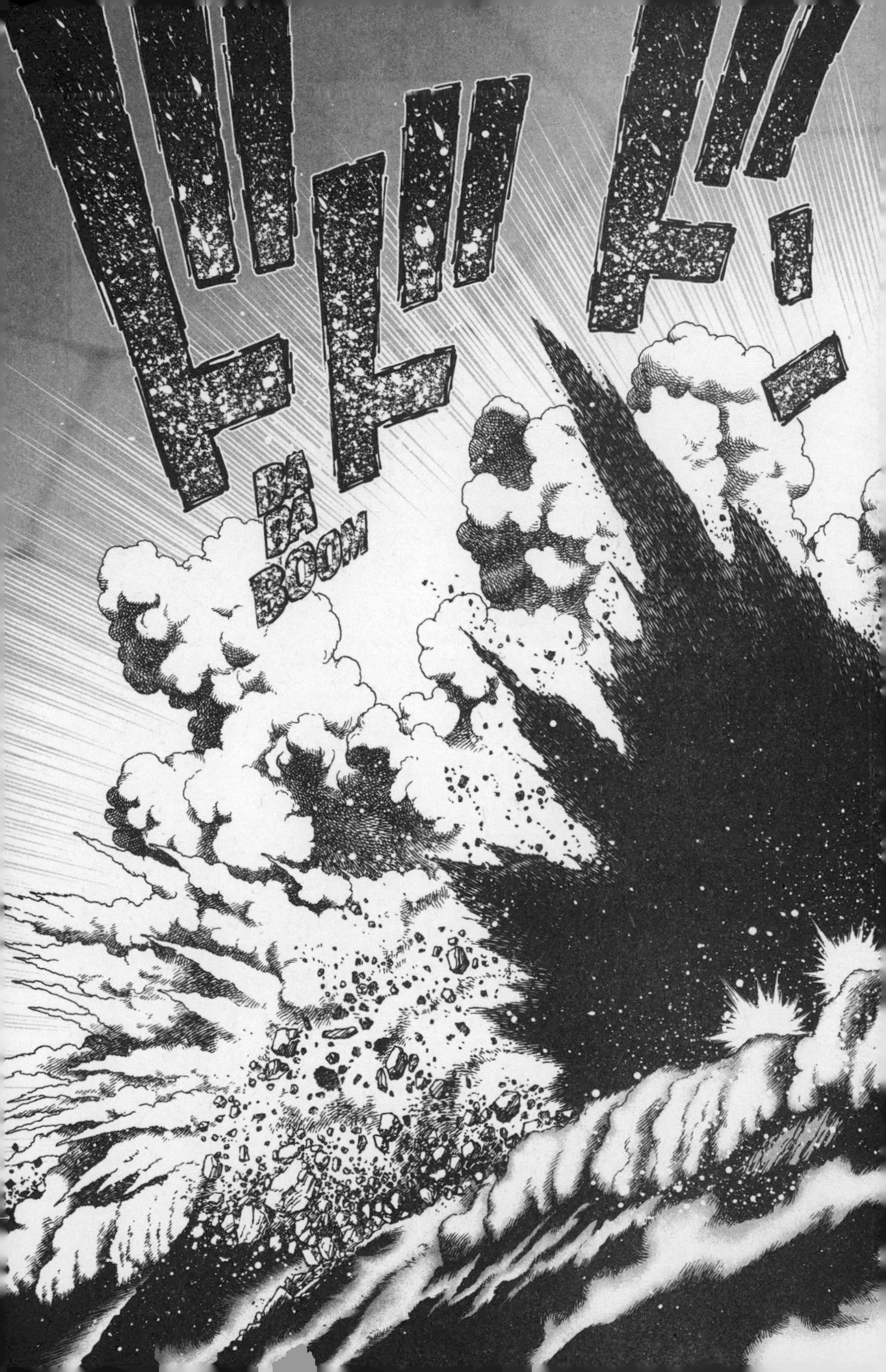
ドドド
DA DA BOOM

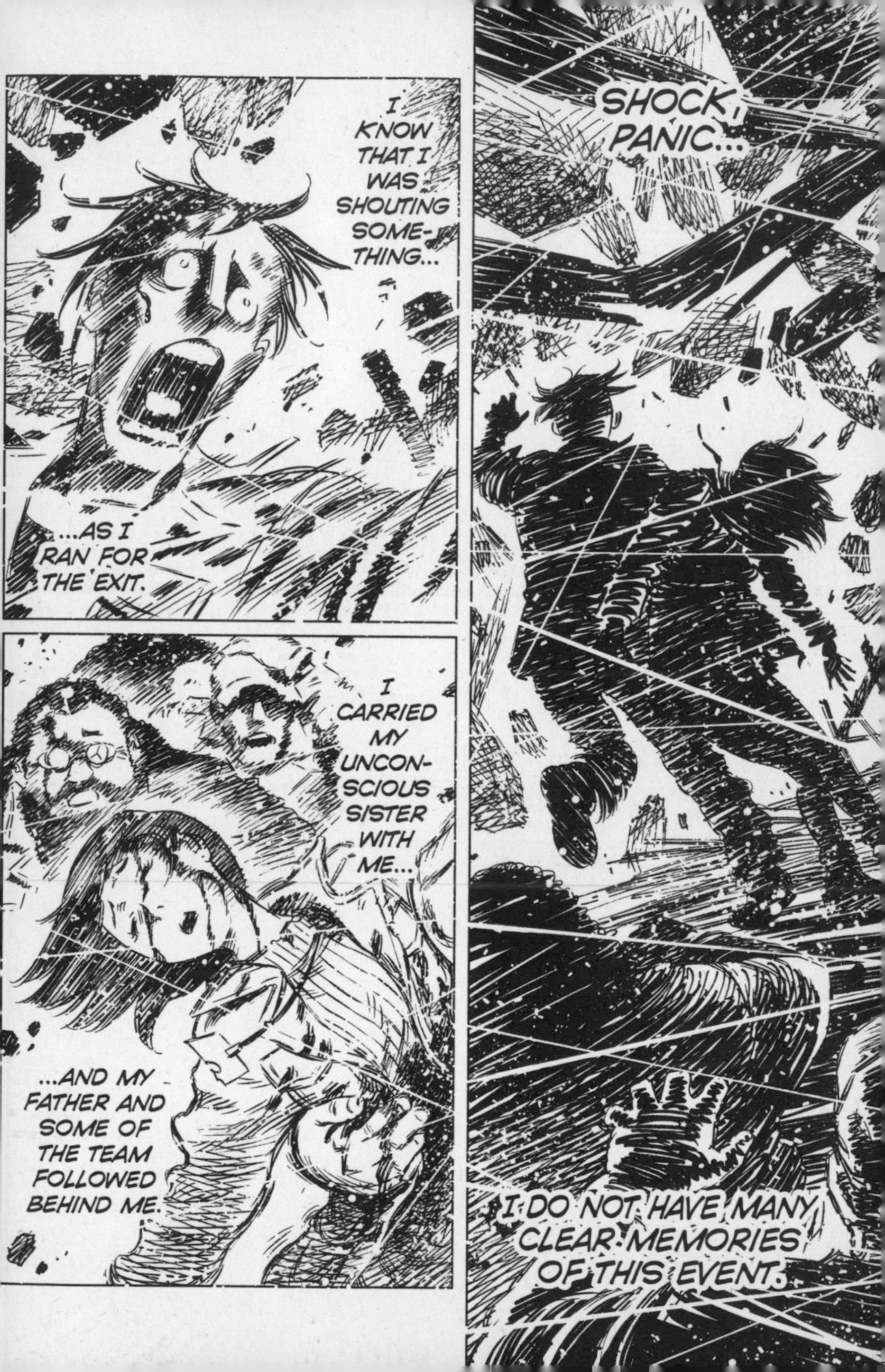
SHOCK, PANIC...
I DO NOT HAVE MANY CLEAR MEMORIES OF THIS EVENT.
I KNOW THAT I WAS SHOUTING SOME-THING...
...AS I RAN FOR THE EXIT.
I CARRIED MY UNCON-SCIOUS SISTER WITH ME...
...AND MY FATHER AND SOME OF THE TEAM FOLLOWED BEHIND ME.

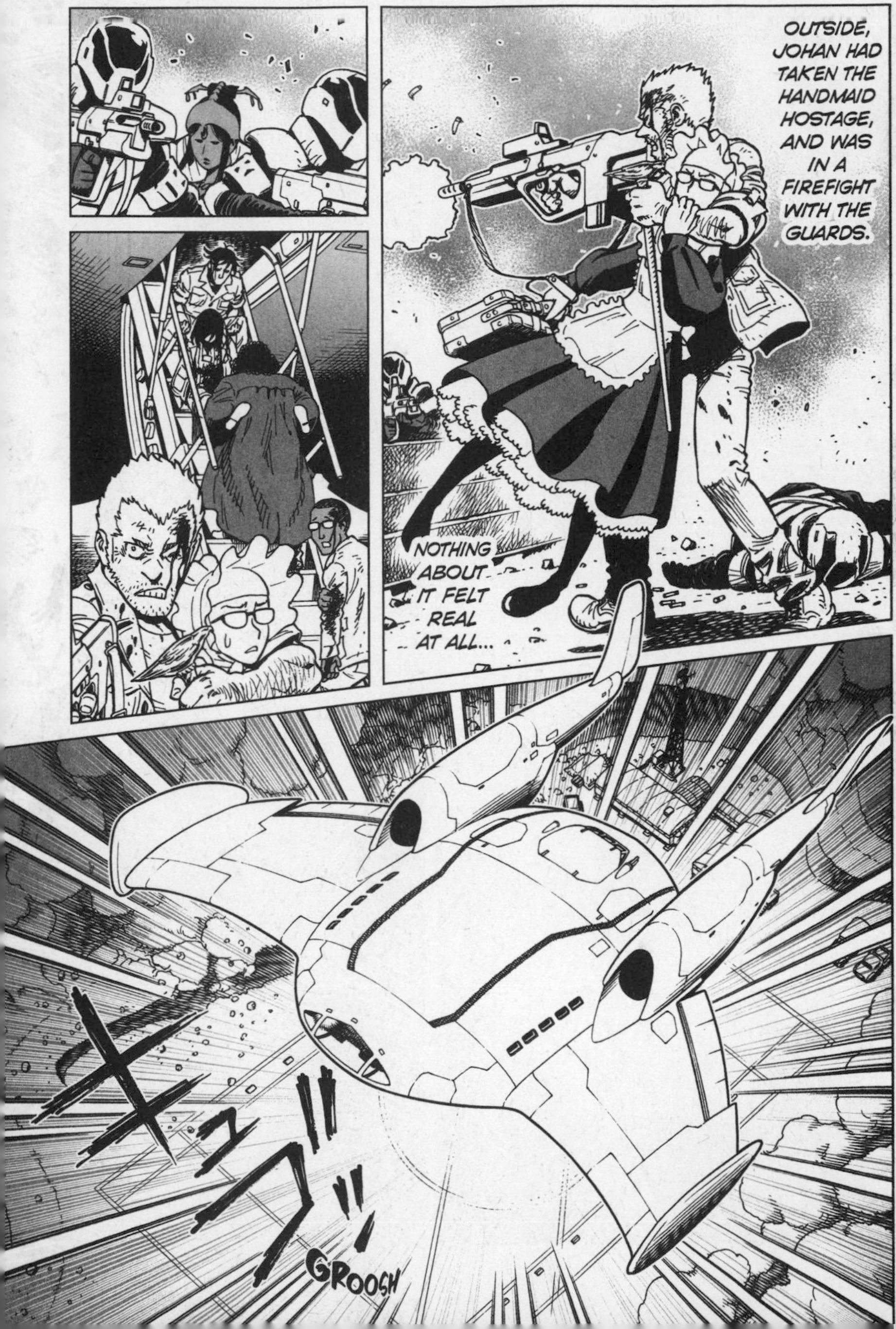
OUTSIDE, JOHAN HAD TAKEN THE HANDMAID HOSTAGE, AND WAS IN A FIREFIGHT WITH THE GUARDS.
NOTHING ABOUT IT FELT REAL AT ALL...
GROOSH

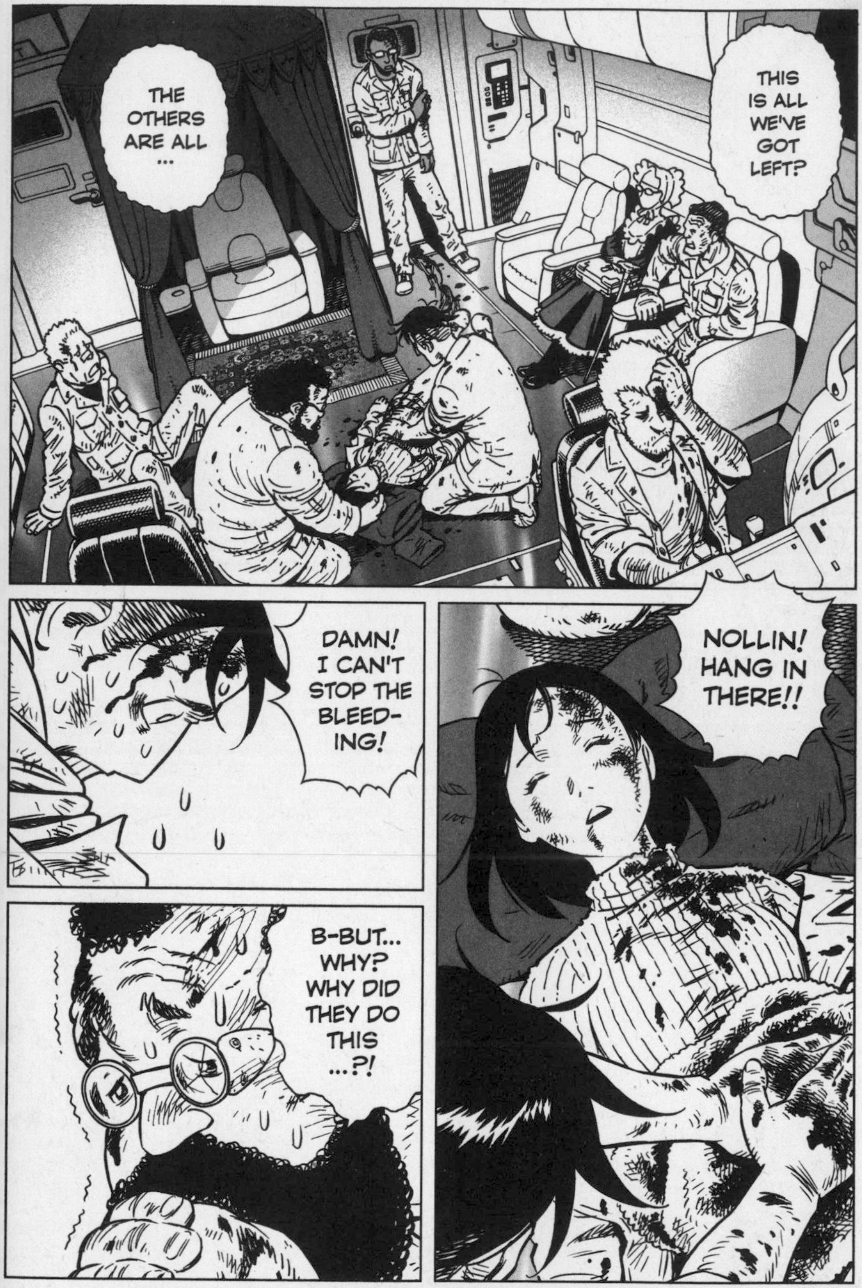
THIS IS ALL WE'VE GOT LEFT?
THE OTHERS ARE ALL ...
NOLLIN! HANG IN THERE!!
DAMN! I CAN'T STOP THE BLEED-ING!
B-BUT... WHY? WHY DID THEY DO THIS ...?!

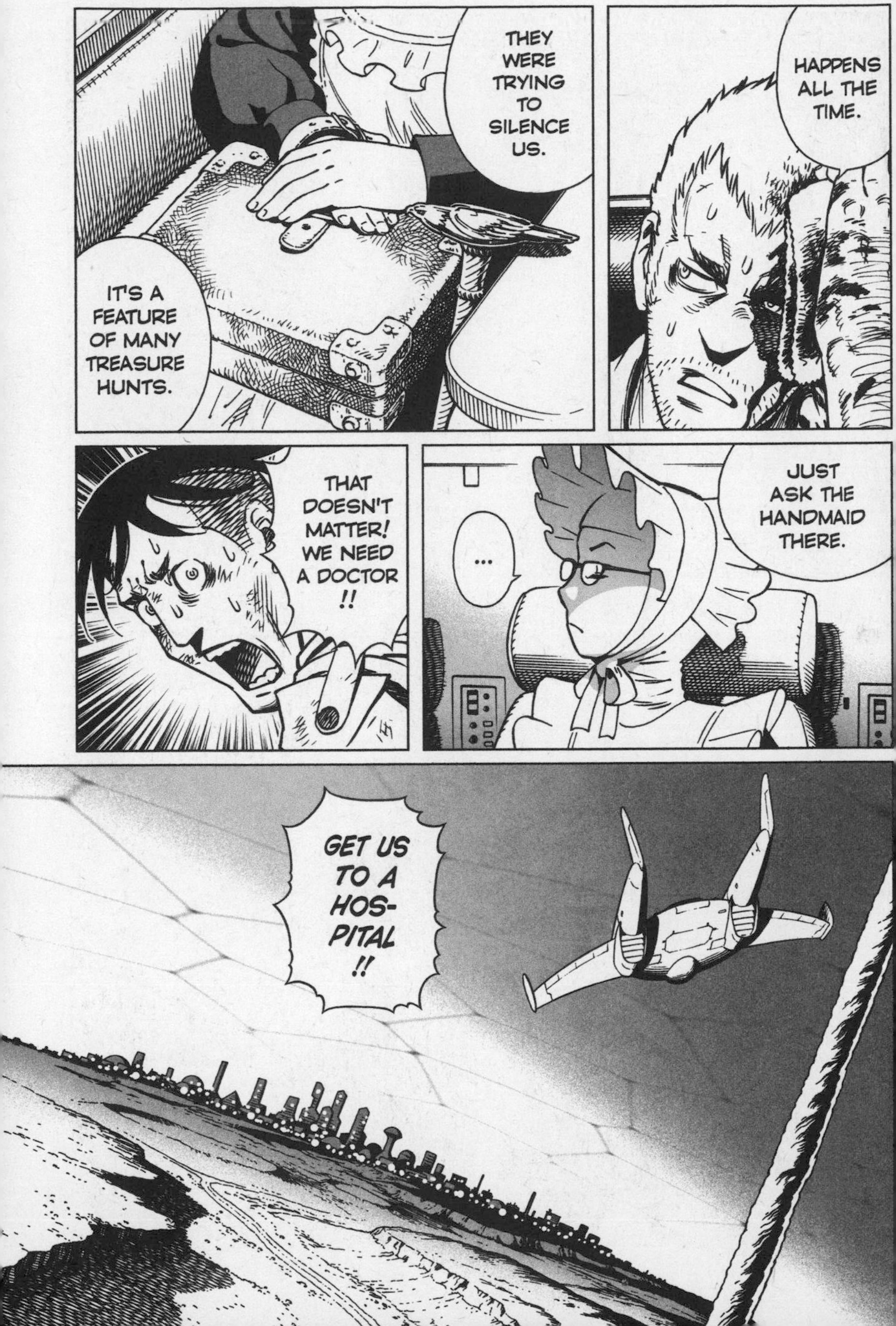
HAPPENS ALL THE TIME.
THEY WERE TRYING TO SILENCE US.
IT'S A FEATURE OF MANY TREASURE HUNTS.
JUST ASK THE HANDMAID THERE.
...
THAT DOESN'T MATTER! WE NEED A DOCTOR !!
GET US TO A HOS-PITAL !!

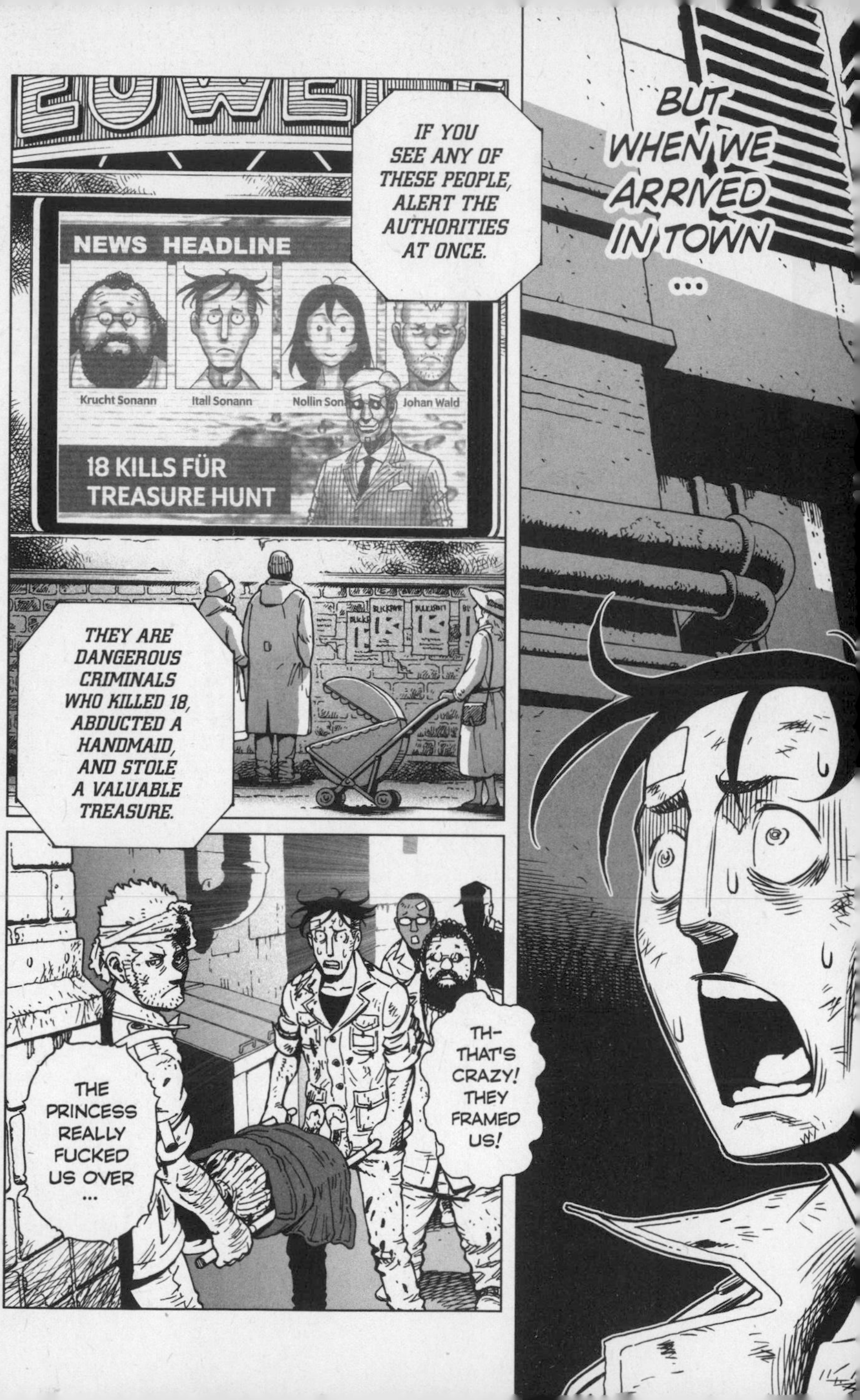
BUT WHEN WE ARRIVED IN TOWN ...
NEWS HEADLINE
Krucht Sonann
Itall Sonann
Nollin Sona
Johan Wald
18 KILLS FÜR TREASURE HUNT
IF YOU SEE ANY OF THESE PEOPLE, ALERT THE AUTHORITIES AT ONCE.
THEY ARE DANGEROUS CRIMINALS WHO KILLED 18, ABDUCTED A HANDMAID, AND STOLE A VALUABLE TREASURE.
TH-THAT'S CRAZY! THEY FRAMED US!
THE PRINCESS REALLY FUCKED US OVER ...

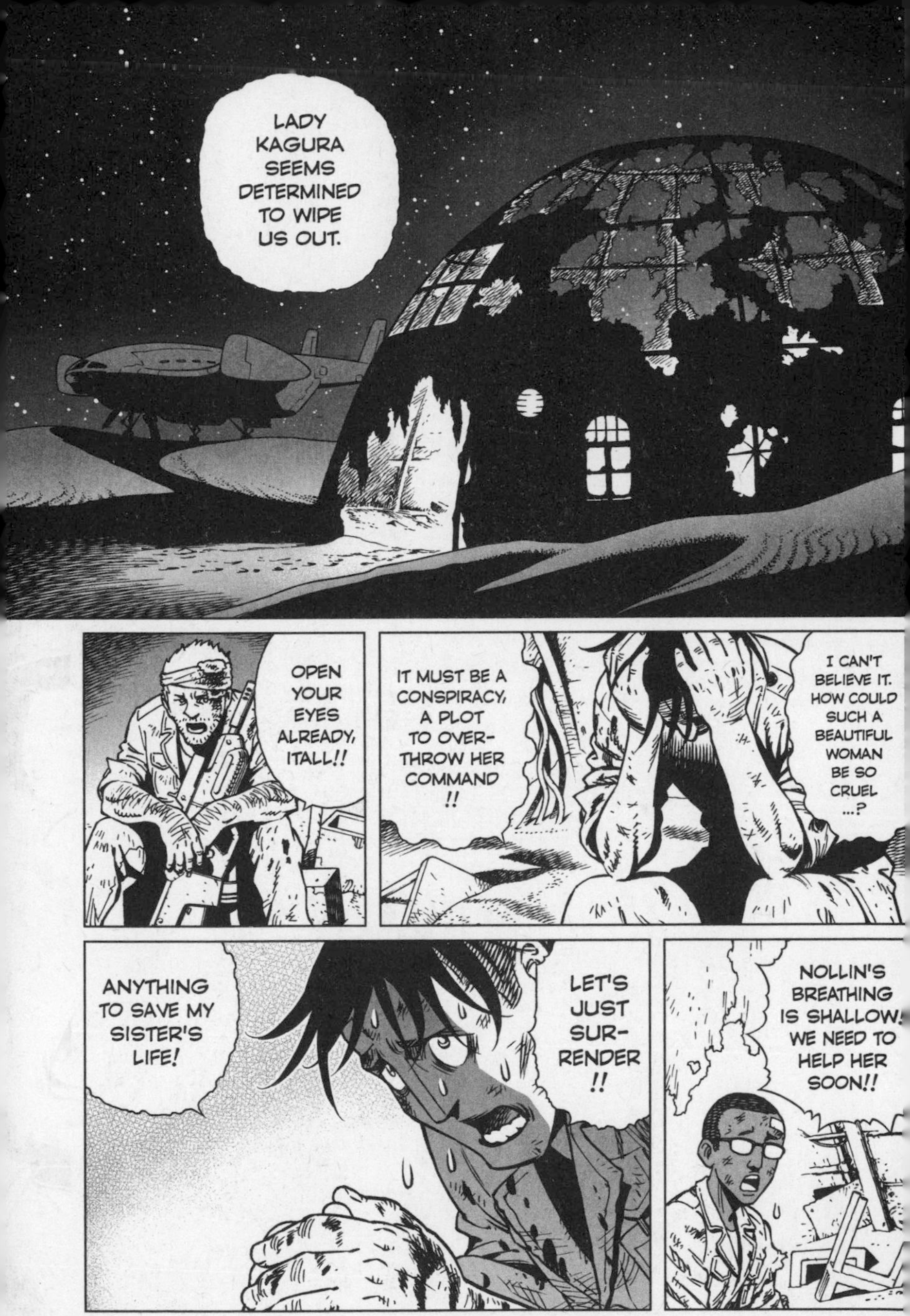
LADY KAGURA SEEMS DETERMINED TO WIPE US OUT.
I CAN'T BELIEVE IT. HOW COULD SUCH A BEAUTIFUL WOMAN BE SO CRUEL ...?
IT MUST BE A CONSPIRACY, A PLOT TO OVER-THROW HER COMMAND !!
OPEN YOUR EYES ALREADY, ITALL!!
NOLLIN'S BREATHING IS SHALLOW! WE NEED TO HELP HER SOON!!
LET'S JUST SUR-RENDER !!
ANYTHING TO SAVE MY SISTER'S LIFE!

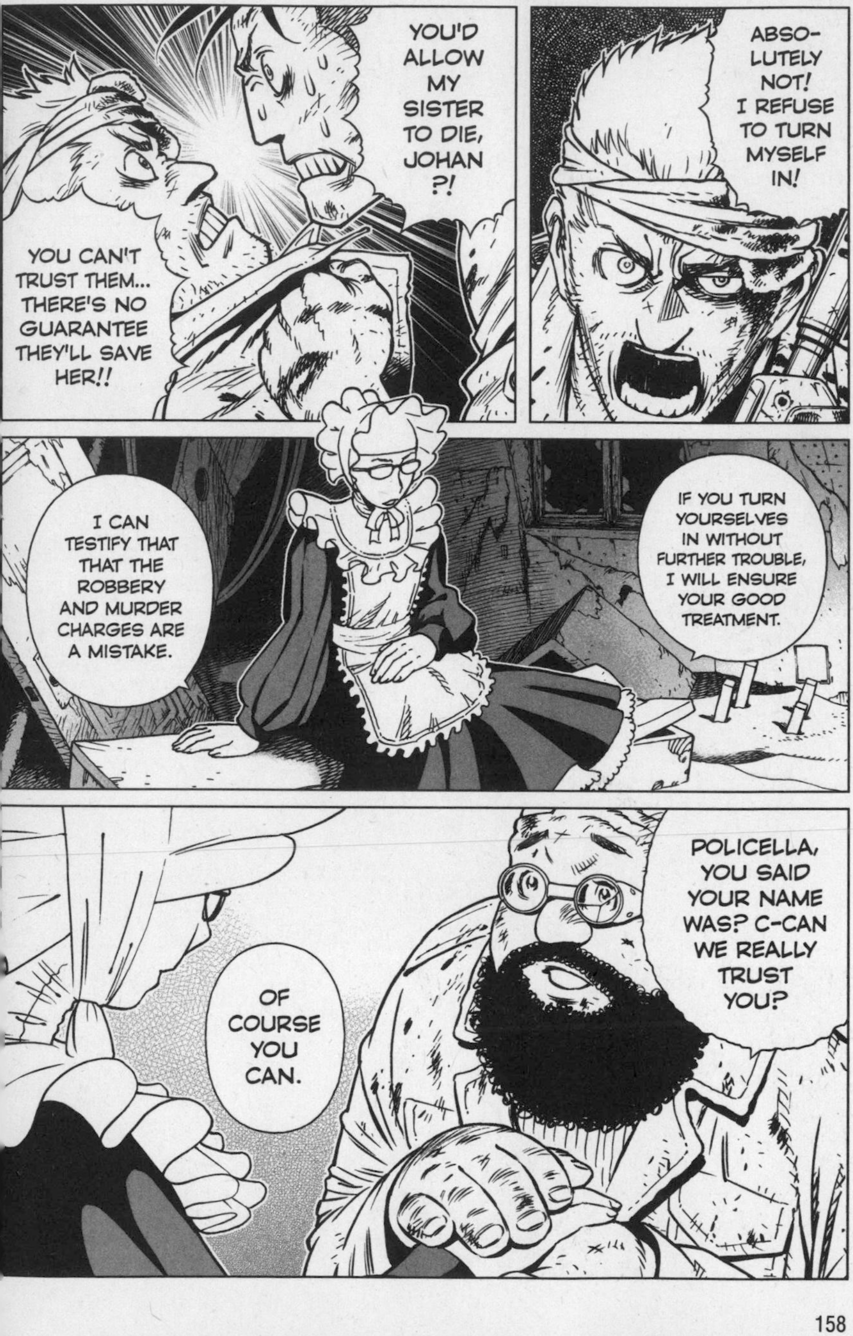
ABSO-LUTELY NOT! I REFUSE TO TURN MYSELF IN!
YOU'D ALLOW MY SISTER TO DIE, JOHAN ?!
YOU CAN'T TRUST THEM... THERE'S NO GUARANTEE THEY'LL SAVE HER!!
IF YOU TURN YOURSELVES IN WITHOUT FURTHER TROUBLE, I WILL ENSURE YOUR GOOD TREATMENT.
I CAN TESTIFY THAT THAT THE ROBBERY AND MURDER CHARGES ARE A MISTAKE.
POLICELLA, YOU SAID YOUR NAME WAS? C-CAN WE REALLY TRUST YOU?
OF COURSE YOU CAN.

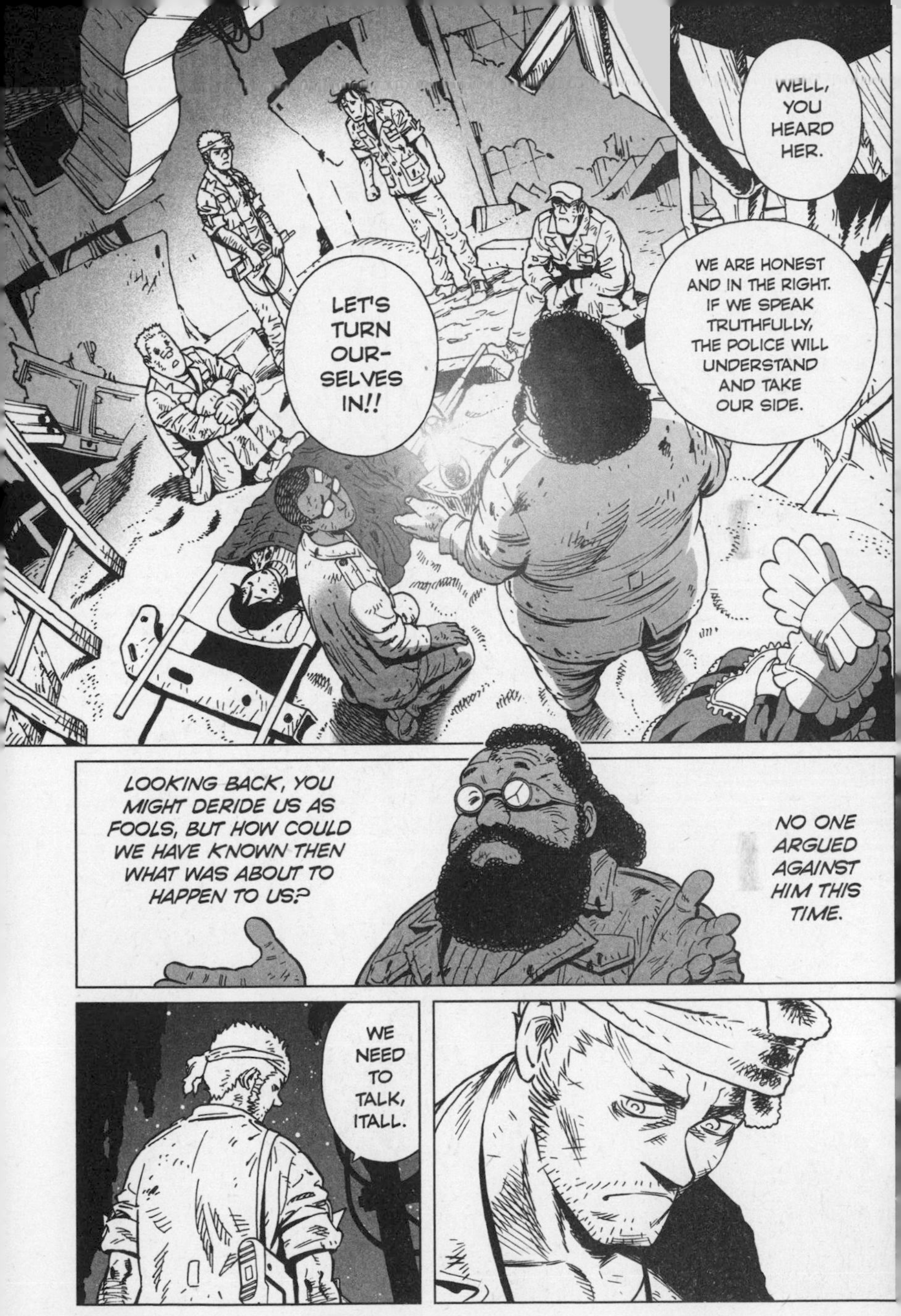
WELL, YOU HEARD HER.
WE ARE HONEST AND IN THE RIGHT. IF WE SPEAK TRUTHFULLY, THE POLICE WILL UNDERSTAND AND TAKE OUR SIDE.
LET'S TURN OUR-SELVES IN!!
NO ONE ARGUED AGAINST HIM THIS TIME.
LOOKING BACK, YOU MIGHT DERIDE US AS FOOLS, BUT HOW COULD WE HAVE KNOWN THEN WHAT WAS ABOUT TO HAPPEN TO US?
WE NEED TO TALK, ITALL.

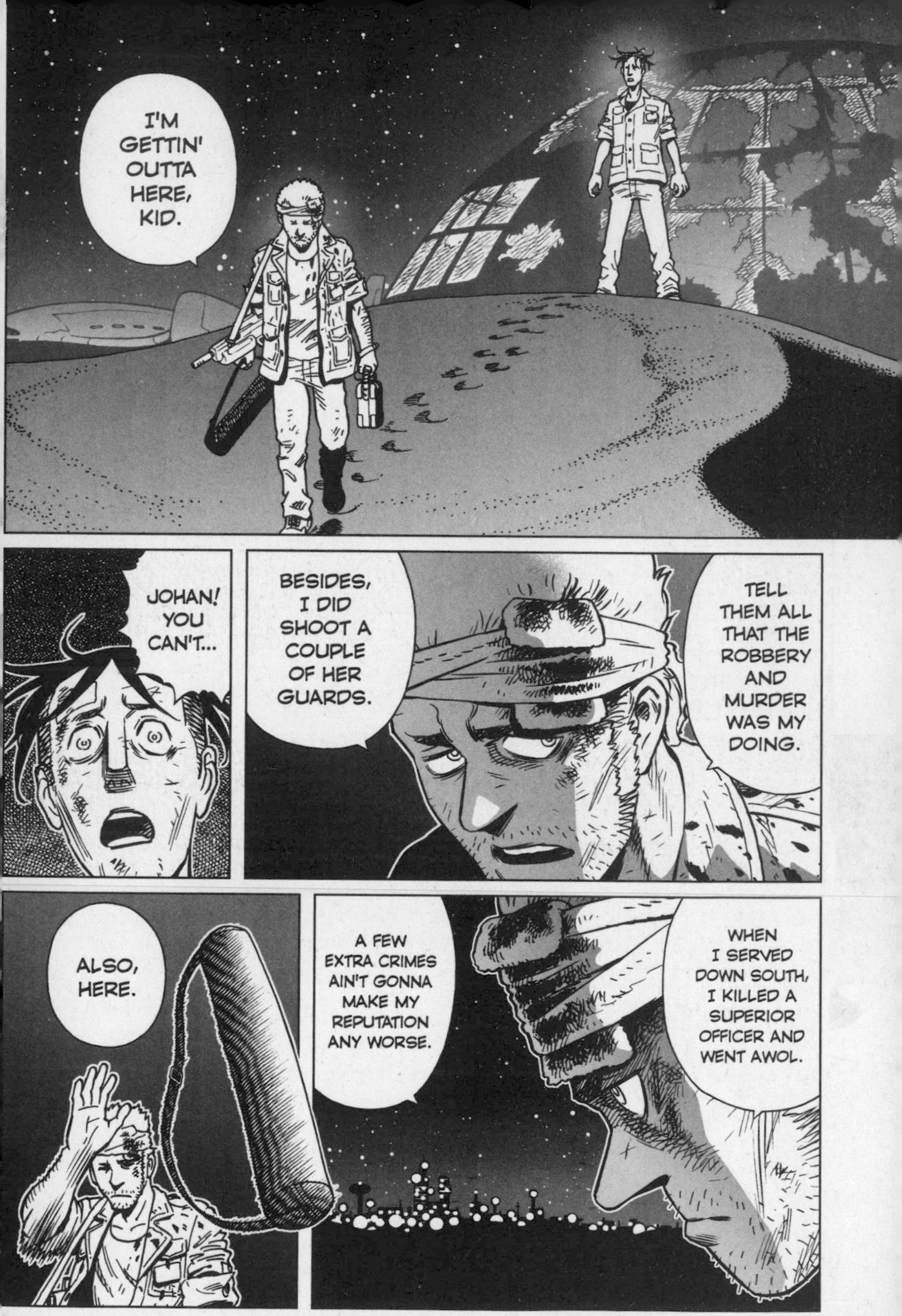
I'M GETTIN' OUTTA HERE, KID.
TELL THEM ALL THAT THE ROBBERY AND MURDER WAS MY DOING.
BESIDES, I DID SHOOT A COUPLE OF HER GUARDS.
JOHAN! YOU CAN'T...
WHEN I SERVED DOWN SOUTH, I KILLED A SUPERIOR OFFICER AND WENT AWOL.
A FEW EXTRA CRIMES AIN'T GONNA MAKE MY REPUTATION ANY WORSE.
ALSO, HERE.

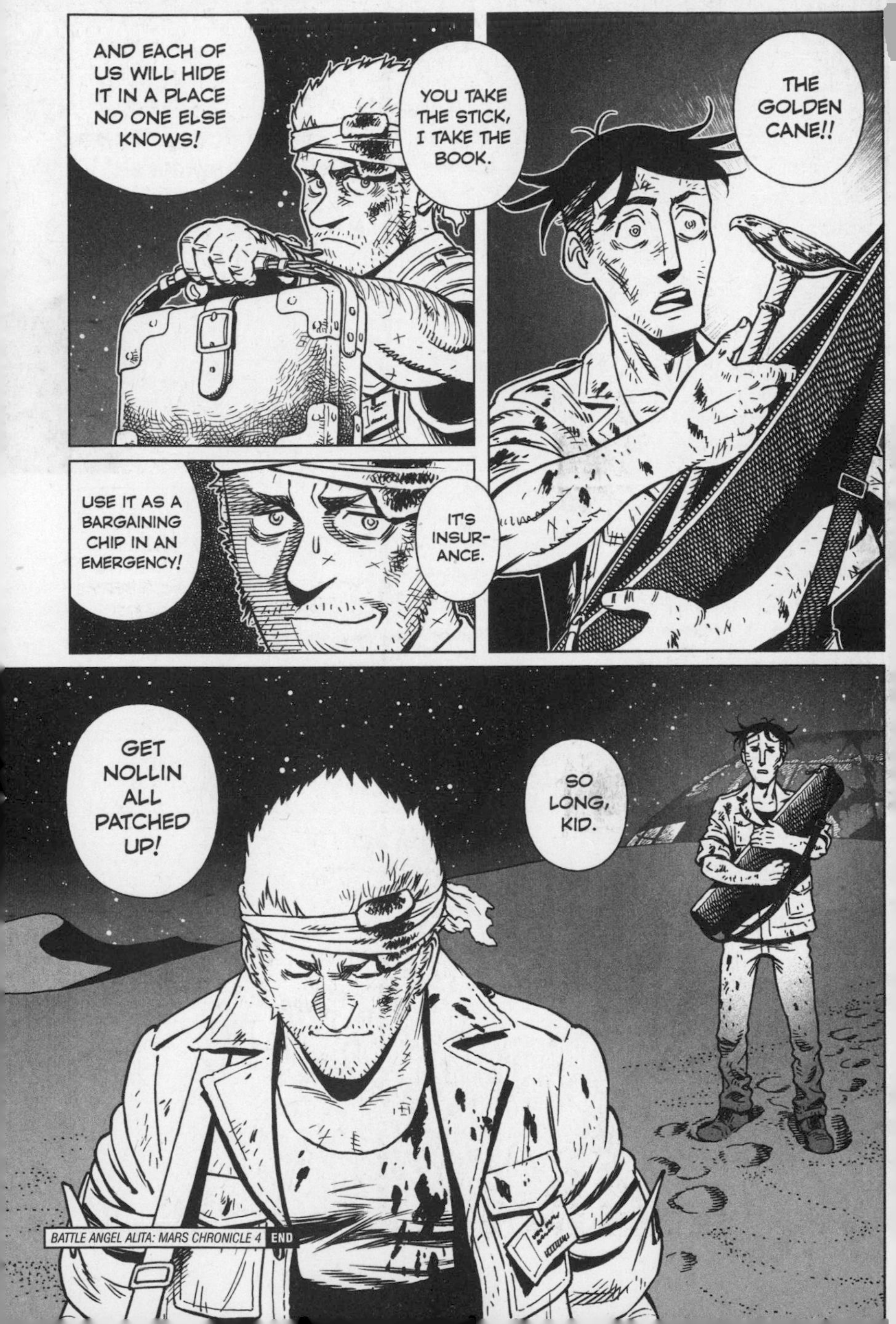
THE GOLDEN CANE!!
YOU TAKE THE STICK, I TAKE THE BOOK.
AND EACH OF US WILL HIDE IT IN A PLACE NO ONE ELSE KNOWS!
IT'S INSURANCE.
USE IT AS A BARGAINING CHIP IN AN EMERGENCY!
SO LONG, KID.
GET NOLLIN ALL PATCHED UP!
BATTLE ANGEL ALITA: MARS CHRONICLE 4 END

RECEIVED
JAN - - 2020
BY:

Battle Angel Alita: Mars Chronicle volume 4 is a work of fiction. Names, characters, places, and incidents are the products of the author's imagination or are used fictitiously. Any resemblance to actual events, locales, or persons, living or dead, is entirely coincidental.

A Kodansha Comics Trade Paperback Original.

Battle Angel Alita: Mars Chronicle volume 4 copyright © 2017 Yukito Kishiro
English translation copyright © 2018 Yukito Kishiro

All rights reserved.

Published in the United States by Kodansha Comics, an imprint of Kodansha USA Publishing, LLC, New York.

Publication rights for this English edition arranged through Kodansha Ltd., Tokyo.

First published in Japan in 2017 by Kodansha Ltd., Tokyo, as *Gunnm: Mars Chronicle 4*.

ISBN 978-1-63236-618-4

Printed in the United States of America.

www.kodanshacomics.com

9 8 7 6 5 4 3 2 1

Translator: Stephen Paul
Lettering: Evan Hayden
Editing: Ajani Oloye
Kodansha Comics edition cover design: Phil Balsman